VOICE OF THE ṚṢIS

यच्चिद्धि शश्वता तना देवंदेवं यजामहे ।

Ṛg. I. 26.6, Sām.1618

Yacciddhi śaśvatā tanā devaṁ devaṁ yajāmahe /

To realise the Truth and to make the body divine, one must repeat constantly – "*Deva, O Deva.*" Thus, *devaṁ devaṁ yajāmahe* is the mantra to enter into the Golden Age and to realise Truth.

ॐ

VOICE OF THE ṚṢIS

An Epilogue to Devāyaṇa, Third Epic of India

A VEDIC REFERENCE BOOK

DR. HAJARI

Edited by

AMITA NATHWANI

New Age Books

ISBN: 978-81-7822-335-3

First Edition: Delhi, 2009

Published by
NEW AGE BOOKS
A-44 Naraina Industrial Area Phase-I
New Delhi-110 028 (INDIA)
Email: nab@vsnl.in
Website: www.newagebooksindia.com

Printed in India
at Shri Jainendra Press
A-45, Naraina Industrial Area, Phase-I, New Delhi-110 028

ॐ

THE HIDDEN DIVINE

The divine romance, surrounding us all,
The unknown fragrance, in which we enthrall.

The illuminating figure, its light so pure,
The mystical sound, in which we mature.

A fragment is this, of the ultimate bliss,
Which few of us know, truly exists.

The awaited is here, with flaming might,
The nameless love, dances in the night.

Prepare yourselves, O souls with sight !
The moment shall come, so unbearably bright.

Open your eyes and see the glorious,
And when He comes, you'll be victorious!

In the musing glow, look through your third eye
And see only, Om Namah Śivaya!

Nishin Nathwani, 2005
13 years old

KEY TO TRANSLITERATION

a	अ	ā	आ
i	इ	ī	ई
u	उ	ū	ऊ
ṛ	ऋ	ṝ	ॠ
lṛ	ऌ	e	ए
ai	ऐ	o	ओ
au	औ	k	क्
kh	ख्	g	ग्
gh	[illegible]	ṅ	ङ्
c	च्	ch	छ्
j	ज्	jh	झ्
ñ	ञ्	ṭ	ट्
ṭh	ठ्	ḍ	ड्
ḍh	ढ्	ṇ	ण्
t	त्	th	थ्
d	द्	dh	ध्
n	न्	p	प्
ph	फ्	b	ब्
bh	भ्	m	म्
y	य्	r	र्

l	ल्	ḷ	ळ
v	व्	ś	श्
ṣ	ष्	s	स्
h	ह्		

ṁ The nasal sound which is marked by a dot and which belongs to the preceding vowel

ḥ A symbol in writing representing a distinct hard aspiration and marked by two perpendicular dots (:) which sounds like h.

Dr. Hajari.
Hearing the Voice of the Ṛsis, 1970

FOREWORD

Real knowledge does not come with reading or chanting mantras alone. It comes only with realisation. In India, we had the Vedas for thousands of years, yet their knowledge and wisdom had receded in the background for centuries. We did not understand them rightly, as we failed to untangle the knots of their symbolic language. The Brahmins chanted them at every religious occasion. It took the form of a ritual. Still, we knew and believed in our innermost being that these visions of the ancient Ṛṣis articulated the Ultimate Truths of our existence. Then the British came to India and colonised the country. They tried to fathom what was in these ancient scriptures. They also failed to understand the symbolic language.

The result was that we suffered pain and humiliation and believed that our culture and beliefs were dramatically inferior to the West. Now we realise that the West was trying to interpret this vast bulk of knowledge of the ancient Seers in an oversimplistic manner. Later on came Swami Dayanand Sarasvati, who showed us how to revere and worship the Vedas in our daily life. A new dimension began to open in front of us. Then came Sri Aurobindo with his dazzling mastery of English and other European languages. He mastered Sanskrit as well and unfolded to us portions of the Vedas in his grandiose poetic style. We glimpsed the secrets of the Vedas in English language and were enthralled. A greater knowledge opened up in front of humanity. We received information for making our lives spiritual. The world realised the reality of a greater being and a bigger power, a grand consciousness and the delight of Its existence came within our reach.

The revered Vedas, the secret book of wisdom, the work of Indian sages and seers who had received the knowledge in their illumined minds, were opened up for us. Still this particular knowledge remained unfolded only to a select few. Since then another century has passed. I feel that we are now ready to receive this secret knowledge with a new light illumining them.

The Voice Of The Ṛṣis by Dr. Hajari is for everyone to understand. Certain parts of the secret knowledge of the Vedic Truth are presented in a simple language. It is an epilogue to Devāyaṇa, the third epic of India, written by Dr. Hajari in which he opens up a new vista. Until now what was obscure, is there to be absorbed by one and all. Never in history before, have so many people around the world expressed their desire to understand the Vedic Realisations, as today. It is simply because the day has come for the Truth to descend, for humanity to march a step forward in the evolution, for the Golden Age to come. This book will prove to be a landmark on this path.

I am grateful to Prashant Khanna of Delhi, who was kind enough to read and elucidate the matter of this book. My sincere thanks are to Prathibha Jobanputra of Mumbai and K.J. Somaiya of Bharatiya Sanskriti Peetham who provided the original Sanskrit texts of the mantras and their references and sources. Amongst those who evinced keen interest in the progress of this book, I must mention the names of my mother, Dr. Indira Sardana, my daughter-in-law Radhika and my nephew Nishin from Canada. Above all, I am indebted to my husband Nilesh for his encouragement and patience during the long hours of silence in which this book was being prepared. I conclude with expressing my deep gratitude to Dr. Hajari who gave me the opportunity to become a part of this enthralling adventure, making it possible for me to dive deeply in the vast ocean of this Vedic knowledge.

AMITA NATHWANI

EDITOR'S NOTE

The divine author and poet, Piṅgala Maheśvara, the Lord of Creation, brought down the epic *Devāyaṇa* to our mortal world. For this monumental task, Dr. Hajari became a human instrument from 14 March 1951 to 8 July 1954, when the last page of this epic was finished. It has been seen that the changing of an age always brings about an epic. During the passage from the Silver to the Bronze Age, *Rāmāyaṇa* manifested. With the transition from the Bronze to the Iron Age, *Mahābhārata* materialised. Now, as the Iron Age is coming to an end and we are approaching the Golden Age, *Devāyaṇa* has come down.

The subject matter of *Devāyaṇa* was circulated as a synopsis in English, French, Bengali and Hindi during the late 50's and the early 60s of the 20th century. It generated widespread interest and many newspapers commented on it. Now, we have updated the synopsis and given it a new title – Glimpses of Devāyaṇa. This has been published recently.

While waiting to publish this magnum opus, Dr. Hajari received innumerable queries on the subject matter of the new epic from interested people. To find an answer to these queries he meditated intensely and went deep within himself. In his intense concentration, the immortal Ṛṣis appeared in front of him in their luminous bodies. They told him to announce the beginning of the Golden Age on the earth. This they said will come through the manifestation of Satyadeva, the Lord of Truth. This book compiles the answers provided

---

* *For more information on this epic please log on to www.devayan.net*

by the Ṛṣis in the form of mantras from the Vedas and the Upaniṣads to the unspoken questions in Dr. Hajari's mind. These references from the four Vedas additionally prove the authenticity of the divine epic. At times the mantras with their meanings and references are included in the text, while elsewhere only the meaning of the mantras has been included in the text. On studying the meanings of the mantras provided by the Ṛṣis, we realise that these mantras have received a more penetrating significance. Also, we receive a new insight into the Vedas and we become conscious that all these truths were there for everyone to see but we were blind.

To welcome the Golden Age, the immortal Ṛṣis gave us the mantra to become liberated from the iron grip of Kali, the sombre Lord of the Iron Age. To prepare ourselves for welcoming the Deva, the Lord of Truth and to realise immortality, the Ṛg and the Sāma Vedas have given us the following mantra:

यच्चिद्धि शश्वता तना देवंदेवं यजामहे ।

Ṛg. I. 26.6, Sām.1618

Yacciddhi śaśvatā tanā devaṁ devaṁ yajāmahe /

To realise the Truth and to make the body divine, one must repeat constantly – "*Deva, O Deva.*" Thus, *devaṁ devaṁ yajāmahe* is the mantra to enter into the Golden Age and to realise Truth.

Although the present edition of this booklet has been edited, the subject matter has remained the same as before. Also Dr. Hajari had given us a few mantras which need to be chanted regularly to purify and to prepare ourselves for the Golden Age. To facilitate this a CD entitled - Welcome to the Golden Age – is attached in this book with these mantras set to music. These may help us to prepare ourselves for the advent of the Golden Age.

AMITA NATHWANI

PREFACE

While waiting to publish the magnificent Devāyaṇa, I sought answers to certain queries that I received from people interested in the new epic. To find an answer to these questions I had to meditate and go deep within myself. Through that meditation, one day, the immortal Ṛṣis appeared in front of me in their luminous bodies. They told me to announce the beginning of the Golden Age on the Earth, which will come about through the manifestation of Satyadeva. They told me that the world was going through a period that was without peace, full of upheavals, fears and great sorrows. They answered all of my innermost questions and provided references from the four Vedas, which in their view would additionally prove the authenticity of the divine epic. The mantras they quoted are known to the learned Brahmins and Pundits, but the meaning that they provided was at once very novel, but also so appropriate that one wonders why we did not see that earlier.

I hereby announce the advent of the Golden Age on the Earth. I call upon all human beings to take refuge in Devāyaṇa from the attacks of vital enemies and hostile forces. Then, mankind would become liberated from all diseases, infirmities and death and enter under the protection of the Lord of Truth, Satyadeva.

To enter into the Golden Age, men need the power of mantras, through which they can be freed from the compulsive control of the dark Kali Yuga. At the previous transition of the Ages, namely from the Silver to the Bronze Age, mankind received the Rāmāyaṇa and the name of Rāma, the Rāma mantra as a protection; from the Bronze to the Iron Age, they received the Mahābhārata and the name of Kṛṣṇa, the Kṛṣṇa mantra. At the end of the Iron Age (Kaliyuga), they received and recited the Hare Rāma, Hare Kṛṣṇa mantra.

Now for the transition into the Satya Yuga (the Golden Age), humanity has received the Devāyaṇa and the name of Deva, the sole mantra to liberate them from the smothering grip of Kali, the Lord of the Iron Age. To come into contact with the golden touch of Deva and to realise immortality, the Ṛg and the Sàma Vedas have given us the following mantra:

यच्चिद्धि शश्वता तना देवंदेवं यजामहे ।

Ṛg. I. 26.6, Sām.1618

Yacciddhi śaśvatā tanā devaṁ devaṁ yajāmahe /

To attain the Truth and to obtain a divine body, one must repeat constantly – "*Deva, O Deva.*" Thus, *devaṁ devaṁ yajāmahe* becomes the mantra to enter into the Golden Age and to realise Truth.

O People of this Earth! O my brothers and sisters! Repeat constantly "*devaṁ, devaṁ*" throughout the day, in all your thoughts and actions to enter into the Age of Truth and meditate in your heart on "a*haṁ-ṛtam*" to attain immortality.

I can see "*Apamayana*" the chariot that the Vasus are pulling down to the Earth. I also see Uṣā, the Divine Dawn making a connection with the fire chariot. There the Vasus are the horses and they are the precursors of the divine dawn. In this chariot, Satyadeva, the golden Puruṣa, the Illumined Being is seated. He is magnificently attired. He has golden earrings in his ears and an imposing crown on his head. The golden crown is inlaid with magnificent precious gems and stones. On his left side is seated the golden Queen of Truth, Suhavā, her whole body ornamented with gold and jewels. On his right side, is the Golden Mother of Truth, Yahvī, even more bejewelled than the Queen. The Lord of Truth is entering the Earth atmosphere through Devāyaṇa, the path of immortality.

One can hear at this moment of advent the Dundhubi, the divine drum, announcing to all and sundry the victory of the Truth. This is the beginning of the Golden Age.

Devāyaṇa is the path that has opened to take us from obscurity to light, from falsehood to truth and from death to immortality.

विमुच्यध्वमघ्न्या देवयानाऽ अगन्म तमसस्पारमस्य ।
ज्योतिरापाम ॥

Yaj.XII.73

Vimucyadhvamaghnyā devayānā' aganma
tamasaspāramasya /
jyotirāpāma //

Devāyaṇa removes the dark obscurity of the Iron Age and eliminates the opposition caused by the dark forces. It opens the path of light, takes us above all darkness and allows us to emerge into the Ocean of Supreme Light.

In this Age, the Creator, Prajāpati Brahman, has ordered death to honour Devāyaṇa

परं मृत्यो अनु परेहि पन्थां यस्ते अन्यऽइतरो देवयानात् ।
चक्षुष्मते श्रृण्वते ते ब्रवीमि मा नः प्रजां रीरिषो मोत वीरान् ॥

Yaj. XXXV. 7

Paraṁ mṛtyo anu parehi panthāṁ yaste anya' itaro devayānāt /
Cakṣuṣmate śṛṇvate te bravīmi mā naḥ prajāṁ rīriṣo mota vīrān //

O Death! With Devāyaṇa opening the path of immortality for mankind, do not lead the people of the Earth into Pitṛyana, the path of obscure mortality; let them enter into the Devāyaṇa with their children. Do not destroy them.

Devāyaṇa like the other two epics has been written in the Anuṣṭubh Chanda. This is really a divine metre. The Ṛṣis have described the metre in the following words.

The power that has descended from the supreme plane to conquer all our enemies, to give us power and heroism, to be liberated from all fears is the Anuṣṭubh chanda, the divine metre.

विषणोः क्रमोऽसि शत्रुयतो हन्ताऽऽनुष्टभं छन्द ऽ ।
आ रोह दिशोऽनु वि क्रमस्व ॥

Yaj. XII.5

Viṣṇoḥ kramo'si śatruyato hantā 'nuṣṭubhaṁ chanda /
ā roha diśo'nu vi kramasva //

The Anuṣṭubh chanda roars like a lion. With the heroic power of Viṣṇu, it conquers all enemies and establishes great power and heroism in humanity.

The Creator Prajāpati Brahman has indicated to the divine powers:

इडाभिरग्निरीड्यः सोमो देवो अमर्त्यः ।
अनुष्टुप्छन्दऽइन्द्रियं पञ्चाविगौर्वयो दधुः ॥

Yaj. XXI.14

Iḍābhiragnirīḍyah somo devo amartyaḥ /
anuṣṭupchanda' indriyaṁ pañcāvirgaurvayo dadhuḥ //

Let the Goddess Ilā increase the power of Agni to call Soma devata, the Lord of Ambrosia to purify the Earth; let the Anuṣṭubh chanda act through the five senses, to receive the inexpressible luminous Truth and to fulfil us with the light, power, joy and purity of Truth.

The place, selected by the Creator at the beginning of the creation for the manifestation of the Truth, is that part of the Earth that aspires for the supramental Truth and wishes divinity for her children and which adores immortality for the whole Earth. It provides room for the Truth to be established for at least ten thousand years. She is *Vīda-Vaṅga* (Bengal). In the Vedas this divine area has been described in the following words:

स्थिरो भव वीडवङ्ग ऽ आशुर्भव वाज्यर्वन् ।
पृथुर्भव सुषदस्त्वमग्नेः पुरीषवाहणः ॥

Yaj.XI.44

Sthiro bhava vīdavaṅga' āśurbhava vājyarvan /
pṛthurbhava suṣadastvamagneḥ purīṣavāhaṇaḥ //

Be still and peaceful immediately, O *Vaṅga*, Home of Truth through realisation of the Deva. Be replete with the riches of Truth in your fields and forests. Let the Truth spread throughout the world from your soil. O Agni! Lord of the Fire! Thou art the bearer of Truth. Bring Truth to Bengal!

Furthermore, the Creator Prajāpati Brahman described the land *Vaṅga*, which has been announced by the Vedas as the home of Truth:

चतुस्त्रिंशद्वाजिनो देवबन्धोर्वङ्क्रीरश्वस्य स्वधितिः समेति ।
अच्छिद्रा गात्रा वायुना कृणोत परुष्परुरघुष्या वि शस्त ॥

Ṛg. I.162.18

Catustriṁśadvājino devabandhor vaṅkrīraśvasya svadhitiḥ sameti /
Acchidrā gātrā vāyunā kṛṇota paruṣparuranughuṣyā vi ṣasta //

The place where Deva the Truth would manifest is *Vaṅga* (Bengal), when she is whole, without fissure and division in her body, when she is one single land, having the length and breadth of 34 horses square (the distance a horse could run in a day). Look at Bengal, full of the joy of Truth and luminous with the light and consciousness of Satyadeva.

Devāyaṇa unveils the realisation that is ultimate, an attainment that is final and an accomplishment that is radical. He is Deva the Truth, the Supreme, the Vast who creates immortality for the Gods.

यच्चिद्धि शश्वता तना देवंदेवं यजामहे ।
त्वे इद्धूयते हविः ॥

Ṛg. I.26.6; Sām.1618

Yacciddhi śaśvatā tanā devaṁ devaṃ yajāmahe /
tve iddhūyate haviḥ //

To achieve the ultimate realisation and to attain the long-term dream of a divine body; we call and repeat constantly, "***Deva,***

O Deva". Chanting this, we give our sacrificial offering to the Deva in the fire of our aspirations.

The Lord of Truth himself announced:

सत्यमहं गभीरः काव्येन सत्यं जातेनास्मि जातवेदाः ।
न मे दासो नार्यो महित्वा व्रतं मीमाय यदहं धरिष्ये ॥

Ath.V.11.3

Satyamahaṁ gabhīraḥ kāvyena satyaṁ jātenāsmi jātavedāḥ ।
Na me dāso nāryo mahitvā vrataṁ mīmāya yadahaṁ dhariṣye ॥

I am "*Satya*" the Truth. I manifest myself in the great Epic. I appear as the Truth through the "*Jātavedā*" Fire. None is above me. I am the Ultimate. O Mahī! Your worship and true adoration I hold with my indomitable power.

And in other words

अहमस्मि प्रथमजा ऋतस्य पूर्वं देवेभ्यो अमृतस्य नाम ।
यो मा ददाति स इदेवमावदहमन्नमन्नमदन्तमद्मी ॥

Sām.594

Ahamasmi prathamajā ṛtasya pūrvaṁ devebhyo amṛtasya nāma ।
Yo mā dadāti sa idevamāvadahamannamannamadantamadmi ॥

I am "Ṛta", the Truth. I was born in the beginning of the creation before the birth of all Gods. The Ṛṣis called me Amṛta.

देवन्देवं वो ऽ वसे देवन्देवमभिष्टये ।
देवन्देवं हुवेम वाजसातये गृणन्तो देव्या धिया ॥

Ṛg. VIII.27.13

Devandevaṁ vo'vase devan devamabhiṣṭaye ।
Devandevaṁ huvema vājasātaye gṛṇanto devyā dhiyā ॥

By chanting *devaṁ devaṁ*, the Gods achieved immortality. To remain in constant touch with the Truth, the Gods continue to chant this mantra without fail. The Seer of Truth, Vajasataye, gave us this japa and meditation to increase power, consciousness and riches brought to us by Satyadeva.

When the Earth feels the touch of light, power, consciousness and purity, then Deva is ready to manifest upon Earth with all Gods and Goddesses. Thus, starts His marvellous journey from eternity to eternity.

Then the divine forces march towards Earth under the command of Satyadeva, the Lord of Truth, to prevail over falsehood, maladies, infirmity and death. Immortality and divinity are established in men for them to enjoy divine life. On the other hand, the obstinate, hostile and evil powers of Falsehood provide a very strong resistance to the divine forces, as they still wish to remain in control of the human body. They try to maintain their control over the ideas and thoughts of human beings so that they continue to remain centred in self-interest and profit. Kali makes a strong effort to oppose the advent of Truth under the excuse of sexual creation and with the ever-present desire for vital enjoyment.

With Satyadeva, the Truth determined to reappear and Kali, refusing to disappear from the Earth, a great battle takes place on the cosmic level and in each and every human being. This struggle for suzerainty brings endless suffering to people until the decisive end comes.

That end comes only when the human will chooses to accept nothing else but the Truth, rejecting ego-centred and sex-related vital enjoyment thoughts. At that time, Man aspires constantly for Truth. Then, the mortal door opens in that human being to welcome Truth. And Satyadeva, the Truth, enters in that being to make it immortal while Kali is forced to withdraw his dark and negative forces. With this, Truth roars its victory in the human being.

With the arrival of Satyadeva together with the Gods and the Ṛṣis, the Golden Age of Truth commences on the Earth in which Heaven embraces the Earth and man appears like God or Superman. All enmity disappears. Everyone becomes friendly, compassionate and loving. One observes the complete manifestation of Devāyaṇa.

O Supreme Truth! Time has come now to announce that the Earth will become peaceful through your light, power and purity. The Vedas announce that only purity is the touch of immortality. Then arises the chant of the Ṛṣis – Victory to the Truth, Victory to the Deva, Victory to Immortality.

O People of the Earth! Look at the Golden Age appearing now on the Earth and realise Deva, the Truth.

In the age of Truth, there will be no avatars or incarnation of gods higher than the human beings. All beings, big or small, will reach the perfection of God.

In this Age, there will be neither democracy nor communism. All beings will have the immortal consciousness shining with the Light, Power and Purity of Truth.

In the Heavens above, there are four beings.

(1) The Ṛṣis, who guard the Vedas, the supreme knowledge and the secret of Truth.
(2) The Gods, who fight against the hostile forces, conquer enemies and establish a divine kingdom based only on the Law and Order of Truth.
(3) The Yakṣas or Gandharvas, those who increase and protect the divine treasury for the use of Gods and the Ṛṣis for spreading Truth. They fight with the Dasyus, the robbers of the riches. They also maintain the treasury.
(4) The Visvedevas, engaged in the construction of creations with art and architecture, sing and dance for the manifestation of the beauty of Truth.

These four divisions of immortal beings would be replicated on Earth during the Age of Truth as in former Golden Ages.

(1) The wise people occupy themselves in studying and spreading the knowledge of the Vedas and the consciousness of Truth. They are the Vipras on the Earth. They will represent the Ṛṣis in Heaven.
(2) The powerful fighters defeat the enemies, administer the Earth and maintain unity and peace on the Earth

through law and the order of Truth. Working under the instruction of the wise Vipras, they are Kṣatriyas on the Earth, who represent the Gods in heaven.

(3) The rich people are those who increase their wealth through trade and cultivation of fields. They maintain different types of animals and are involved in the collection of earthly metals and jewels. They are always under the protection of Kṣatriyas and use the treasury under the guidance of the wise Vipras. On Earth, they are called Vaiśyas, who represent the Yakṣas and Gandharvas of Heaven.

(4) The workers – engineers, artists, architects, labourers, cultivators etc. – work to develop the beauty of the Earth with the support of Vaiśyas, the protection of Kṣatriyas under the guidance of the Vipras. They represent the purity, love and beauty of truth. They are the Śūdras on the Earth and are like the Visvedevas of heaven.

All individuals remaining immortal will be unified during the Age of the Truth through their different activities. This will be the manifestation of heaven on Earth. Men will appear as Gods and as Supermen.

When one visualises the human society as a single human being, the wise Vipras will appear as the head or the brain, the Kṣatriyas as the arms, the Vaiśyas the trunk or thighs and the Śūdras as the feet. This body will then appear as a body full of supramental consciousness. This will be the manifested body of Satyadeva that will include all people. This will be the peace and truth as described in the Vedas. Nārāyaṇa Ṛṣi described his realisation of the Deva in these words:

ब्राह्मणोस्य मुखमासीद्बाहु राजन्यः कृतः ।
ऊरू तदस्य यद्वैष्यः पदभ्यां शूद्रो अजायत ॥

Yaj. XXXI .11

Brāhmanosya mukhamāsīdbāhū rājanyaḥ kṛtāh /
Ūrū tadasya yadvaiśyaḥ padbhyāṁ śūdro ajāyata //

Brahmans or wise Vipras are His face, powerful Kṣatriyas or Rajanyas the arms, rich Vaiśyas the thighs and the Workers, the Śūdras, the feet.

चन्द्रमा मनसो जातश्चक्षोः सूर्यो अजायत ।
श्रोत्राद्वायुश्च प्राणश्च मुखादग्निरजायत ॥

Yaj. XXXI.12

Candramā manaso jātaścakṣoḥ sūryo ajāyata /
Śrotrādvāyuśca prāṇaśca mukhādagnirajāyata //

The Moon is His mind, the Sun is the eyes, Indra and Agni devata the mouth and Vāyu, is the life force.

नाभ्याऽ आसीदन्तरिक्षꣳ शीर्ष्णो द्यौः समवर्तत ।
पदभ्यां भूमिर्दिशः श्रोत्रात्तथा लोकां २ अकल्पयन् ॥

Yaj. XXXI.13

Nābhyā' āsīdantarikṣaṁ śīrṣṇo dyauḥ samavartata /
Padabhyāṁ bhūmirdiśaḥ śrotrāttathā lokāṁ akalpayan //

The antarikṣa, the vital plane is the navel, dyauh, the heaven is His head, this land is His feet and the sky above is His ears. This is the meditation on Deva the Truth.

यज्ञेन यज्ञमयजन्त देवास्तानि धर्माणि प्रथमान्यासन् ।
ते ह नाकं महिमानः सचन्त यत्र पूर्वे साध्याः सन्ति देवाः ॥

Yaj. XXXI-16

Yajñena yajñamayajanta devāstāni dharmāṇi prathamānyāsan /
Te ha nākaṁ mahimānaḥ sacanta yatra pūrve sādhyāḥ santi devāh //

The Deva, who appeared through the sacrifice and from the sacrificial flame, is manifesting now on the Earth with the glory of Heaven. The devotees and sadhaks of Truth will see and realise Satyadeva before other human beings.

When Satyadeva descends on the Earth, we will see a united world, without any division. We will also observe the entire humanity leading a peaceful life. When Kali reigns then the world is broken up into many countries, parties, societies and religions. The knowledge that removes the Falsehood of Kali and brings back the Truth of Satyadeva, that is Devāyaṇa. The whole humanity is His body, their combined lives is His life. When He is visible to us all, then the Age is called the Satya Yuga or the Golden Age. This was also mentioned by Sri Aurobindo in his magnum opus "Savitri"

"And heaven shall grow native on mortal plane."

The manifestation of Devāyaṇa on the Earth, announces the commencement of the Golden Age. O humanity! Look at the Supreme Divine. Satyadeva, the Lord of Truth, has descended on this Earth. He is appearing gradually through the Devāyaṇa. Observe the path of immortality, realise the Truth and enter into the Golden Age.

DR. HAJARI

CONTENTS

1

REVELATION OF THE VEDAS

By the grace of the Supreme, I became conscious that the epic Devāyaṇa is the revelation of the Vedas. As if through a miracle, the Veda revealed itself in front of me with its own divine light and power. The letter *Akṣarabrahman*, that had disappeared from the earthly consciousness several thousand years ago, again appeared in front of me. I asked myself the reason for the revelation at this time. Promptly, the answer came that as the period of the manifestation of the Supreme Truth approaches; it is ready for the manifestation of "*Ṛtaṁ*" the Age of Truth. The Golden Age with all peace, joy and *ānanda* will pour its immortal bliss and purity on all of us. I will continue now on the discovery of the eternal secret.

I heard the great epic Devāyaṇa continuously for more than three years in the words of Piṅgala Maheśvara. These celestial words I have described in detail in the vast Epic Devāyaṇa. However, the revelation that flashed in front of me now made it clear that the manifestation of the Devāyaṇa is the magnificent reappearance of our lost Vedas. As I heard the greatest epic that would open a new age through the voice of Piṅgala Maheśvara, I felt that the Vedas had in reality manifested again.

Initially on hearing the sound of *OM*, the sound Brahman, which was coming from my navel, I entered into the sound of eternity and received the complete knowledge of humanity's past, present and future. In the same way, I became immersed in divine rapture on observing the astonishing shape of *Oṁkar*, ॐ, which was blazing as the symbol of the supreme soul.

Gazing at the incredible shape of the *Oṁkar*, I lost consciousness of my earthly existence and entered into another breathtaking plane. In front of me, I saw a wide, shoreless eternal ocean, resplendent with sunlight, pulsating, full of bliss with a singularly beautiful rhythm and a sweet melody that left me astonished and without words. I cannot say for how long I remained in that trance-like state. But, on hearing the following words, "O Seer! What are your questions?" I came back to myself. I saw the immortal Ṛṣis standing around me. Many questions came to my mind. I wondered how I came to the bank of that ocean and, moreover, what the nature of the ocean was. I could however not utter a single word from my mouth. The Ṛṣis, themselves, started answering my mental queries with a serene smile.

O Child of the Earth! You could be a seer now. Whatever you are seeing here is the one and only reality. You are seeing the Truth, the Vedas. We sang the mantras from the Veda Saṁhitas, which exist on the Earth; the mantras are there to prove the authenticity and purity of the spiritual experiences according to the ancient scriptures. These secret mantras can be known neither by reading nor by recitation, nor by analysis and translations; they can be known only through direct realisation and particularly by the revelation of the Vedas. This revelation comes rarely and then only when Truth is about to manifest on the Earth. It is only in the Golden Age that the Vedas reveal themselves.

Listen, my child. The Vedas are the Truth. They reveal themselves only in the Age of Truth. Piṅgala Maheśvara, the Lord of Time, spoke to you about Deva in the Devāyaṇa. In that Epic, the Truth has manifested, or in other words, the Vedas have revealed themselves. The Deva is Satyadeva. The Atharva Veda mentions,

य एतं देवमेकवृतं वेद

Ath.XIII.4.22

ya etam devameka vritam veda,

which means that there is a Deva existing throughout the Vedas. Now see for yourself the source of the Deva, His life, His character and activities as told by Piṅgala Maheśvara. The Vedas, "the water of letter", is visible as an Eternal Ocean. Above the Ocean, a powerful Sun is penetrating the Ocean with several thousand rays. The name of this Sun is Aditya. He appeared from the unmanifested eternity and established Himself in the *paramvyom*, the supreme Heaven. He is the Supreme Truth and was called, "*Rtaṁ*." He announced to us His Glory with this famous couplet,

अहमस्मि प्रथमजा ऋतस्य पूर्वं देवेभ्यो अमृतस्य नाम ।
यो मा ददाति स इदेवमावदहमन्नमन्नमदन्तमद्मि ॥

Sām. 594

Ahamasmi prathamajā ṛtasya pūrvaṁ devebhyo
amṛtasya nāma /
Yo mā dadāti sa
idevamāvadahamannamannamadantamadmi //

I am the Truth. I came into existence, even before the birth of Gods. The Ṛṣis called me Ṛta and gave me the name Amṛta. Truth appeared in the very beginning. The ocean is the Aditi-Sindhu, but different sages have called it Bliss-Sindhu, Kśīr-Sagara, Brahma-Sindhu etc. In the centre of the Aditi-Sindhu, you can see the eternal beautiful creation not visible before. This is the highest Heaven, the Supramental Plane. All the Gods – Indra, Candra, Sūrya, Bṛhaspati, Agni, Vāyu and Mitra-Varuṇa have their own palaces where they were born, where they grew up and where they live. From that plane, they influence creations that worship the Truth, the *Ṛta*, who exists above them. With the identification of the Truth, they achieve immortality. They drove out the Asuras with the power of

Truth. Both the Gods and the Asuras existed in the same plane in the beginning.

The Earth saw that the Supreme Heaven had identified itself with the Truth. Entering into immortality, the Gods aspired for the supramental and achieved it with Truth. This is the ancient history of the world. The Yajur Veda said:

परो दिवा परऽ एना पृथिव्या परो देवेभिरसुरैर्यदस्ति ।
कं स्विद गर्भं प्रथमं दध्र ऽ आपो यत्र देवाः समपश्यन्त पूर्वे ॥

Yaj. XVII-29

Paro divā para' enā pṛthivyā paro
devebhirasurairyadasti /
Kaṁ svid garbhaṁ prathamaṁ dadhra' āpo yatra
devāḥ sampaśyanta pūrve //

The supreme Heaven is the supramental plane and this is the mortal Earth. In the supreme Heaven, the Gods and Asuras were living together before a power struggle arose. To settle that conflict, the Asuras used the immense power at their command. The Gods sought the assistance of Satyadeva. He appeared before them and conquered Heaven for the Gods. When Earth came to know about it, she worshipped Heaven with the Truth to become supramentalised.

Look at the immortal Heaven, the supramental plane, enlightened with the light of Truth. It is full of melodious music, divine rhythm and bliss. The homes of the enlightened Gods are beautifully ornamented with gold and jewels. Each palace is adorned with various types of jewels to worship the glory of the individual God. The Gods constantly remain with the beauty of their immortal golden body, immense powers, glorious riches and their ever-peaceful smiling faces. The Goddesses always remain youthful with their beauty and softness, ornamented with gold and various jewels. They bloom with a divine splendour, playing in their spiritual garden, walking, singing and dancing. Look at the Heaven, at the beautiful play of love, which is constant and incessant.

Gods and Goddesses are beyond fatigue, need no sleep and suffer neither from pain nor sorrow nor grief. Death or diseases do not exist there. With the power of Truth, they remain in a state of constant and divine joy, vibrating with bliss. In Heaven, all the riches, beauty, light and love are under the power and the influence of Truth. They have achieved the highest status in the creation and for this they were called Deva. Surrounding the Heaven, there is an ocean, the Bliss-Sindhu, the Eternal Ocean, radiating light, power, peace, love and purity. With joy, bliss and unity, the rhythm of songs and dances has become melodious. Above in Heaven and in the eternal plane, Truth glows with its power, light, consciousness and bliss, showering the Heaven and Ocean and becoming united to protect them from hostile attacks of negative forces. At times, Truth descends into Heaven to play with Gods. Know that the Truth, Heaven and Bliss-Sindhu, the Ocean are combinedly the Vedas. Realise that the Vedas are eternal and they have no author. They are the self-manifested supreme knowledge of the Ultimate Truth.

With mounting astonishment I saw the creation of the word, ॐ, which is at the root of all creations and the reason for the creation of the Divine Mother Aditi. I was blessed with immortal bliss. The Gods and Ṛṣis, the Seers of the Vedas, the Poet Kavi, Singer of the Vedas, gave me an equal status with them. I felt overjoyed and overwhelmed.

Then the Ṛṣis said, "O Child of Earth! You have seen the Truth! Do not become overwhelmed with divine joy and bliss. Free yourself from this." My heart was troubled due to the pain and sorrows of the Earth. I was seeking Truth to alleviate the pain and sorrows of Earth. This had been my wish in the road to spirituality and my only desire since birth. The Ṛṣis read my innermost thoughts and told me to forget my worries. They also had the same aspiration. In the past, they had also sought peace for the Earth. Their aspiration led them to the Truth and they became Seers. With these words of the Ṛṣis, I gained confidence.

They continued – When the Earth suffered under the influence of the hostile forces, a few men felt her pain and sorrows. They tried to search for a solution. If the moment for the manifestation of Truth had arrived, they received the message of Truth for the Earth. At other times, the questions disappeared and became absorbed in the plane of Truth. Listen, O Child of Earth! If you become mute after seeing this vision of Truth, or you feel anxious about the conditions on the Earth, then you have to undertake some measures to prepare the ground. The time for the manifestation of Truth has come. It is very near. Listen to the inner voice of Time.

The Vedas comprising the Satyadeva with all other Gods and the complete Heaven will manifest now on the Earth. I asked the Ṛṣis how was that possible as the Vedas were already present on the Earth. How would they again manifest? They replied that the Veda Samhita presently existing in the world is merely a scripture. The Eternal Vedas that are needed for the realisation of the Truth and the efforts that mankind has to make for immortality are not present. Even though, the Vedas exist in the form of a scripture and mantras, the secret knowledge of the Vedas has vanished from the human mind. Now the time has come, when truth will become apparent to all. The period of revelation has arrived. The revelation of the Vedas means that Satyadeva with His supreme light and consciousness, the Gods with their immortal beauty and their play of love and bliss will again manifest on the Earth. Earth will become transformed into Heaven. The Gods will take residence in human beings and men's body will become similar to those of the Gods. There will be no disease, pain, sorrow and death. Mankind will live in eternal bliss.

2

VOICE OF THE ṚṢIS

I was delighted to hear this message from the Ṛṣis. I became disturbed as I worried about the effects of the immortal touch of Truth on this Earth, which was reeling under the unbearable burden of pain, sorrows, diseases and death. I wondered how the Earth could be liberated from the iron grip of attachment, māyā, consisting of ignorance and falsehood. I was concerned about how the Earth could receive the knowledge of immortality in her present state. The Seers read my innermost thoughts and dispelled my worries.

Look at the high Heaven, O Child of Earth! Deva, together with other immortal Gods and Ṛṣis is living on Akṣrapa, the Ocean of the Vedas. There, the creation of letters is absorbed in the Supreme Will. That is the eternal spiritual plane where the enlightened souls remain ablaze like stars. Look below on the Earth where the same immortal souls descend from Heaven, receive a physical form and take birth on Earth but come completely under the power and influence of great Time, Mahākāla. On taking a human birth, they lose their clear vision and consider themselves mortal. They undergo pain, diseases and suffering. They cry and appeal to the Gods to be liberated from their sorrows and look for peace and rest. Think of the pitiful condition of these beings! They are immortal, but are constantly shivering from fear of diseases and death. Total ignorance has enveloped their immortal soul through the power of attachment. They have even forgotten that they are immortal.

Then, look at the supreme Heaven, the supramental plane, where souls remain immortal, immune, enlightened and replete with never-ending joy. On Earth, the same souls suffer from maladies, pains and sorrows. Fear of death is hovering constantly over them. This terrible condition of humanity is mainly due to their wrong way of thinking. In former Ages, advanced souls like the Sages, Saints and Mahātmās knew this secret; they communicated it to some of their close disciples. With tapasya and austerities, they were liberated from ignorance and became aware of their immortality. They achieved fulfilment in their lives. However, these realised souls were few in number. As sages and great men, they influenced limited areas of the world and gave their teachings to a few. The remaining population was under the evil influence of the ruler of the Iron Age, Kali. In this Age, every being is defeated at the moment of death while taking the last breath. Time remains the most important factor. Time makes the Sun rise. Birth and death are all ruled by Time. All works are accomplished in Time. Thus, Time is all-powerful. No embodied being, not even the Avatars, can transcend Time.

In eternity, Time has two aspects, one that is auspicious and the other that is inauspicious. The auspicious time opens the path of Truth starting the journey of the Gods towards mortality. This is called Devāyaṇa. In contrast, the inauspicious time opens the road to darkness and falsehood. It leads mankind to diseases, suffering and death and the creation becomes mortal, governed by birth and death, as at present. This is called Pitṛyana.

When Mahākāla Śiva leads this creation towards destruction, he takes the form of Rudra Maheśvara. In the destructive phase of the cyclic movement of time, Kali expands the area under his dominance right from the Silver, through the Bronze to the Iron Age. In the present Age, Kali's reign is supreme. When Mahākāla Śiva wishes to take this Earth towards a new creation, he takes the form of Piṅgala Maheśvara. In the new creative and cyclic movement, Satyadeva acts to bring the Iron Age to an end and opens the golden door of the Age of Truth. That is Devāyaṇa. This secret of auspicious time was announced by Prajāpati in the following words:

Yajurveda says,

> ये देवा देवेष्वधि देवत्वमायन् ये ब्रह्मणः पुरऽएतारो अस्य ।
> येभ्यो न ऽ ऋते पवते धाम किञ्चन न ते दिवो न पृथिव्या ऽ
> अधि स्नुषु ॥
>
> Yaj. XVII.14
>
> *Ye devā deveṣvadhi devatvamāyan ye brahmaṇaḥ pura' etāro asya /*
> *Yebhyo na'ṛte pavate dhāma kiñcana na te divo na pṛthivyā' adhi snuṣu //*

The Brahman wills that the Earthly creation, charmed by Māyā, achieve liberation from it and guides mankind to enter into divinity, so that the Earth becomes like Heaven and is enlightened. That is why we always pray for the Advent of Satyadeva and other Gods so that we may become purified.

This is the Supreme Will. For its fulfilment, there is a determined moment when Satyadeva, descends upon the Earth, with other Gods to remove ignorance, diseases and death prevalent here. These will then be replaced by immunity and immortality through His power, light, purity and consciousness. The Earth is destined to become immortal. There is absolutely no doubt that the Earth will be liberated from pain, suffering, diseases and death. No power can stop it. Earth will also imbibe nectar as Heaven.

Kali, the notorious Time, received the boon of suzerainty over humanity for a limited time period, through his penance and intense meditation. He became the leader of the creation. Soon afterwords, he started to effect his nefarious plans. The Brahman then experienced the pain that Kali would bring to the Earth. Poverty would become widely prevalent and the Earth would undergo manifold pains and sufferings. A Thought and a Will arose from Him to free the Earth from the grip of

Kali. To fulfil that Supreme Will, Satyadeva, together with the other Gods will manifest again upon the Earth to remove the Earth's suffering. This is inevitable and no power can hinder it. This is the indomitable and inevitable advent of Truth.

To welcome Satyadeva, the Earth will have to purify and prepare herself to be able to sing a welcoming ode. When the people of the Earth realise this fact, they will prepare themselves and become ready to receive the Truth. At present, the Earth is covered with the deepest darkness of Kali, the root cause of all suffering. Everyone has to realise that Kali will be forced to withdraw from this creation when confronted with the indomitable advent of Truth. The long-awaited moment has come when mankind will be liberated from the clutches of Kali. Your task, O Child of Earth, is to ensure that men prepare themselves to realise the Truth. That is the only aim and fulfilment of human life. Humanity will then experience immortality, peace and Heavenly bliss. Without Truth, nothing is of any value. Truth is the ultimate treasure and source of all fulfilment.

Kali holds sway over humanity through man's ignorance, selfishness, pride, desire for fame and honour. A determined will and an aspiration to be identified with the divine are important to be rid of these dark forces. Let everyone become aware of this. O humanity! The advent of Truth is inevitable. Prepare yourself to receive the Truth. Make a determined attempt to be free from the grip of Kali. Be ready to welcome Deva, the Lord of the Golden Age and to reject Kali, the Lord of the Iron Age. The Deva will appear at a pre-determined time. If you are not ready when the Truth manifests then you will face destruction and fall into the abyss together with Falsehood. Reject materialism, which teaches you to neglect the soul. This is your task. The rest will be done by Satyadeva and the other Gods. This will be a great help to the divine.

In Heaven, the spiritual world, the delightful *akṣaras* or souls are absorbed in true bliss, while this world is mired in ignorance, pains and sufferings caused by materialism.

Between these two planes, there is the mental world that spreads its light on both sides as far as it can. On one end it goes from the level of the individual to the highest superconscient and on the other end it goes from the individual to the deepest subconscient. This is the basis of all our reflections, thoughts or manifestations, good or bad, divine or undivine. It is very important that human beings select their thoughts. They have to make a choice. Do they wish for Truth or Falsehood, Deva or Kali, Divine or Antidivine? That is the only task in front of mankind. As they decide for either the divine or the antidivine, the positive or the negative powers will become active in them. Their decision, be it for positive or negative thoughts, will determine their level of consciousness. When they are aware of the choice in front of them, they will be able to make the right decision.

3

THE STATUS OF MIND

We know the mind with its thoughts and judgements. It receives ideas from unknown sources and acts mechanically on it. These are known as thoughts. One part of the mind reaches above to the infinite from where we receive higher thoughts. This part encourages discoveries of certain secrets in the ever-changing strange world or leads us to enter into divine bliss.

The other part of the mind reaches far below to the inconscient or the subconscient. From there, we receive devilish thoughts concerning vital desires, or lewd, dirty, nasty thoughts that lead to the destruction of divine purity and immunity. Observe the extremely wide range of thoughts at the command of the mind from the highest to the lowest. The individual decides which thoughts to choose and which to reject. These individual thoughts are always influenced by Time. This is the reason why birth, death and other actions are guided by Time. Individual thoughts are under the control of Time, which then decides whether one should or should not do certain actions. During the Iron Age, the vital thoughts become harmful and dangerous. This results in mankind taking wrong decisions at crucial times of human history, leading to catastrophic events and resulting in mass destruction and an extremely negative frame of mind.

In the Iron Age, Kali, the Lord of Darkness, acts on individual beings through negative and dangerous ideas and concepts. He unleashes powerful negative forces like desire, anger, envy, greed etc. that make a person prey to diseases and death. Human life degenerates into depression and pains. It becomes full of sorrows, resulting in a completely troubled condition. When Satyadeva guides ideas and thoughts, then His light, power, love, purity and consciousness lead us into a life full of joy, immunity and immortality. We have a divinised life; an everlasting youth with divine beauty, strength and power. Life on Earth becomes joyful and peaceful.

This is the secret that we wish to disclose now. In each mind, through individual thoughts – birth, death and diseases build their base to work on the human beings to satisfy their hunger and thirst. If the individual being becomes conscious about the dark forces and closes his mind to such ideas, then the earthly forces will not be able to lead him to destruction. That human being will be completely protected. Additionally, if the individual becomes increasingly conscious about the divine light and truth and opens his mind to such ideas, then Truth with its immortal purity will act in the sensorium and his thoughts would lead to meditation for the Truth.

Your task is to universalise this secret message in the human society. Tell humanity that there is neither birth nor death. Sickness, sorrows, pain, grief, repentance should not be allowed to have a negative impact on a human being. Everyone should ensure that these forces do not enter into them. One should recognise these forces (desire, anger, greed etc.) for what they are and declare to them, – "O life torturing enemies – leave me immediately. I am the son of immortality; I am the sparkle of Truth." At the same time, mankind should concentrate on Satyadeva, surrounded by the other Godheads (eternal source of peace, joy, divine beauty, bliss and youth), the giver of immortality and immunity. To escape the iron grip of Kali or to remove his dark influence on yourself, chant loudly with determination,

> O Deva! Thou art the Truth. Thou art the immortality and giver of immortality and immunity. O Deva! Adored by all, the ever beautiful, pure Deva! Thou art in the heart, Thou

art in the mind, Thou art in the Heaven and Thou
art in the Sun with your eternal light.

The Yajur Veda says the same in the following mantra:

हृदे त्वा मनसे त्वा दिवे त्वा सूर्याय त्वा ।

Yaj.VI.25, XXXVII.19

Hṛde tvā manase tvā dive tvā sūryāya tvā /

Concentrate your mind on this mantra.

Repeat constantly the mantra *Ahaṁ-Ṛtaṁ*. This is the mantra that contains the essence of the eternal consciousness, light, peace and power, just as a seed contains a big tree in its tiny form. This is the seed mantra for the Golden Age. The seed mantra for the Silver Age was *Hari, Hare-Rāma* for the Bronze Age and *Hare Rāma, Hare Kṛṣṇa* for the Iron Age. To enter into the Age of Truth, we have *Ahaṁ-Ṛtaṁ* as the seed mantra for the approaching new Age, the Age of Immortality. Let us explain the seed mantra and its formation. As the Sāmaveda says,

अहमस्मि प्रथमजा ऋतस्य पूर्वं देवेभ्यो अमृतस्य नाम ।
यो मा ददाति स इदेवमावदहमन्नमन्नमदन्तमद्मि ॥

Sām.594

Ahamasmi prathamajā ṛtasya pūrvaṁ devebhyo amṛtasya nāma /
Yo mā dadāti sa idevamāvadahamannamannamadantamadmi //

This mantra means – I am the Truth, born in the very beginning, before all creations, even before the birth of Gods and my name is Amṛta. In the short form, this mantra is *Ahaṁ-Ṛtaṁ*, (I am the Truth). When this mantra is repeated as a *japa* the *Ahaṁ-Ṛtaṁ* will turn into *Amṛta,* the heavenly nectar. Even in our thoughts, slowly the I, the ego, will dissolve and then only *Ṛtaṁ* will remain. With this mantra, individuals will reach the immortality in each being and life will be transformed into divinity. In this way, truth will have a direct influence on the individual being. That will be the advent of truth in life. Through this mantra, the Earth will escape the control of Kali and enter into Truth. Then life will become replete with Truth and it will become the life divine. This is the only way for an individual being to enter into truth or divinity.

"The creator of this mantra is Prajāpati himself, the rhythm is Gāyātri, tune is Sharaja and the God is Satyadeva. Let the Earth become full of Truth and Divinity with this chant."

I heard these words with amazement. The mantra *Ahaṁ-Ṛtaṁ* echoed in my ears. This is the mantra to banish Kali and to enter into Truth. *Ahaṁ-Ṛtaṁ* is the mantra, the Deva is Satyadeva, the Ṛṣi is Prajāpati, the chanda is Gāyātri, the svara-Sharaja all this increased my astonishment.

The Ṛṣis began again: Why are you so amazed? Leave your doubts, O Child, remain pure and hear,

मन्त्रे तीर्थे द्विजे देवे दैवज्ञे भेषजे गुरौ ।
यादृशि भावना यस्य सिद्धिर्भवति तादृशि ॥

Mantre tīrthe dvije deve daivajñe bheṣaje gurau /
Yādṛśi bhāvanā yasya siddhirbhavati tādṛśī //

This means that one is as one thinks. The "I" is always present in everyone. We hear often people saying that I am sad, I am sick, I am unhappy, I am poor, I am helpless; my birth, my death, and my life are full of suffering. Others say, I am happy, I am strong, I am healthy, I am rich and then in course of time, my fate changes and then I have to suffer. That is why in everybody, this "I" is how each person views this world. This "I" when influenced by Kali forgets its own reality and accepts that he was born to suffer and to die. This is the ego that conceives and preserves birth and death, diseases and sufferings. When "I" unites with Ṛta, the false formation of ego dissolves and it turns into truth. When this "I" enters into the Truth consciousness, then there is neither birth nor death. Diseases and sorrows do not affect the "I". Then we say I am alive in eternal bliss – *ānanda*. I am immune and immortal. In short, when the "I" becomes identified with *Ṛta*, the Truth, then the individual achieves immortality.

Thus when the ego is liberated from the false formative ego by the touch of Truth, it becomes pure, joyful and peaceful. Allow *Ṛta*, Truth to touch each breath, each movement of blood, each thought where the slight indication of "I" remains. Let it constantly be dissolved and divinised. Let Truth touch actions in the various organs, such as the sight, the hearing, the smell, the speech, the touch, the power to walk, to eat, and to pass the faecal, the semen and urine. For all these movements when Ṛta is remembered in place of ego, these become immortal. He who is Ṛta was called Amṛta by the Ṛṣis of yore. Experience Ṛta and enter into immortality. For this, we tell you to chant "*Ahaṁ Ṛtaṁ*" as a constant japa for realising the immortal or divine life. Now we will tell you more about meditation on the Deva Immortal.

4

MEDITATION ON DEVA, THE TRUTH

As the Vedas – Yajur, Sāma and Atharva – say: The Deva who is Agni-netra, meaning whose eyes are like fire, powerful and ablaze, let Him stand in front of me. The Deva who is Yama-netra, meaning whose eyes demonstrate constant determination and are full of power, let Him stand on my right side. The Deva who is Viśvedeva-netra, meaning whose eyes contain the world, the Gods and the creation, let Him stand behind me. The Deva who is Mitra and Varuṇ-netra, meaning whose eyes show unity, peace, harmony and unique power, let Him stand on my left side. The Deva who is Soma-netra, meaning whose eyes are full of grace, compassion and sweetness of heart, let Him stand above my head.

The Deva was born in the family of Aṅgirās Abhivarta. He held the Kālacakra, the Wheel of Time, to maintain immortality in the creation. He is absolutely pure, is surrounded by a dazzling light and is ablaze like the Sun. I meditate on Him.

He is the power of light in the Sun, the all-conquering power in Indra, the power of moulding in Agni, and the intelligent will power in Bṛhaspati; on that Deva I meditate.

The Deva who is eternally identified with the all revered Hari; to Him I offer my adoration. As Hari stands in front of Him, let Hari appear by clasping Vajrābahu who was born in the family of Purandara in his self-sacrifice. I meditate on Him.

Through the help of the Deva, all Gods had achieved immortality, grown up into their divinity and achieved their fulfilment. For that reason, all Gods pray for his constant presence and aspire that his purity increases and spreads everywhere. They wish to be strengthened through his power and riches. On that Deva, I meditate.

O Lord of the World! O Lord of the Mind of the World! O Lord of the Word of the World! O Lord of the Words of the World! Bless us with true hearing, establish into us the religion of Truth and give us the capacity to identify with the Truth. Let our food and drink be pure and divine by which we may always eat divine food. Let the aspiration of our heart burn as the fire of Vitihotra, let it be identified with the Truth; by which we can enter into immortality and immunity. Let the whole Earth be covered by His purity and sweetness. On Him I meditate.

Above the Earth, beauty, peace and bliss exist in a triangular room. In that fully enlightened powerful and purest home, Lord Viṣṇu drinks *soma* (nectar). All our actions, our thoughts and all that we do on Earth, go to the Supreme Palace, where Deva, who is the Truth and Consciousness, exists. O Indu! We call him Deva-Satya or Satyadeva. O Indra! He is the Supreme Truth. I meditate on Him. Just as Indra and Indu devata have seen the Satyadeva and entered into immortality, so I meditate on Satyadeva to take us from diseases to immunity and from mortality to immortality.

Look at the most beautiful creation blazing like the Sun. Therein you can see the still greater Sun shining in all its glory. That is the purest light of the Supreme Truth, showering blessings on this creation. Through these all the hostile forces will be removed and destroyed. That light and power of Truth, was called "*Mahas*", the Supramental. I meditate on him.

Like the eternal Sun, the Vedas (the supreme knowledge) exist eternally. Therein Deva is supreme himself. Light and Darkness, Truth and Falsehood, Divine and Undivine, appear with the movement of the Veda-Sūrya (Sun). This is called the Mahān Ayana. When the Sun (*Veda-Sūrya*) is in front of the creation for immortality, bliss and peace; and Deva the Truth is there as "The *Vibhu*", then the Divine Supreme manifests himself with an aurora of beautiful light. The Supramental manifests.

When this Earth identifies itself with the Truth, at that moment humanity achieves a divine beauty. They receive beautiful bodies like Gods, they hear the voice of Truth and experience Truth directly and liberate themselves from all falsehood. They talk sweetly with each other. That is the manifested Golden Age on the Earth.

The entire Heaven with Satyadeva is ready to manifest upon this Earth. Aspire, O Earth, as Truth is ready to manifest upon you with the eternal divine creation. Pray for the Vedas, which have been revealed before you.

O Deva, Thou hast manifested before, appear again in all Thy Glory. Hold the Kālacakra, the Wheel of Time and guide us with your unique power. Appear with Thy purity, power, light and love, where lives are under constant attacks of the hostile powers.

O Deva! Thou art ablaze with power like the Sun. Thou art Soma Devata radiating pure love like the Moon. O Truth! In this Earth, protect Thy home, Vaṅga with Thy purest powerful light.

O Deva! O Truth! Manifest with great delight. Thou art Soma Devata, Giver of Immortality. We worship Thee to realise riches and beauty for the whole humanity and to be liberated from all bondages to enter into a new consciousness.

O Deva! Guard us with your golden protection. Thou art Soma Devata, Lord of the Divine Nectar! Remain in immortality. Thou art Varuṇa, the Honourable! Lead us to divine victory. Descend, O Deva, on this Earth to immerse all mankind in eternal bliss.

There is only the one Deva who exists in all the Vedas. In front of the manifested Vedas, bow down and utter these words of peace and repose.

"O Vedas, you are the source of supreme knowledge, bring peace and respite in this peaceless and troubled world. Enlighten us with eternal knowledge. Like an axe, cut and destroy all ignorance and stupidity. Establish in us the knowledge of Truth and provide us with a haven of peace."

5

MODERN AND ANCIENT CIVILIZATION

As I heard the prayer and meditation of the Ṛṣis for the Vedas and for the Deva, one question still remained in my mind. That was the burning question how the Vedas and Deva would manifest upon this Earth. I could not conceive even in my wildest imaginations how the Earth would become divinised.

The Ṛṣis understood my query without a single word being uttered. They continued, O Child of Earth! You wish to know the way. The Truth that you have seen is the manifestation of the Deva during the auspicious time to guide this creation towards immortality. How the Deva will manifest, remains hidden from us all. When the time comes, the Deva will be visible upon the darkest Earth to enlighten it with His Truth, Light and Consciousness. How will the Earth be able to bear the Deva's presence, His Purity, Light and Power if it is a sudden advent with a rapid transformation? The knowledge, the sincerity required for preparing the Earth, to bear the presence or advent of Truth, has to be taken care of now. Work for the preparedness of the Earth at the present time. If the Earth is unprepared and the Truth descends here with its uncompromising heroic power and purity to defeat the hostile powers, then she will be shattered into pieces.

Look at the Eternal Heaven, where the Deva reigns supreme. How will the Earth be able to bear the pressure of Truth, when humanity is under the complete control of the dark powers of Kali? In the case of such a sudden advent, beings controlled by the devilish forces will be crushed just as Hirṇyakaśipu was destroyed by the appearance of Narasiṁha Hari. Preparation of the Earth is important. Manifestation requires faithful devotees and sincere followers, particularly those who have committed their lives completely to Deva, just like Prahlāda. These sincere faithful beings will become the base for the advent of Truth. They will be the standard bearers of Truth in the world and be its desireless, fearless instruments. They will be the foundation stone for the Age of Truth, the Golden Age. On this foundation will then be constructed the victorious palace of Truth with the ultimate divine victory. At that moment, the Manifested Truth will become visible to the common people.

Which fortunate place on the Earth has been chosen to serve as the base for the Advent of Truth? As this query arose in my mind, the Ṛṣis told me, O Child of Earth! Look towards the East. Every morning, the Sun rises in the East and sets in the West, followed by dusk and then the dark night. Next morning, the Sun rises again in the East. This is the natural rhythm of day and night. Together with the movement of the seasons, we call it Ṛtāyana. In the same way in an aeon, there comes Deva and Kali, its opposite in the creation as the divine day and night, which we call Devāyaṇa. During the course of the Devāyaṇa, the Golden Age, the Divine Day of Truth dawns from the East. From there Truth scatters its rays throughout the creation. For this reason, the Age of Truth starts from the East and ends when it reaches the West. The Day of Truth will manifest when the divine civilization will be amongst us.

With this descent, we will have the knowledge of the soul, the secret knowledge of Gods, the Heaven and Truth. This would be based on the knowledge of Brahman. Humanity will be without diseases and death, relieved from pain, sorrows and depressions, as well as repentance and grief. Men will live like Gods on the Earth. Life would be always full of joy, with unalloyed peace in the heart, without fear. Men would be direct, straightforward, faithful to Gods, sincere, modest, radiating joy on their faces, with love and mercy in their eyes, hearing a divine melody in their ears. They would eat food, thinking of the divine through which every morsel would taste like nectar. Through the divinisation of the Earth, humanity would have a life full of constant pleasure, with a pleasant smell in the nose and a delicious taste on the tongue. They will hold conversations full of love, experiencing a constant touch of pleasure on the skin. Everything will be accomplished with divine pleasure – working with the hands, walking with legs, eating to nourish the Gods and maintaining purity of body through cleaning the body, approaching the spouse for a child to fulfil the Will of the Brahman, without desire, greed and ego and thus achieve the purest, most magnificent divine life. Peace would reign everywhere. In the Day of the Truth, the divine civilization would manifest which is in reality the ancient civilization. This civilization would bring a divine race on the Earth, which is the manifestation of the Golden Age. When the Divine Will influences humanity, then nationality will vanish from the Earth and it will be the period of the divine dawn upon the Earth.

Furthermore, when the human ego dissolves, Gods would guide all our senses. The false ego would be replaced by the Truth. A true individual "I" would remain for accomplishing the works of Gods resulting in a life dedicated for the Truth. Every action will be done for the Truth and the Gods will be the main actors. Sūrya for the eye sight, Candra for the mind, Vāyu for life energy, Agni for the tongue and to take food, Rudra for the hearing, Vanaspati for the touch, Mitra-Varuṇa for the unity and harmony of life, Bṛhaspati for the intellect, Viṣṇu for maintaining longevity, Aśvinīs for clearing the body by eliminating the waste materials and increasing beauty, Brahmā for creating progeny, and Dharma-Yama for the departure of the soul from the body. Indra with other Godheads would organise the body according to the divine rules, to maintain the work of Gods and to protect it from all opposition. Identified with his eternal friend, Hari, Lord Indra would establish the Kingdom of Truth and provide divine law and order and establish the divine nationality upon the Earth. These are the Godheads who are active in different organs of each human being. For example, when Sūrya is active in the eyes of an individual, He is also active in the eyes of each and every being. Similarly, all the other organs will be guided by the other Godheads universally.

When this mortal life is guided by Deva, the Lord of Truth, various Gods in different parts of the body become active and human life would be divinised. In this way, the present functioning of the body would then be transformed. Life that was guided so far by the mental ego would then be under the control of the Supramental Godheads and thus be supramentalised.

As people start coming under the influence and guidance of Deva the Truth, they will be called the divine or supramentalised race. Such people will continue to increase in number among the common people. When humanity came under the influence of the vital plane during evolution and existed in the vital world, some people achieved intellectual greatness. Similarly at this time, there will develop a beautiful race of divinised intellect, having the divine greatness of a superman. But this divine greatness will not remain forever. Human beings existed like animals in the world until now. In the course of evolution, when the human figure was finalised, Gods approved of it and chose it as a beautiful instrument for their manifestation. Then evolution came to a standstill.

The divinisation of the human being comes through the ayana, by the movement of the aeon. This period is the Supramental or the Golden Age. Also known as the Satya or the Deva Yuga. During this period, man becomes a divine man or superman. And the Earth becomes like the immortal Heaven. That is the manifested day of Truth, a beautiful play of Gods with purity reigning all around. Life is then united, peaceful, joyful and full of heavenly riches. This continues for approximately ten thousand years.

The Ṛgveda says,

शतमिन्नु शरदो अन्ति देवा यत्रा नश्चक्रा जरसं तनूनाम ।
पुत्रासो यत्र पितरो भवन्ति मा नो मध्या रीरिषतायुर्गन्तोः ॥

Ṛg.I.89.9, Yaj.XXV.22

Śatminnu śarado anti devā yatrā naścakrā jarasaṁ tanūnām I
Putrāso yatra pitaro bhavanti mā no madhyā rīriṣatāyurgantoḥ II

This means that the Deva will exist in this earthly creation for a hundred times hundred autumns that is ten thousand years. During this period there will be no diseases and old age in the body, thus it will remain ever young. Fathers will remain like their young sons; there will be no old age until the end of the aeon comes to this creation.

On the last day of the Truth, that means at the end of the Golden Age, the activities of the Gods, the presence of Truth or Brahman, the knowledge of the soul with the divine civilization and the Vedas will disappear in the fore-ordained way. The divine race then will withdraw back to Heaven. Then the dark influence of Kali will become evident in the course of the ayana, on the eve of this creation. Day by day, the sense of belonging to the divine race will vanish and the feeling of a human nationality will increase with a plethora of humanitarian activities. In the course of time, a shade of darkness appears from the West to cover the Earth with the sense of individuality and undiluted egoism. Humanity suffers again from birth, death and diseases. This peaceless divided consciousness spreads as the dark night over this creation. Human civilization splinters into many, resulting in the formation of numerous nations, several religions and innumerable languages with an unbelievable increase in individual egoism. Thus in the human civilization, self-knowledge will be on the basis of the body and vital consciousness, without any knowledge of soul. Men will search for fulfilment in this life, instead of concentrating on divine activities and looking for Heaven, through analytical discussions of nature and natural elements. This will be done primarily for vital pleasure and the satisfaction of an egoistic sense of pride through scientific research. They will decide that immunity from diseases, immortality, Gods and Heaven are all the creation of a poetic fantasy, which do not have any solid foundation.

In this stage, humanity remains distant from divine *ānanda*, peace and light, due to their egoistic pride. The motto of each person is to maintain a healthy body, enjoy life and live on the Earth as long as possible. This is a false delusion. It results in men having argumentative natures, who are always afraid of death and diseases. Such a society remains without unity or harmony and is full of discord, diseases and sufferings. Men remain continuously unhappy. They feel that they are missing out if they do not experience everything in the world, while nursing fear and restlessness in their hearts. They treat each other very roughly, have no good words for each other and have unaccountable desires, with unsurmountable pride and selfishness. Thus, they become full of desires and greed, remain faithless to Gods, become worshippers of falsehood and live with an unknown fear that makes them feel helpless.

They feel that enemies surround them everywhere. For this, they invent weapons that can kill at a distance. They become passionate, proud and arrogant in nature. These beings wear a cruel smile on their faces, having no love and affection for others. Their talk is dry and rude, with their ears always ready to hear the vilification of others. They feel perennially unsatisfied, eat food without any taste and have a bad smell in their nose. This makes them feel tired. In addition, they become very sensitive in their nature, with zero tolerance. Their bodies become hypersensitive to cold and heat as climate changes and they find life a constant burden.

This results in human beings suffering from an egoistic pride, desire and anger, who nourish their greed through eating different types of foods which should not be eaten, resulting in an impurity of being, with unclear bowels, bladder and secretive glands. This gives rise to various diseases and creates the fear of death in them. To satisfy their passion, they give birth to children. Human life in this modern civilization makes man believe that he, himself, is the Lord of the Universe, however, with the realisation that he has no control on birth, death and on love in marriage.

Towards the end of the Kaliyuga or the Iron Age, the modern Western Civilization increasingly influences the East. It is as if the deep dark night covers the daylight of the East. Kaliyuga is figuratively like the deep dark night upon the Earth furthering a divided consciousness. In the divine civilization, the "I" comprises the Truth and Gods who are active, conversely in the modern civilization, a false "I" becomes active in the senses which are ego-based with the Ṛpus (desire, greed, anger, etc.) controlling them. These are manifold results of Kaliyuga as the spiritual night upon Earth. Work is undertaken only to achieve pleasure for the self. This also forms a basis for efforts that are good for the human civilization and are in the name of humanity. Men become blind due to selfishness. They work for their own pleasure, are proud and egoistic and are engaged perenially in their own enjoyment that can lead them even into insanity. This forms the basis for the modern civilization, resulting in unending pain and sorrows. This is the dark time that signals the beginning of Kali, in the human civilization. This starts from the West, spreading finally to the East.

This period can be divided into three phases. In the Silver Age, with the touch of Kali on the enlightened human race, the Vedas and Deva disappear into the vast Heaven. The Rṣis make a concerted effort to retain the Truth and the Vedas and maintain the connection between the Earth and Heaven. Subsequently, the Gods and the Ṛṣis withdraw themselves gradually from the Earth. At the same time, in other parts of the world, desire and greed become very powerful. This results in a spiritual darkness covering a portion of the world.

The second period, the Bronze Age, is when attempts made for sacrifice and spiritual austerity vanish and individual efforts to this end constantly decrease. The Vipras are doing self-sacrifice by burning the fire with their own efforts to retain a link with Gods and Heavens. Truth and the Vedas remain distant from them. At that time, sacrificial offerings are made to Gods through Agni (the Fire). Efforts are made by mankind to enter into Heaven with the help of Agni. During this period, spiritual darkness covers half of the world. Jealousy and anger together with desire and greed become very powerful and Gods and Heaven remain distant from humanity. We call this the Bronze Age, when there is no possibility of immortal life.

The third period arrives when the creation is totally covered with darkness. This is the Iron Age or Kaliyuga. This Age also could be divided in three.

The first part is when the one united Earth is splintered into many countries and states, with many languages, races and religions. There is the formation of a separate character for each country, language, race and religion under the form of a separate nationality. Ignorance becomes very powerful along with jealousy, anger, greed and desire. Spirituality remains limited to hearing the stories of Gods and visiting their places of activities (tirthas), as well as the wish to reach Heaven at the end of life.

The second part is that the Earth becomes further divided into smaller states, resulting in a world without peace. Even families become divided and the individual ego continues to increase and become monumental. Spirituality is restricted to fate, that is guided by the Gods and to attain Heaven is difficult.

The third part results in further divisions among families, resulting in greater chaos in the social structure. This tendency goes so far that magnified egos cause an ever-increasing antagonism even between men and women. People have no faith in Gods and thus do not believe in the existence of Heaven. Spirituality is restricted to calling down the spirits of the departed human beings.

Then comes the end of Kaliyuga in the world, which is without peace, unity, hope and help. From there, mankind starts to develop with its own efforts and tries to bring back peace and unity in the human society. This is the modern civilization. Man studies matter, the elements and the forces existing in nature. Through the discovery of material forces and the combination of elements, mankind undertakes scientific research to solve problems and to battle against diseases, death, pains, sorrows and sufferings in the various countries. Through these individual efforts, many "isms", parties and groups take formation. These drive the world further into turbulences, discord and disunity. At that moment, to remove Kali by the cyclic movement of an aeon, the Truth-Light touches the Earth again.

6

NECESSITY OF GREAT EPIC

The Day of Truth starts from the East and that is the ancient divine civilization. Following this, the dark night appears from the West and that is the modern human civilization. To start again the Golden Age and the ancient civilization, the pre-ordained place remains the same just as in the ancient times.

Now look towards the East. The divine civilization appears from the East to relieve the Earth from the influences of the Western civilization and to remove the dark rule of Kali so that humanity could become divine. The fire of aspiration was kindled for invoking the truth in Bengal. That fire of psychic aspiration, named *Vitihotra* by the Ṛṣis was kindled to call Deva, upon the Earth. The aim was to bring back the ancient peaceful civilization and thus regain the lost divinity or immortality for the Earth in this modern civilization that exists without the divine. To reopen the Day of Truth and to herald in the Golden Age came the Seer, Sri Rāmakṛṣṇa from the supramental plane to kindle the *Vitihotra*, the aspirant fire. He lit the fire of aspiration through his worship, sādhana, and made an effort to remove all divisions caused by Kali in the various religions. His aim was to achieve the Truth and he prayed for unity and peace for the whole humanity. He accepted the one Mother Śakti (power) for all and he sought to release motherhood from all sorts of vital enjoyment. Swami Vivekānanda, his disciple, announced his findings to the whole world and cemented the call of Truth and the adoration of the Mother-Śakti for all religions.

Then followed another Seer of Truth, Sri Aurobindo, from the Supramental plane, at the same place. His sacrificial rite, *havyāhūti,* came at a time when the country was aflame with the fire of aspiration. He wanted to lead his country towards political and spiritual freedom. At the time when humanity was going through its worst sufferings, he opened the way towards the supramental plane and announced the life divine. His gospel of truth for the supramentalisation of the human race aimed to bring back the Golden Age upon the Earth. He rejected totally the modern civilization and tried to recreate the ancient civilization of the Ṛṣis. He also told the world about the Divine Mother and established her to take humanity towards divinity by the surrender of ego and desire to be transformed in nature under her guidance.

It was only in the heart of Bengal that this psychic aspiration was kindled as the *Vitihotra* and the Seers of Truth were also born in Bengal. The fire of aspiration, *Vitihotra,* called down the Deva, to descend in this world once again to re-open the age of immortality. And the way opened by the cyclic movement of time (ayana) for bringing down the Deva, is the monumental epic Devāyaṇa given to us by Mahākāla Piṅgala Maheśvara. This would open once again the divine age upon the Earth. The pre-ordained place where the *Vitihotra* had been lit and from where two great Seers have pulled the Truth down towards the Earth is Bengal. This is the reason why the Vedas have been revealed in the Devāyaṇa in the Bengali language to teach us more about the divine civilization and to establish the foundation of the Age of Truth.

As the great epic Devāyaṇa has manifested to take humanity to divinity, the Yajur Vediva Kāthaka says:

यः पन्था विततो देवयानश्छन्दोभिर्विगृहीत एति ।
तेनातिष्ठ दिवमन्तरिक्षं यज्ञं गृहीत्वा सुकृतस्य लोकम् ॥

Yaj.kāt.sam.39.17

Yah panthā vitato devayānaśchandobhirvigṛhīta eti /
Tenātiṣṭḥa divamantarikṣaṁ yajñaṁ grīhītva
sukrutasya lokam //

The wide road that has opened with the rhythm (chanda) to be identified with the Truth and the Gods through the sacrificial flame (Yajña) takes us to the eternal Heaven of purity that is the Devāyaṇa.

Now, let us discuss the nature of this Devāyaṇa. What is the secret character of this ancient and at the same time, new Epic (*mahākāvya*) of India? Is this an imaginary story describing events without any foundation in history, with some beautiful lines of knowledge and some magnificent descriptions ornamented with vivid examples? No, absolutely not. It is the Truth, the Vedas that have been revealed by the great Epic. It is more real than history. History is a narration of facts that have happened in the past, a dead past which does not repeat itself. Also, persons reporting history might pen a biased account according to their own wishes or bowing down to their rulers' wishes. The great Epic is instead the full manifestation of Truth in this Age of Falsehood. It describes the divinity in human life, the movement and activities of Gods on the Earth and their impact on humanity.

Look at the two ancient great Epics, where Lord Viṣṇu himself manifested in human form as the *avatāra* or an incarnation with some other Gods. They lived as ideal human beings and although they have left this Earth now, they still exist near this earthly consciousness from ancient times until now. The Yogis can see them vividly and talk with them, as they are present near the Earth plane. For example, Lord Rāma and Lord Kṛṣṇa still appear before their devotees when they meditate on them. Thus, the Epics are living pictures of the Truth, while history is a dead mixture of facts and imagination. The Epic manifests for the change of an Age to give an ideal life to the human society in the coming aeon.

This present Epic recounts the history of the kalpa or an aeon lasting 26,000 years on the Earth. During the previous Golden Age, the Earth was divinised, became immortal, immune and continued thus for ten thousand years. Due to the cyclic movement of Time, this Age disappeared together with the Vedas and the divinised human being. Gradually, the sombre forces of Kali started to influence mankind. To protect humanity, the Gods and the Seers made certain efforts according to the rules of Truth. To keep the memory of the manifested Vedas on the Earth and the fact that life is immortal the grandson of Varuṇa, Kavi*, collected Vedic history, which described the activities of Gods and Ṛṣis. He put the Vedas in writing in four parts (Ṛg, Sāma, Yajur and Atharva) for the benefit of this Earth. Kavi was the first great poet to collect the Vedas, which were only in the memory of the ancient Ṛṣis. When Kavi was compiling the Vedas, his son, Uṣana and his disciples with other Ṛṣis of different dynasties helped him in this great work. The result was that the Earth received the scriptures of the Vedas.

Kavi was such a selfless great Seer, that he gave the names of different Ṛṣis to various parts of the Vedas. The same was with the hymns to the different Gods. He announced that although he had compiled the eternal voice of Truth, still he was not the author of the Vedas. He said, "Hear! O Earth! We are the channels of the voices of the Supreme and the stream of eternal Truth flows through us. We are the Seers of Truth and the Vedas have revealed themselves as the eternal, infinite, ever-existing Truth."

In the great works of Kavi, Uṣana-Kāvya gave a full chapter on Immortality, known as the Hymns to Soma Devata. For this reason, Uṣana became very famous amongst all Ṛṣis, but the main poet was Kavi. He was so great that to this date his name signifies a poet. Thus, Kavi was the second great poet of the Silver Age to maintain the knowledge of Truth in the cyclic movement of Time.

With the further advance of Kali, Vedic knowledge became too complicated for mankind to grasp. Kavi's brother Cyavana

* *Kavi was the son of Bhrigu Ṛṣi, Lord Varuṇa's son. For this reason, he is also called Kavi-Bhārgava. Uṣana is the son of Kavi-Bhargava, also known as Uṣana-Kāvya.*

had a son named Ratnākar. Ratnākar under the name of Vālmiki became the third great poet, at the end of the Silver Age (Treta Yuga). He composed the great epic Rāmāyaṇa, which would inspire the approaching Bronze Age (Dwāpara Yuga). He told the story of Lord Rāma, which he chose among many Gods. Lord Viṣṇu would descend in the human figure as an avatāra, namely Sri Rāma. He would be the saviour of all, even of the Gods. To worship him was to become liberated from all bondages. He was known as the third great poet of the Bronze Age.

Towards the end of the Bronze Age with Kali becoming all-powerful, there appeared another great poet, Dwaipāyana. He was the descendent of Lord Mitra. The son of Lord Mitra was Vaṣiṣṭha-Maitra-Varuṇi. Son of Vaṣiṣṭha was Śakti and his son was Parāṣara. Dwaipāyana Vyāsa was the son of Parāṣara. He aspired for Lord Viṣṇu to descend once again as avatāra in the form of Sri Kṛṣṇa-Vasudeva. He described the life of Lord Kṛṣṇa upon this Earth, as the Lord, friend, brother, husband and a guide to become an ideal for the whole humanity. His advice was to surrender mortal life and works to Him, as He is the saviour of all. Mankind would become liberated from all bondages on remembering Him till the end of Kaliyuga. Thus, Vyasa became the fourth great poet at the end of the Bronze Age (Dwāpara Yuga). His great epic Mahābhārata with Kṛṣṇa Lilā remained as the inspiration for the approaching Iron Age. He also wrote down the Bhagavad Purāna and seventeen other Purānas in which he compiled the stories of former Ages to serve as a history for the people during the Iron Age. At the end of the Kaliyuga, the previous Kalpa finished. With the cyclic movement of the Kālacakra, the Wheel of Time, a new Golden Age started with the commencement of the new Kalpa. The new Kalpa or the cycle begins with the Golden Age with the help of the Great Time (Mahākāla).

Mahākāla Piṅgala Maheśvara himself became a poet to open the new Age of Truth. He, himself, is the creator of the new epic. He discloses the wide road of immortality for the Earth, that is the Devāyaṇa, the great Epic, to manifest a new divine race upon the Earth. Devāyaṇa is the journeyings of men towards the Deva and the journeyings of Gods to the men of the Earth. This is the whole ayana, from one Golden Age to the next. Piṅgala Maheśvara opens the path of immortality or divinity to men and leads them to light, consciousness, power and purity of Truth.

Then, during the course of the ayana and for facilitating the work of Kali, Mahākāla, the Lord of Time, becomes Rudra Maheśvara, his destructive form. He throws the whole creation into darkness and leads it to destruction. Mankind becomes helpless in the hands of negative forces having no peace and experiencing great pain from the fear of death and birth. This happens to the immortal soul, which is above experiencing any kind of pain, suffering, birth, death or diseases. Rudra in his destructive mood creates this illusion that results in chaos in the creation so that the immortal soul believes that it dies and suffers from pain, sorrows and diseases. The same Mahākāla, to bring into existence the works of Deva, becomes Piṅgala – Maheśvara, in the course of the ayana. He, himself, becomes the Poet of the new creation and opens the path of Gods. He manifests the Truth and brings down the revelation of the Vedas, which is the Devāyaṇa and thus Piṅgala Maheśvara himself becomes the first Great Poet.

About Piṅgala Maheśvara, Atharva Veda said to the Ṛṣis that there were many enlightened souls, who have meditated for the new creation. In the Shandilya Upaniṣad we read that Atharva says – O Shandilya! The Supreme Brahman is immobile, eternal and formless. This is the Truth, but this formless Brahman still has three attributes, one with form, the other without form and the third being both with and without form. He is immobile, pure, very subtle, even more than the minutest atom, beyond knowledge and eternal. He possesses myriads of faces. Truth, knowledge and *ānanda* are his formless conditions. In the form and formless nature of the Brahman, where the ignorant Māyā, consisting of Sattwa, Rajas and Tamas, exists there is also the luminous being called Piṅgala Maheśvara.

The Vedas have stories of many Gods and Goddesses but in the second and third great Epics, there are only a few Godheads for the change of an Age. Lord Viṣṇu, Indra, Marut and Agni from the Vedas are active with some other Gods. However, without Deva, they have less power and they can remain active only for a short period. As mentioned in the Ṛg and Atharvaveda,

मम देवा विहवे सन्तु सर्व इन्द्रवन्तो मरुतो विष्णुरग्निः ।
ममान्तरिक्षमुरुलोकमस्तु महयं वातः पवतां कामायास्मै ॥

Ath.V.3.3

Mama devā vihave santu sarva indravanto maruto viṣṇuragniḥ /
Mamāntarikṣa murulokamastu mahyaṁ vātah pavatām kāmāyāsmai //

Without our Deva to guide this Earthly creation; Indra, Viṣṇu, Marut-Vāyu and Agni behind us or from within us, can maintain purity in our lives by the removal of our desires and selfishness for a certain period only.

Let us look at the past Ages. At the end of the Silver Age, this Earth was gradually becoming increasingly sombre under the influence of Kali and impurities were entering into the earth atmosphere. To save mankind from the evil influence of Kali, the above-mentioned four Godheads became active during the time of the Rāmāyāṇa. Lord Viṣṇu came as Sri Rāma, Indra as Sugriva, Marut as Marut-Hanumān and Agni appeared as the power of sacrifice to conquer the opponents and to secure the divine victory. Few other Godheads were also in action, Sūrya as Bali; Mitra-Varuṇa as Nala and Nila; Aśvinīs as Gaya-Gavaksha; Bṛhaspati as the Jambuvan and Dhanwantri as Sushena.

The same occurred in the Mahābhārata with a little difference. The activities of Lord Viṣṇu as Sri Kṛṣṇa, Indra as Arjuna, Marut-Vāyu as Bhīma and Agni who acted as the power to establish Dharma and to conquer the opponents as Kapidhwaja for the divine victory. A few other Godheads were also actively supporting their efforts, Dharmaraja-Yama as Yudhisthira, Aśvinīs as Nakula-Sahadeva, Sūrya as Karna, Vasu as Bhiśma etc.

We saw during these Ages that without the Deva; Viṣṇu, Indra, Marut and Agni were only partially effective and that too for a short period during the transition to the next Age. They also kept the ideal alive for the approaching Age. Rāmāyāṇa manifested at the end of the Silver Age and remained as an ideal for the Bronze Age. Mahābhārata manifested at the end of the Bronze Age and remained as an ideal for the Iron Age. With the ending of the Iron Age, the previous Kalpa has come to an end.

At present, we are going through a transitional period from the Iron to the Golden Age, when the transcendental being Satyadeva will descend upon the Earth to open a new Kalpa with the Golden Age. In this Age, Satyadeva together with all the Godheads will be fully active on the Earth and that will be the full manifestation of the Vedas. This is described in the great Epic Devāyaṇa that has come down for humanity. For this Epic, we chanted the mantras from the Vedas in previous Kalpas. Listen!

7

HYMNS TO THE DEVĀYAṆA

Look at the Eternal Ocean where the vast light glitters rhythmically with joy, bliss, purity and peace, empowered by the power of the sacrifice of thousands of Ṛṣis. That is the Supreme Truth. His eternal glory increases with the efforts and meditations (tapasya) of the Sages, with his fame and grandeur manifesting through the Vipras, the wise people. Truth announced its own manifestation to the Earth in the following words:

O Mahī! I am the Transcendental Truth, I manifest through the Jātaveda, the Fire in the great epic. Hear, O Earth! None is above me, I am the unique Lord, I receive your adoration through my indomitable heroism.

विधुं दद्राणं समने बहूनां युवानं सन्तं पलितो जगार ।
देवस्य पश्य काव्यं महित्वाद्या ममार स हयः समान ॥

Ṛg. X.55.5

Vidhuṁ dadrāṇaṃ samane bahūnāṁ yuvānaṁ santaṁ palito jagāra I
Devasya paśya kāvyaṁ mahitvādyā mamāra se hyaḥ samāna II

Vidhu – the Moon God gave eternal youth to Heaven. This is the reason why the Vasus were free from any sort of deformities related to old age. They remained ever young and immune to diseases and death. You too, Mahī! You have received the Divine Epic, Devāyaṇa. You can see the wide road of immortality and immunity that was disclosed by the Vasus. This Path we call Devāyaṇa for the journey of the Deva.

प्रकाव्यमुशनेव ब्रुवाणो देवो देवानां जनिमा विवक्ति ।
महिव्रतः शुचिबन्धुः पावकः पदा वराहो अभ्येति रेभन् ॥

Sām.524, 1116

Prakāvyamuśaneva bruvāṇo devo devānāṁ janimā vivakti I
Mahivrataḥ śucibandhuḥ pāvakaḥ padā varāho abhyeti rebhan II

This transcendental knowledge has been disclosed by Uṣanakāvya (son of Kavi), in the divine Epic. This comprised the unknown secrets of Satyadeva, his birth and activities together with secret knowledge. He has, in addition, narrated the spiritual austerities, *vrata,* of this Earth to achieve supreme purity with the help of the *pavaka* Agni, the pure fire.

Ye te aryaman vahave Devayāṇa panthano rajan diva acharanti, Te bhirne adya pathibhisanugebhi raksha channe adhi cha vruhideva.

The Godhead Aryama carries the Devāyaṇa and opens the royal road from Heaven to this Earth for us. We pray to Thee, O Deva! Protect us from hostile powers, which attack us as we progress through the enlightened road towards immortality.

Be free from all tinges of the dark night through the enlightened path of the Devāyaṇa and advance towards the eternal Heaven. As long as we are with the Deva, in full purity of the mind, we stay on the plane of Truth. This is the path of the seventeen hymns called the Sarasvatī-path. When Māyā-Śakti, the power of illusion, ignorance and stupidity is dividing the plane of Gods and Asuras, there the Satyadeva manifests himself for the Gods.

Realise today that the path opened before us by the glorious Deva, the Lord of the Truth, is the Devāyaṇa. O Worshippers of Truth, offer your sacrificial rite to Agni, the Fire, existing in your heart.

O Fire, *havyavahu*, pull down the adored Satyadeva, to the sacrificial altar. O Fire! You know the Satyadeva and you know how to offer yourself and to become one with Him.

विमुच्यध्वमघ्नया देवयानाऽअगन्म तमसस्पारमस्य ।
ज्योतिरापामः ॥

Yaj.12.73

Vimucyadhvamaghnyā devayānā' aganma
tamasaspāramasya /
Jyotirāpāmaḥ //

Remover or redeemer from the opposition of the dark forces, Devāyaṇa removes all darkness (unconsciousness) and establishes us in the plane of light or Truth. In other words, Devāyaṇa takes us from ignorance to light and knowledge; from unconsciousness to consciousness; and from mortality to immortality.

आरोह पथो जुहु देवयानान् यत्रर्षयो जग्मुः प्रथमाः पुराणाः ।
हिरण्यपक्षाजिरा संभृताङ्गा वहाँसि सा सुकृतां
यत्र लोक उत्तमोऽहं भूयासमधरे मत्सपत्ना : ॥

Yaj.kāt.sām. 31-34

Āroha patho juhu devayānān yatrarṣayo jagmuḥ
prathamāh purānāḥ /
Hiranyapakṣājirā saṁbhṛtāñgā vahānsi sā sukṛtaṁ
Yatra loka uttamo'haṁ bhūyāsamadhare matsapatnāḥ //

O Juhu! You are our first Mother. You were there at the beginning of this creation, when the eternal stream of life had become too narrow and without any space. O Mother! Open the stream of life and push us towards the royal road of Devāyaṇa. Take us to the secret lonely place surrounded by the golden light from where all these creations have come out! That is the divine "I" who is in the life water swimming like a fish.

यः पन्था विततो देवयानश्छन्दोभिर्विगृहीत एति ।
तेनातिष्ठ दिवमन्तरिक्षं यज्ञं गृहीत्वा सुकृतस्य लोकम् ॥

Yaj.kāt.saṁ.39.17

Yaḥ panthā vitato devayānaṣchandobhirvigṛhīta eti I
Tenātiṣṭha divamantarikṣaṁ yajñaṁ gṛhītva sukṛtasya lokam II

Devāyaṇa is the wide road that has been opened through the rhythm of eternal sound to become identified with the Truth and the Gods, where the sacrificial flame (Yajña) has been lighted to lead us to the eternal Heaven of purity.

O Abhi! King of the Ṛṣis! You have realised the Supreme Lord of Light by chanting the enlightened word and have received him as your son Deva, Lord of the Manifested Supreme, the Transcendent Light.

When men repeat and meditate upon the word Brahman constantly, then the inner fire is lit and the supreme knowledge surrounds them as the ring surrounds the wheel.

In former times, Indu, the Moon God had taken birth as a young poet, Amitouja. At that moment, Indra, the Vajri, maintained the activities of this world and harmonised, protected and controlled the works, which are not to be done by holding his unique weapon, Vajra.

Opening a new Age by the purification of the Word is to enter into the Truth through the stream of nectar, with a beauty and sweetness that reveals a supramental image with magnificent descriptions. There we listen to the eternal stories and come to know the ancient history of Truth. And, that is the manifestation of the divine epic Devāyaṇa.

The Earth was happy and pleased with Akṣa when he had cultivated this land. She gave a huge quantity of gold and other metals with corns of various varieties. For this she was named Bhūmi. Eight Vandhus (son of Gopavana and Lopamudra) unitedly called and pulled the divine chariot with which Satyadeva decided to descend on the Earth to transform her. Then the world became happy, pure and peaceful. This means that when Deva moved towards the Earth due to the change in the time cycle, the world entered into purity, peace and joy.

Formerly, our Ṛṣis, Seers and Poets had arranged the eternal tunes, rhythms and melodies with words in such a way that when chanted properly they can easily lead us to immortality. To develop this knowledge they have decided upon the feet of the rhythms and words. They have also included secret spaces and time of rest in between by which Satyadeva's immortality can manifest in this human society.

Without anyone's knowledge, the baby grows secretly in the womb of the mother, increases and becomes fully developed and ready for delivery. Similarly, the tongue moves groups of words in different rhythms and tunes in various ways. The true import of the words increases and becomes fully developed in course of time, out of everyone's sight. Similarly, in this world, the chosen persons through their secret meditation on Truth, unknown to others, will increase their will and aspiration for achieving Truth and attain self-fulfilment.

As Sri Aurobindo has so well described in his magnificent epic "Savitri":

> A few shall see what none yet understands;
> God shall grow up while the wise men talk and sleep;
> For men shall not know the coming till its hour
> And belief shall be not till the work is done.
>
> *Sri Aurobindo, Savitri, Canto IV*

Thus the Devāyaṇa increases the will and aspiration for the achievement of Truth in the normal human beings without anyone becoming aware of it and gives them the ability to enter into Truth for their fulfilment.

8

THE POWER OF MANIFESTATION OF THE GREAT EPIC

The rhythms in which the divine Epic manifest in are Chandas, seven in number. They have come out from the mouth of Parabrahman, as Prajāpati himself mentioned to Ṛṣi Atharva –

गायत्र्युष्णिगनुष्टुब् बृहती पङक्तिस्त्रिष्टुब् जगत्ये ॥

Ath XIX.21.1

Gāyatryuṣṇiganuṣṭub bṛhatī panktīstriṣṭub jagatyai //

In short, Gāyātri, Uṣṇik, Anuṣṭubh, Bṛhatī, Panktī, Triṣṭubh and Jagati are the seven chandas, metres that have emanated from the Parabrahman for the manifestation of the Vedas. Among these seven chandas, he chose Gāyātri to manifest the Vedas. This was mentioned thus –

स्तुता मया वरदा वेदमाता प्र चोदयन्तां पावमानी द्विजानाम् ।
आयुः प्राणं प्रजां पशुं कीर्तिं द्रविणं ब्रह्मवर्चसम् ।
महयं दत्त्वा व्रजत ब्रह्मलोकम् ॥

Ath.XIX.71.1

Stutā mayā varadā vedamātā, pra codayantāṁ pāvamānī dvijānām /
Āyuḥ prāṇaṁ prajāṁ paśuṁ, kīrtiṁ draviṇaṁ brahmavarcasam /
Mahyaṁ datvā vrajata brahmalokaṁ //

O Mother of Vedas, Giver of boons! I worship thee. Thou art giver of purity, sincerity and consciousness to those who are intellectually wise (Vipras). Thou increasest their longevity, life, progeny, domestic animals, fame and honour when they adore Thee. Nourish them constantly with Thy Grace. I am the Creator of the whole Universe, I say to Thee, "O Gāyātri, stay with me eternally in this Brahmaloka and guide all the words (Vedas and the Truth) for the universal creation. Remain with me as the mother of Brahmaloka and work here with thy glory."

Gāyātri, the great Power of manifestation of the Vedas, the *Mahāśakti* was worshipped and honoured by the Creator Brahmā for her work. When she observed the fire of psychic aspiration "*Vitihotra*" burning in the secret cavern of the heart of the Earth, she gave a boon to the Earth. She was very pleased with this land, which was invoking Truth and immortality through the adoration of the great Worshippers of Mother Power namely, Sri Rāmakṛṣṇa and Sri Aurobindo. She accepted their birthplace "Vīda-Vaṅga" as the Home of Truth to be glorified with her rhythms to receive again the Vedas with the Truth upon Earth.

Through her great compassion, she has arranged the words of the Brahman in the language of Bengal in the Anuṣṭubh metre, to express the Vedas in the form of Devāyaṇa. For the manifestation of Truth, she has sent down the Anuṣṭubh metre on the Earth to Vaṅga with her light, power, purity and *ānanda*. This would surcharge humanity with the power to enter into divinity.

The power descended from the supreme plane "Brahmaloka" as the Anuṣṭubh chanda, the divine rhythm, with the Godheads acting through the Anuṣṭubh chanda on this Earthly consciousness. The Gods and Ṛṣis have always adored this chanda. As Prajāpati said in the Vedas,

उदीचीमारोहानुष्टुप् त्वावतु वैराजं सामैकविंश स्तोमः
शरदृतुः फलं द्रविणम् ॥

Yaj. X-13

Udīcīmārohānuṣṭup tvāvatu vairājaṁ sāmaikaviṁśa stomaḥ
śaradṛtuḥ phalaṁ draviṇam //

O Anuṣṭubh! Thou art the worshipper of Truth. Let thy power vibrate in men in all your sounds through the third tune, transform their unconscious self to consciousness and help those who have fallen to rise up again. Along with Anuṣṭubh, O Viraja! Thou art the poet. Move with thy power through the fifth tune for the Hymns to the Deva by chanting the mantra of Sāmaveda; Through this autumn will be pleased to give us a huge quantity of riches (corns, fruits and flowers).

विश्वे त्व देव वैश्वानर आच्छिन्द्रन् त्वानुष्टुभेन छन्दासङ्गिरसवत् ।

Yaj.Vāj.Saṁ-11.65, Kāt.S.16.6

Viśve tva deva vaiśvānara ācchindran tvānuṣṭubhena chandāsaṅgirasavat /

O Deva! In this world, (Vaiśvanara) the Fire, with the help of Aṅgirāsas, worships and welcomes you to descend on this Earth through the Anuṣṭubh chanda.

विष्णोः क्रमोसि शत्रुयतो हन्तानुष्टुभं छन्दऽ आरोह दिशोनु विक्रमस्व ॥

Yaj XII.5

Viṣṇoḥ kramosi śatrūyato hantānuṣṭubhaṁ chanda' āroha diśonu vikramasva //

With the power of Lord Viṣṇu, let the Anuṣṭubh chanda roar against enemies with an all-conquering heroism that vibrates in the air and spreads far to the horizon.

अनुष्टुभेन त्व छन्दस् सदायामि

Anuṣṭubhena tva chandas sadāyāmi

O Lord of Immortality! I establish you on this Earth by the Anuṣṭubh chanda (the Anuṣṭubh rhythm)

अनुष्टुप् छन्दो लोकम् त इन्द्रम्

Anuṣṭup chando lokaṁ ta indram

Where the Anuṣṭubh chanda is, is the world of Indra. In other words, it manifests the divine kingdom with the divine riches.

Let the fire of aspiration call and worship Somadevata (the Moon) for receiving the Truth of the Great Heaven with the Anuṣṭubh chanda by his power in the five senses (the eyes, nose, ears, tongue and skin). Let the Truth be manifested with his light, power, consciousness, bliss and purity.

Let the Aśvinīs remain in the eyes as the eyesight and Sarasvatī stay in the vitality as the power and strength of life. Let her take her seat on our tongue, to control and work through the other senses by the Anuṣṭubh chanda.

With the Hymns of the Ṛṣis, Fire (the divine Priest – Agni *devata*) goes to the *Vṛtrahanta* (slayer of the Asura, Vritra), Indra and they combinedly call upon Somadevata, to increase the longevity of our life. O Humanity! Pray to the Divine Priest, Agni through the Anuṣṭubh chanda. It will blaze more powerfully towards Heaven; with the result that the power of Agni in the five senses will increase the power and strength to enter into increased longevity.

The Dawn (Uṣā) and the Night (Rātri) are empowered by the Divine Indra and Satyadeva, the Lord of Truth is increasing the holding power of Indra. The all-powerful Indra in our five senses increases the power, longevity, strength and enthusiasm by the Anuṣṭubh chanda. I invoke you, O human spirit; sing your songs through the Anuṣṭubh chanda to achieve these divine riches.

Through the Anuṣṭubh chanda, the combined powers of Viṣṇu, Indra, Agni and Vāyu act and join with the activities of Sarasvatī, Aditi, Uṣā, Rātri, Somadevata and the Aśvinīs. When we recite our verses, these powers act through our five senses to increase the power of action of these Godheads. They also join their power with the nature, the seasons, etc. and time brings about a transformation in our human nature so that we are able to enter into immortality. In other words, Anuṣṭubh stands as the medium between mortality and immortality. By chanting the Anuṣṭubh, we rise towards immortality. O human being! Chant constantly the Anuṣṭubh chanḍa and enter into divinity.

9

PLACE FOR MANIFESTATION OF TRUTH

In the sacrificial flame (Yajña) of the heart, I perform my sacrificial rite and offer the mind as (ghṛta) the clarified butter. With the sacrificial rite, let the Fire be lit as the Vitihotra to clasp the Truth and let us enjoy the advent of Truth.

O Fire! Take your seat on the soul of Vaṅga and call down Deva. This is your eternal seat to call and pull down the Truth upon the Earth. By your aspiration, let Truth be manifested with all the Godheads in the world.

Bengal (Vaṅga) was the place decided upon from the very beginning of the creation for the manifestation of Truth. With the movement of the time cycle (ayana), the moment came when Piṅgala Maheśvara brought down to the world the great epic Devāyaṇa, written in the language of Bengal. The great Seers of Bengal, like Sri Rāmakṛṣṇa Paramhaṅsa and Sri Aurobindo, lighted the Vitihotra, the psychic aspirant fire. These Seers had selected Bengal that is the Home of Truth on the Earth, for taking their human birth, for leading their lives and their yogic sadhana for the manifestation of Truth. Their worship was known to the world. For completing their adoration of Truth, the *Vitihotra*, the Fire of Aspiration, that they had lit up in Bengal, is still very much alive. Their main aim was that the humanity should achieve immortality to enter into divinity. The time has finally come. Satyadeva is now ready to fulfil the Will of the Parabrahman, the Supreme, that the Earth be liberated from ignorance, pain and suffering and become immortal.

In former times also, Bengal was the chosen land from where the divine light spread in the whole world. When the Deva wished to begin the Kalpa and to open the Golden Age (Satya Yuga), he descended and manifested only in Bengal. For this reason we adored Bengal as the Vīda-Vaṅga (*Vīda* means the home of Truth and *Vaṅga* is Bengal). Thus Bengal is the home of the Lord of Truth, Satyadeva.

In the Vedas, the Ṛg, Yajur and the Atharva, you can read the mantras about Vīda-Vaṅga. We worshipped and chanted them in former Golden Ages. Deva had manifested Himself in Bengal many times and the time is approaching again now. One can observe that the revelation of the Vedas, elaborated in the great Epic Devāyaṇa with the description of the life, character and activities of Deva as well as of other Gods in subtle forms has been done through the language of Bengal, *i.e.* in Bengali.

Once more this *Vīda-Vaṅga* will be worshipped by the whole world, when the Golden Age commences with the full manifestation of the Truth.

Devana priyam dhama bhavati tasya prachyam dishi– the most favoured home of the Deva exists in the East. When the divine civilization descends on the Earth, the light of the Vedas will be showered throughout the world. In the beginning, for the divinisation of life and the human nature, *Vīda-Vaṅga* will wake up with the manifestation of the Truth. Her language has now been identified with the Truth. With the Anuṣṭubh chanda, Bengali has received the power of expression from the "Brahmaloka", the plane of the Brahman, to describe the activities, mode of work and character of Deva. With this, the Bengali language has become divinised. With the grace of Mahāśakti, the Bengali language has become divinised with the movement and dance of the divine rhythm of the Anuṣṭubh rhythm.

Vīda Vaṅga means that Bengal is the home of Truth. Therefore, it is only natural that in the course of time, Deva will come to his Earthly home. For this reason, the Ṛṣis have chanted the mantras on *Vīda-Vaṅga*, which was then collected in the Vedas (in the Ṛgveda; in the Yajurveda Vajaseniya branch, Kaṇva branch, Taitteriya branch, Moitrayani branch, Kathaka branch; and in the Atharvaveda). These hymns to *Vīda-Vaṅga* we shall disclose now again. When the people of Bengal show their true respect to their motherland and become conscious and express their homage to their country as the home of Truth, then we, the Ṛṣis, shall chant again with the Bengalis. We shall chant the hymns to Vaṅga by moving and playing on the fine strings of their hearts. The songs will then appear through their voices and tunes:

वनस्पते वीड्वङ्गो हि भूया ऽ अस्मत्सखा प्रतरणः सुवीरः ।
गोभिः सन्नद्धो असि वीड्यस्वास्थाता ते जयतु जेत्वानि ॥

Yaj. XXIX 52

Vanaspate vīdavaṅgo hi bhūyā asmatsakhā prataraṇaḥ suvīraḥ /
Gobhiḥ sannadho asi vīḍyasvāsthātā te jayatu jetvāni //

O Vanaspati! Let our ever-beloved friend Satyadeva come and establish himself in Vaṅga, the home of Truth, again with his all-conquering power and divine riches. Let all places in Vaṅga become enlightened through his purity and pure light. Let her forests and fields become filled with fruits, flowers and corn. Manifest yourself to sing the songs of the victory of Truth and become famous throughout the world.

स्थिर भव वीड्वङ्ग आशुर्भव वाज्यर्वन् ।
पृथुर्भव सुषदस्त्वमग्नेः पुरीषवाहणः ॥

Yaj. XI. 44

Sthiro bhava vīḍavaṅga āśur bhava vājyarvan /
Pṛthurbhava suṣadstvamagneḥ purīṣvāhaṇaḥ //

Be tranquil and peaceful, O Vaṅga, Home of the Truth! Be happy and full of riches in all your fields and forests. Let these riches spread throughout the world. O Agni, you are the bearer of Truth to this earthly home at Vaṅga.

शिवो भव प्रजाभ्यो मानुषीभ्यस्त्वमङ्गिरः ।
मा द्यावा पृथिवी अभि शोचीर्मान्तरिक्षं मा वनस्पतीन् ॥

Yaj.X1.45

Śivo bhava prajābhyo mānuṣībhyastvamaṅgiraḥ /
Mā dyāvā pṛthivī abhi śocīrmāntarikṣaṁ mā vanaspatīn //

O Aṅgirā! Let men become like Śiva; let the Earth be purified by unification with Heaven and the Antarikṣa (the vital plane) as well as by the appearance of Vanaspati to receive the Truth.

चतुस्त्रिं शद्वाजिनो देवबन्धोर्वङ्क्रीरश्वस्य स्वधितिः समेति ।
आच्छिद्रा गात्रा वयुना कृणोत परुष्परुरनुघुष्या विशस्त ॥

Yaj.XXV.41

Catustriṁ śadvājino devabandhorvaṅkrīraśvasya svadhitiḥ sameti /
Āchidrā gātrā vayunā kṛṇota paruṣparuranughuṣyā viśasta //

The area of *Deva-Bandho*, the home of Deva the Truth is *Vaṅga* (Bengal), without fissure and division in her body. This occurs only when she is united into one, having the length and breadth of 34 horses square (the distance a horse can run in one day multiplied by 34. The length and breadth would be similar). Look at Bengal appearing radiant with joy and shining with the light and consciousness of Truth.

महि त्वाष्ट्रमूर्जयन्तीरजुर्यं स्तभूयमानं वहतो वहन्ति ।
व्यङ्गे भिर्दिद्युतानः सधस्थ एकामिव रोदसी आ विवेश ॥

Ṛg.III 7.4

Mahi tvāṣṭramūrjayantīrajuryaṁ stabhūyamānaṁ vahato vahanti /
Vyaṅge bhirdidyutānaḥ sadhastha ekāmiva rodasī ā viveśa //

When Tvaṣṭā gave an artistic shape to this creation, at that moment, Mahī appeared resplendent with a divine beauty. Her constant prayer was being carried by Agni towards the high Heaven. Then the divine grace came back to the Earth through which Bengal started glittering with divine beauty and was adorned with the purest light of Truth. In the whole Earth and Heaven, Bengal alone achieved the most beautiful and artistic appearance.

We have found the ancient references from the Vedas that disappeared several thousand years ago, which reveal the reality of the Age of Truth or the Golden Age. When the people of Bengal become conscious and aware of their divine destiny to receive Deva; at that moment five Gods, Prastoka, Sarjaya, Vanaspati, Apānapāt and Tanunāpat will become active in Bengal to clean and to prepare it for the advent of the Truth as well as embellish the land with riches to welcome Deva.

Before calling upon these five Godheads, we shall seek that Bengal be prepared. O Bengal! Aspire for the Truth. O Suffering Humanity! Tired of constant battles and scarred with many injuries. O Divine Land! Be conscious. Remember that you are already surrounded by the Truth. This is your eternal history. O Devi! Throw away your entire fatigue and silence and pray firmly: "O Divine Guru Bṛhaspati! Open the royal road by which Truth can come to me quickly, to relieve me of my pains as He is the redeemer of all sufferings."

O Divine Land! Day by day, prepare yourself to give a cordial welcome to the Deva. He will be pleased and there will be a glorious advent in your heart; and the Night spread by the dark Ignorance will pass away. The appearance of Deva will be like the day of pure divine light. Then you will enter into the joy of peace and bliss, through His presence and His activities.

Then we will call upon the five Godheads, one by one, O Prastoka! Come and worship here in Bengal and bring all the deeply desired divine royal riches. Through your worship, ten kinds of riches, powers and weapons of the divine King Indra will re-appear. You are the divine worker at the beginning of the Day of Truth. O Servant of Truth! O Divine

Guest to the Mortal world! We worship you alone in this land to achieve undisturbed peace, immense wealth and riches, eternal youth with immunity and the power to change the body only through the Will.

Bring us ten kinds of powers, weapons, riches and dresses. Fill the land with ten sorts of foods and ten forms decorated with gold, jewels and gems for the Truth. O Discloser of the Day of Truth! O Servant of Truth! Disclose those ten rules and items of truth in this land of Bengal.

O Prastoka! Manifester of divinity in Bengal. Re-open the ten homes of Satyadeva and renew the dwellings of Truth. May the hundred forms and strength of the mantras of Atharvaveda act in the people of Bengal to increase their willpower to conquer disease, old age and death!

With Prastoka active in this land, we will then call upon the Godhead Sarjaya.

O Sarjaya! Worship the all-desirable Truth in Bengal for the whole Earth and bring fulfilment and peace to entire humanity. By this mantra of Bharadavāja, the land will be enlightened and fruitful.

Next we shall invoke Vanaspati – O Vanaspati! In the home of Truth; let Satyadeva become established with ten types of riches and divine *ānanda*. He has always been our intimate friend and the conqueror of all opponents. To make Bengal glitter with the pure light of Truth, fill up and decorate this land with flowers, fruits and corns in the fields, forests and gardens. Sing the songs of victory for the Truth and be famous on the Earth.

Then we shall call Tanunāpat – O Tanunāpat! You know the asuric, undivine and hostile forces as well as the Lord of Truth, Satyadeva, as you are his personal attendant. Open and observe the royal avenue of Truth by which Satyadeva can come to this Earth. You also prepare food with *ghṛta*, the clarified butter and *madhu,* honey to offer the feast of Deva.

Finally, we shall call Apānapāt – O Apānapāt! This is the auspicious land of Bengal, the land that is glittering with gems.

Spray with divine fragrance her trees and creepers, flowers and fruits of her forests, the different types of plants, paddies and berries of her fields, the fountains, the rivers and the winds. With the pure divine aroma, the people of this land will become absorbed into meditation of truth with a joyous heart. They will gradually be liberated from diseases and old age and attain longevity with divine health and purity.

When those five Godheads will become active in this land of Bengal, a close contact will be established with the Deva. At that moment, we shall chant the songs of "Bharat" India and spread the news of the advent of Truth upon the Earth throughout the world.

10

HYMNS TO AGNI FOR THE LAND OF INDIA

We shall chant with "Agni-devata" the Fire in front of us.

उदग्ने भारत द्युमदजस्रेण दविद्युतत्
शोचा वि भाह्यजर ॥

Ṛg.VI.16.45

Udagne bhārata dyumadajasreṇa davidyutat
Śocā vi bhāhyajara //

Manifest, O Fire! With your all purifying power burst into flames in Bharat (India). With your all cleansing touch, let India achieve divine purity. Let her enter into immunity through the rejection of negative forces and become liberated from disease, old age and death.

त्वां दूतमग्ने अमृतं युगेयुगे हव्यवाहं दधिरे पायुमीड्यम ।
देवासश्च मर्तासश्च जागृविं विभुं विश्पतिं नमसा नि षेदिरे ॥

Ṛg.VI.15.8

Twāṁ dūtamagne amṛtaṁ yugeyuge havyavāhaṁ dadhire pāyumīdyam /
Devāsaśca marfāsaśca jāgṛviṁ vibhuṁ viśpatiṁ namasā ni ṣedire //

O Agni! O Fire! You are the Herald of Immortality in every Age. O Havyavāhu (Fire)! The Hymns to the Truth, chanted by Payu Bharadavāja, are the mantras that you are carrying to the Deva. You are the only power who can take our prayers before Deva the Truth, who has given consciousness to us. O Lord of the World! Take our adoration and prostration to the Supreme.

O Fire! Remain in front of the human being as the symbol of Truth. Pull down the Truth constantly for us. Give the Seeker of the Truth, the indomitable Will and remove their bondages from birth and work. Increase their *ānanda* by flashing the pure light of Truth.

चित्तिं जुहोमि मनसा घृतेन यथा देवाऽ इहागमन्वीतिहोत्राऽ ऋतावृधः ।
पत्ये विश्वस्य भूमनो जुहोमि विश्वकर्मणे विश्वाहादाभ्यं हविः ॥

Yaj.XVII.78

Cittiṁ juhomi manasā ghṛtena yathā devā'
ihāgamanvītihotrā' ṛtāvṛdhaḥ ।
Patye viśvasya bhūmano juhomi, viśvakarmaṇe
viśvāhādābhyaṁ haviḥ ॥

In the sacrificial flame of the heart, we offer our mind as the *ghṛta*, the sacrificial offering, by which the Fire reaches the high Heavens as Vītihotrā, the psychic aspirant fire of Truth. Then Deva clasps it while descending down on the Earth plane. Who is the Lord of this Earth, who frees humanity by removing all impurities and contaminations and brings in peace? He is Darbhya, the divine man upon Earth. O Viśvakarmā! We are offering our sacrifice, (the *havi*) clarified butter, in the fire of the heart. You provide the shape to divinity in this auspicious work.

उतो हि वां दात्रा सन्ति पूर्वा या पुरुभ्यस्त्रसदस्युर्नितोशे ।
क्षेत्रासां ददथुरुर्वरासां घनं दस्युभ्यो अभिभूतिमुग्रम ॥

Ṛg.IV.38.1

Uto hi vāṁ dātrā santi pūrvā yā
purubhyastrasadasyurnitośe ।
Kṣetrāsāṁ dadathururvarāsāṁ ghanaṁ dasyubhyo
abhibhūtimugram ॥

Awake, O Mother India! Remember your past glorious history, when the Emperor Puru with the help of his weapons drove out and killed the *dasyus*, the hostile forces existing between Heaven and the Earth. He reestablished the unity between Earth and Heaven, which earned him divine honour and garlands.

At that moment, O India! Earth and Heaven were united into one. Remember your glorious past to be reunited with Heaven! Aspire for the Truth! Pray for the destruction of the evil forces that have separated Earth from Heaven and forced the Earth constantly towards the deepest and darkest Ignorance.

पुनर्नो असुं पृथिवी ददातु पुनर्द्यौर्देवी पुनरन्तरिक्षम् ।
पुनर्नः सोमस्तन्वं ददातु पुनः पूषा पथ्यां या स्वस्तिः ॥

Ṛg.X.59.7

Punarno asuṁ pṛthivī dadātu punardyaurdevī punarantarikṣam /
Punarnaḥ somastanvaṁ dadātu punaḥ pūṣā pathyāṁ yā svastiḥ //

Let the Earth offer her sacrificial rite again to the Heaven! Let the Goddesses of Heaven, the divine powers act upon the Earth again! Let the *antarikṣa*, the vital plane, help in the aspiration for the Truth. Let Somadevata disclose the adoration and hymns to the Truth again! Let Pūṣā open the divine royal road for your rest and peace.

शं रोदसी सुबन्धवे यह्वी ऋतस्य मातरा ।
भरतामप यद्रपो द्यौः पृथिवी क्षमा रपो मो षु ते किं चनाममत् ॥

Ṛg X.59.8

Śaṁ rodasī subandhave yahvī ṛtasya mātarā /
Bharatāmapa yadrapo dyauḥ pṛthivī kṣamā rapo mo ṣu te kiṁ canāmamat //

Yahvī, the Mother of Truth, is the transcendent power. She is like a friend, who ties the knot of divine love between the Earth and Heaven to make them into one. With this India, Bharat, became famous to establish perfect unity between

Heaven and Earth. It is in India that our duty lies and that is our aim.

> अव द्वके अव त्रिका दिवश्चरन्ति भेषजा ।
> क्षमा चरिष्ण्वेककं ।
> भरतामप यद्रपो द्यौः पृथिवी क्षमा रपो मो षु ते किं चनाममत् ॥
>
> Ṛg. X.59.9
>
> *Ava dvake ava trikā divaścaranti bheṣajā*
> *Kṣamā cariṣṇvekakaṁ* /
> *Bharatāmapa yadrapo dyauḥ pṛthivī kṣamā rapo mo ṣu te kim canāmamat* //

In this country, by pounding two or three times the creeper of *soma*, people became identified with Heaven and attained the *kṣama-śakti*, the power of tolerance and forgiveness. With that they established one world throughout the Earth. For this the land of India was very famous. Our duty lies in India and this is the goal we have to reach.

> समिन्द्रेरय गामनड्वाहं य आवहदुशीनराण्या अनः ।
> भरतामप यद्रपो द्यौः पृथिवी क्षमा रपो मो षु ते किं चनाममत् ॥
>
> Ṛg.X.59.10
>
> *Samindreraya gāmanaḍvāhaṁ ya āvahaduśīnarāṇyā anaḥ* /
> *Bharatāmapa yadrapo dyauḥ pṛthivī kṣamā rapo mo ṣu te kiṁ canāmamat* //

We bowed our heads and folded our hands before the divine King Indra. We adored Him and sought his all powerful divine rule and order on the Earth as well as his power of tolerance and modesty. Through this power, there would be one united kingdom throughout the whole of the Earth. Formerly, India became very famous as it had established unity between Heaven and the Earth. Today, in India our duty for action lies in the attainment of this aim.

मा नो रक्षो अभि नड्यातुमावतामपोच्छतु मिथुना या किमीदिना ।
पृथिवी नः पार्थिवात् पात्वंहसोऽन्तरिक्षं दिव्यात्पात्वस्मान् ॥

Ṛg.VII.104.23

Mā no rakṣo abhi naḍyātumāvatā ma pocchatu mithunā yā kimīdinā /
Pṛthivī naḥ pārthivāt pātvaṁ haso'antarikṣam divyātpātvasmān //

O Deva, Son of Abhi! If we do not have your protection in the inanity of life and in constant vital enjoyment, then where is our safety and security? The Earth is engaging us in vital enjoyment and increasing our daily sufferings. Antarikṣa, the vital plane, is pushing us towards vulnerability and the abyss and Heaven is beckoning us through divine enjoyment. We are in this peaceless, strange and grave condition without you, O Satyadeva! Who else is there to save us and to establish us into the immortal *ānanda*.

Awake, O Divine Land! You were ornamented with gold and jewels, remember your glorious past by the identification of Earth and Heaven. In this land which is for both Truth and Falsehood, we pray to you to drive out Falsehood and ask Deva the Truth to manifest for the Earth to enjoy immunity, eternal youth and peaceful divine rest.

Look at the beautiful divine chariot, which is carrying the divine Vasus and drawing the Virsha Ṛṣis from the East to the West. The Aśvinīs are chanting the Hymns to Uṣā, the Divine Dawn, who is sitting in the chariot to manifest throughout the Earth. That divine chant one can hear even till the West. O Mādhvi India, hearken our voice and the chant of the Aśvinīs.

By the chant of the Aśvinīs, this dark and sombre period will vanish slowly and the individual ego of this world will disappear. The adventurous Uṣā, the Divine Dawn, through its golden avenue will announce the secret of the golden Puruṣa, through the way of Suṣamma, the surrounding ocean. Listen, O Mādhvi India! To our voices and the chant of the Aśvinīs.

The Aśvinīs chanted the Hymns to Uṣā, the Divine Dawn, to present us with vast divine riches and they themselves entered into eternal youth through their chanting. The all-conquering power of Rudra (the Rudra-Śakti) announced the news of the delightful golden path by which wealth and riches filled up the creation. Listen, O Mādhvi India! to the voices and the songs of the Aśvinīs.

11

UṢĀ - DAWN OF GOLDEN LIGHT

Uṣā, the Aurora, drank the divine wine, became golden red and entered into purity. She is bringing the Truth-Consciousness, the hidden knowledge of light, down to the Earth and telling us the news of the golden path "Devāyaṇa" as well as the secrets of Satyadeva in the antarikṣa, the vital plane.

O Agni! O Fire! Present your divine adoration before the Truth Sun, and the magnificent appearance of the golden Aurora. O Jātaveda Fire! Give the meditation and prayer to us so that Uṣā and Satyadeva appear here.

या दस्रा सिंधु मातरा मनोतरा रयीणाम् ।
धिया देवा वसु विदा ॥

Ṛg. I.46.2

Yā dasrā sindhu mātarā manotarā rayīṇām /
dhiyā devā vasu vidā //

Who was called the Mother of the Ocean of the Golden Light? Who gives us the desired wealth and riches and the meditation for "*Satyadeva*" the Truth? That meditation was received by the Vasus and then given to us.

एषो उषा अपूर्व्या व्युच्छति प्रिया दिवः ।
स्तुषे वामश्विना बृहत् ॥

Ṛg. I.46.1

Eṣo uṣā apūrvyā vyucchati priyā divaḥ /
Stuṣe vāmaśvinā bṛhat //

O Uṣā, you are scattering the wonderful golden light! Come here and manifest yourself in the land of Truth. O Beloved Daughter of Heaven! Remover of dense sleep! Let us become conscious with your soft-sweet touch. O Uṣā! The Aśvinīs have chanted the Hymns to You to manifest the truth of eternity.

उषासानक्ता बृहती बृहन्तं पयस्वती सुदुघे शूरमिन्द्रम् ।
तन्तुं ततं पेशसा संवयन्ती देवानां देवं यजतः सुरुक्मे ॥

Yaj.XX.41

Uṣāsānaktā bṛhatī bṛhantaṁ payasvatī sudughe śuramindram /
Tantuṁ tataṁ peśasā saṁvayantī devānāṁ devaṁ yajataḥ surukme //

The great King of Gods, Indra, existing in the *Maharloka* – the supramental plane, adores Satyadeva to attain Truth-immortality. He has made all preparations. There Uṣā, the Divine Dawn, is milking the Night as the Cow. With this milk, she prepares the divine feast for the Deva. While she was milking, a wonderful strand came out through her efforts. This has now started spreading. The Gods are weaving the ever-widening thread to prepare the divine clothes and garments to worship and receive Deva the Truth.

नक्तोषासा समनसा विरूपे धापयेते शिशुमेकं समीची ।
द्यावाक्षामा रुक्मो अन्तर्विभाति देवाऽअग्निं धारयन्द्रविणोदाः ॥

Yaj.XII.2, XVII.70

Naktoṣāsā samanasā virūpe dhāpayete śiśumekaṁ samīchī /
dyāvākṣāmā rukmo antarvibhāti devā' agniṁ dhārayandraviṇodāḥ //

The Goddess Dawn "Devi-Uṣāsi" runs towards the Lord of the Night "*Nakta*" angrily, as the mother runs irritably towards her naughty child to control him. With the power of Truth, she removes the darkness and blemishes caused by the influence of Night and enlightens the Heaven. To help her in her work, the Lord of Fire, Agni devata burns the pollution and gives in its place divine purity. Finally, Draviṇoda clears the resulting ashes to increase the light and beauty of Heaven.

Similarly, O Draviṇoda! On this Earth, be active to clean the dirt and contamination of Nakta, the Night, which has been removed by Uṣā and burnt by the Lord of the Fire. Clean the path of the Deva and open it so that he can give fulfilment to the people of the Earth. Remove the filth from the path of the Deva. Purify it by showering divine water on it and decorating it with divine flowers, incense and light to welcome Deva upon the Earth.

Through the hymns to the divine land, Bengal will become self-conscious and by the activities of Prastoka, Sarjāya, Vanaspati, Tanunāpat, Apānapāt and Draviṇoda, the land will regain its purity when the destruction and dislocation caused by Kali is made good. When Bengal is again full of wealth and riches, corns and gems; when its fruits, flowers, milk and honey give a divine fragrance, when it has become affluent with the ten riches and the ten weapons, then the land will look like the ten-handed Durgā, the Divine Mother. With the wealth and jewels, fruits and flowers, milk and honey, Bengal will prepare the offering for the Deva. Fire will start the sacrifice for the Deva to worship immortality. The Ṛṣis will chant mantras of Yajña through the dumb throat of Bengal in the Anuṣṭubh chanda.

The Anuṣṭubh was preceded by the Gāyātri and came down to the Earth from the Brahmaloka with the power of truth. Through the work of Uṣā, the Dawn and other Godheads, Bengal will be purified from the deep darkness of Kali. At that moment, the Anuṣṭubh will roar with the power of Hari. As the lion roars in the forest, so will the Anuṣṭubh roar through the Bengali language in the divine epic Devāyaṇa, which will become a divine language among all the other languages on this Earth.

The divine Epic Devāyaṇa will become very prominent in the life of Bengal with the power of the Great Godheads. Also, as in the previous great epics, Agni will become active to increase the aspiration of mortality for Heaven, Vāyu to bring vital purity and devotion, Indra by his unique weapon Vajra to remove injustice and to re-arrange the divine rules and orders; and Viṣṇu by his weapon, the Cakra, to destroy the opponents of Truth and to re-establish peace upon Earth.

In the former two epics, Agni, Vāyu, Indra, Viṣṇu, these four Godheads were active partially and temporarily with a few other Godheads to change the Age. In these two epics, Lord Viṣṇu was the Hero. But at present, the former Kalpa comprising the four Ages is coming to an end and a new Kalpa will begin with the Golden Age. Now all Gods and Goddesses will fully manifest with their power to transform and divinise the people of the Earth, to identify Earth with Heaven. The hero in the epic Devāyaṇa is the Satyadeva, the Supreme Truth himself, the Puruṣa Vedamāyā, who will manifest with the four Vedas and all the Godheads. The Aditi–Sindhu has already manifested in the subtle form in the intermediate plane, the Antarikṣa.

हिरण्यकर्णं मणिग्रीवमर्णस्तन्नो विश्वे वरिवस्यन्तु देवाः ।
अर्यो गिरः सद्य आ जग्मुषी रोस्राश्चाकन्तूभयेष्वस्मे ॥

Ṛg.I.122.14

Hiraṇyakarṇaṁ maṇi grīva marṇa stanno viśve varivasyantu devāḥ /
Aryo giraḥ sadya ā jagmuṣīrosrāścākantū bhayeṣvasme //

I aspire for Deva, Him with the golden ears, with gems around his neck, having a huge and wide golden body. I aspire to receive him here in this world. He is always sweet-spoken and has the best words. His head touches the Heaven when He places his feet on the Earth. On seeing Him the weak ego in us becomes frightened that it will exist no more.

The Deva who appears as the eternally pure supreme soul gives purity to us; there the Devi Pavamani Suhavā (his power of purity) showers us with a thousand streams.

12

THE ṚṢIS CALL FOR THE TRUTH

Just before the appearance of the spiritual Dawn, when the twilight was still spread over the Earth; we, the seven Immortal Ṛṣis worshipped the Lord of Truth, *Satyadeva*, to ask Him to descend down on the Earth. As in the previous Kalpas and to start a new Golden Age, we, the Ṛṣis again offered our worship to Deva for His descent on the Earth.

Ṛṣi Bharadavāja said:

The stream of *soma* that purifies us is glittering like molten gold. In the place of manifestation of the Divine Truth, where there were huge wealth and riches, the hostile powers are taking away the divine purity and riches. O golden Puruṣa, Satyadeva! Appear there again to control these hostile powers.

Then Ṛṣi Kaśyapa added:

The purest stream of *soma*, called the best "havi" – clarified butter, we offer as a sacrifice for the worship of Truth. This enlightens the inner vital forces of humanity. This stream of nectar or ambrosia is falling from a quiet immovable mountain to purify all of us.

Also Ṛṣi Gautama told us:

This wide stream of *soma* is falling down from an immovable mountain and is flowing everywhere in our human society. Look, it is reaching all the houses, inside and outside, near and far away in the forest. on the fields and is spreading everywhere.

Furthermore, Ṛṣi Atri spoke:

From the eternal ocean of *soma*, a stream is coming out. O Deva! O Gauribiti! Receive that flow of *soma* and drink it. After drinking *soma*, when both of you experience extreme *ānanda*, at that moment there will be a flow of honey from the honeycomb. From that very sweet honey, create a most beautiful creation for this Earth.

Ṛṣi Viśvamitra said:

O Deva! By drinking *soma* create a force like the Sun which abolishes the darkness. The Sun would be here like Hari, with His calm and quiet face having a sweet smile, for a creation full of great heroism. By His power and force, this Earth can be liberated from the deepest Ignorance and the Gods can perform their own tasks.

Ṛṣi Jāmdagni said:

I pray for your friendship, O Indu! Drink *ṣoma* and day by day, let us increase our friendship. Move towards the home of Eternal Truth. O Great Friend of Mankind! O Wise One! You know the secret of Truth, gradually fill the thirst for sweetest *soma* in this human heart.

Finally, Ṛṣi Vaśiṣṭha added:

O Abhi! *Soma* increases the longevity of life and then one achieves divine purity. By the joy of purity take us to the Eternal Ocean of *ānanda* to be absorbed there. The sages are swimming in the Ocean of *ānanda* like fishes. Their egos are completely dissolved.

Then appear flashes of the Golden Dawn on the sky of the Far East and the dormant souls awake. At that moment, other Ṛṣis start to chant the Hymns to the Deva and they commence the Deva-Yajña.*

---

* *The Deva Yajña is a sacrificial fire to be kindled to bring about a change in the earthly nature and transform it into the divine nature. The individual sacrificial flame in the heart is the Vitihotra, but when a collective effort is made to transform the earthly nature then it is the Deva-Yajña.*

A golden fountain is flowing from the immovable silent mountain. That golden water, *amṛta,* is the pure stream of *soma* that Satyadeva together with the other Gods are drinking. This gives them purity and joy. In the pure and peaceful home of the heart, the vital priest is offering and praying to Truth to drink the pure and Heavenly *soma.*

A son of Vaśiṣṭha, Indrapramati said:

By singing the songs of truth and by worshipping the Truth, Soma devata and the Moon God, the Sages attained the purest, all blissful, divine honey (nectar) in the golden pot.

Another son of Vaśiṣṭha, Parāśara said:

That transcendent stream of immortality is falling upon the Earth as the pure semen to form a divine child. From the body of the Deva, the stream of immortality when falling down offers its adoration to the Indra as the divine ruling power, to the Sun as the divine creation, to the Moon as the light of divine purity.

The son of Nahuṣa, Yayāti said:

The all purifying sweetest divine honey is filled up in golden pots, protected by Indra, the Divine King and is established in the eternal sound and letter. O Satyadeva! Take that into the eternal *ānanda* and immortality.

The son of Viṣvamitra, Renu said:

Three rays from each cow, like that we milk seven cows. In other words, we meditate above our head on the transcendental Heaven, where the Truth exists. There, O Aryama! Be a helpful worker to manifest the Truth in this determined, harmonious, cyclic movement of the three universes.

Then, the son of Alandan, Vatsapri said:

In the deepest shrine of the heart exists the most enlightened Deva, the child of immortality; O Indu! Give Him the divine *soma* to drink. By drinking *soma*, let the beautiful Deva enter into divinity and be conscious of his own immortality. And let him guide us with his pure sweet voice to purity and *ānanda*.

Moreover, Apsava Manu said:

O Indu! Let the Deva and Biti be purified by the stream of the enlightened powerful *soma*. Hand over the golden pot full of divine honey to Biti for the manifestation of the new Truth-Creation. Let Satyadeva also become pleased by drinking *soma*.

The grand daughter of Vaśiṣṭha, Gauribiti said:

I offer first *soma* to Somadevata, O knower of sacrifice. By drinking *soma*, be content and then let us be happy and purified by that honey of intoxicated *ānanda*. Let the Earth also become purified and released from her sufferings under the dark ignorance.

Then the son of Vaśiṣṭha, Śakti said:

O Deva! Through the most divine purity, let the transcendental light from your body spread over the Earth to manifest as the divine creation and let it be openly announced to all that immortality can be attained through it.

The son of Aṅgirā, Urdhvasadma said:

O Ishaspati! You are the Herald of the Truth! Surrounded by the light of Abhi, the famous transcendental Deva is his light above this creation. You should be guided by him for manifestating the purest Age of Truth to open everlasting youth, in other words open the path of immortality.

13

THE BEGINNING OF DAWN AND THE DESCENT OF THE DEVĀYAṆA

As the Divine Dawn moves towards the Earth, the darkest night of Kali passes away slowly. The awakened souls start remembering their past glorious days of immortality. We, the Ṛṣis, sing the songs of transcendental Truth through their memories.

य एतं देवमेकवृतं वेद ।

Ath.XIII.4.22

Ya etaṁ devamekavṛtaṁ veda .

There is only one Deva, who exists throughout the Vedas.

He said to us: I am above, I am beneath and I am in the core of all creations. The past is my father; I am the present like the Sun. I am seeing the past and the present from the secret cavern of the Deva.

In the home of Truth (*Vīda-Vaṅga*) let the pure light of Truth reappear. Becoming liberated from the bondage of work, I wish to place myself in a quiet transcendent condition. For reaching that fulfilment, I make a sacrificial rite to the *Deva* with the word svāhā. In other words, I concentrate on "Devāya svāhā" in place of the egoistic "I". O Truth! Replicate thyself upon the Earth.

O Deva! Come again with your power "the *Devi-Śakti*" at the place that you had left before. Come, O Supreme Puruṣa! with the pure and beautiful features, establish yourself on this

Earth with your eternal *dharma* (the eternal rules) and Heaven. With this word "Svāha", I adjust my prayer and offer my sacrificial rites. O Fire! Go quickly before the Deva and ask him to come here soonest.

Now we are conscious about the advent of Truth, O Manasaspati! Return to this world, return here again and perform the Deva Yajña with the word Svāha.

O Deva! You became very powerful and forceful with the Uṣṇik chanda. At that time, you entered into your favourite Gods, Agni and *Soma* and partook of the mortal feast, offered by the Earth. O Deva! Indra and *Soma* are your favourites, as you partook of the feast offered by the Heaven. O Deva! *Soma* and Viśvedeva are very dear to you, as you accepted the feast offered by Antarikṣa, the vital plane.

O Deva! To increase the riches of sacrifice with the manifestation of the immortal light, come down upon the Earth. Establish unity on the Earth and Heaven and manifest with your pure light. O Deva, when you appeared in the family of Abhivarta, they were enlightened. Enlighten us on this Earth in the same way.

The Deva appeared before the Gods from the sacrificial fire "Yajña" as a giver of sacrificial fruits, by churning the sacrifice. We remember him today, as we did before the sacrificial rite. O Deva! Accept our sacrifice and drink the ghṛta and madhu (clarified butter and honey) that we are offering to you.

Prajāpati has told us about an incredible feature of Deva in the sacrifice during the Yajña. The Supreme Truth, whom no one recognises, has existed throughout all creations. All the creations are dangling on his chest on the thread of his Yajña. With his purity, Satyadeva is delightfully scattering his white rays. O Fire! The Lord and the Protector of the Yajña is the Deva. Offer this sacrifice to Him.

The transcendent Deva, remains in the Sun as a power of consciousness with joy, light and heroism. He has manifested everywhere, in Indra and Agni as the light and power and in other Gods. In Bṛhaspati, he has manifested as intelligence. We worship Him.

Hari, worshipped by all, is identified with Deva the Truth. We aspire for Him to realise Deva the Truth. We offer our sacrificial rite for this purpose and worship the omnipotent Hari. By this, Hari might come with the descendent of Purandara Vajravahu, each clasping the other, to receive our offering to the Deva. Let them also manifest in this Yajña.

O Guru of Devas, Bṛhaspati! People of this Earth are becoming conscious with the light of the Sun. However, in their innermost being they are still unconscious. In fact, they live only to experience vital pleasure and to attain more prosperity. To enable humanity to enter into the bliss of Satyadeva. give the mantra of Deva, the Truth to this Earth. Teach them to be conscious of the Deva and guide them affectionately towards the Truth.

As Prajāpati said in Yajurveda:

देवं बर्हिरिन्द्रं सुदेवं देवैः वीरवत् ।
स्तीर्णं वेद्यामवर्धयत् ॥

Yaj.XXVIII.12

Devaṁ bahirindraṁ sudevaṁ devaiḥ vīravat /
Stirna vedyāmvardhayat //

The Deva is the one transcendental Truth; through his activities he received three forms and three names, Satyadeva, Sudeva and Vasudeva. For the moment, think that the Deva is one. He is one for all activities through all Godheads.

Satyadeva is standing on the Indra-Varhi (the sacrificial seat in the human heart). The Deva is here, by scattering his own power and light, He is increasing our self-knowledge in his three manifestations.

1. He is called Satyadeva, the Transcendental Truth, when he gives guidance to all creations. He holds the *Kālacakra* (the Wheel of Time) in his hands to drive out Kali from this creation, to bring about a change at

the end of the Iron Age. He ushers in a new Kalpa with the glorious Golden Age.

2. When the Deva guides individual beings to make a union between the Earth and the Heaven, he is called Sudeva.
3. When the Deva guides the whole humanity he is called Vasudeva. The Deva is one and the same, only with differing activities he is known as Satyadeva, Sudeva or Vasudeva.

Satyadeva guides us from above as the leader of the Golden Age and the Lord of Activities of all Gods; Vasudeva from the outside, who removes all divisions, discords and disharmonies and unites the human race on a peaceful Earth; Sudeva from inside, as the psychic being or the soul willing to be identified with the Earth and Heaven.

But the Deva, is the One Transcendental Being.

14

AGNI OPENING THE PATH FOR THE DESCENT OF DEVA

We come to know more about the Deva in the following ślokas.

As the Vedas say:

देवं देवं वोऽवसे देवं देवं अभिष्टये ।
देवं देवं हुवेम वाजसातये गृणन्तो देव्या धिया ॥

Yaj.XXXIII.91

Devaṁ devaṁ vo'vase devaṁ devaṁ abhiṣṭae /
Devaṁ devaṁ huvema vājasātaye gṛṇanto devyā dhiyā //

With Satyadeva's help, all Godheads are developing and attaining their divine fulfilment. That is why all the Gods are aspiring for His constant touch. They are always calling upon Him to be present amongst them. Satyadeva increases their meditation, assists them in proliferating their activities and makes them dominant with his power, light and riches.

यज्ञेन यज्ञमयजन्त देवास्तानि धर्माणि प्रथमान्यासन् ।
ते ह नाकं महिमानः सचन्त यत्र पूर्वे साध्याः सन्ति देवाः ॥

Yaj.XXXI.16

Yajñena yajñamayajanta devāstāni dhārmāṇi prathāmanyāsan /
Te ha nākaṁ mahimāṇaḥ sacanta yatra pūrve sādhyāḥ santi devāḥ //

When the manifested Deva undertook sacrificial activities, with his own "*dharma*", then these were called the "*Satya-dharma*", the Truth activities. These activities shed the brilliance of Heaven on the Earth. This is when the worshippers and the Gods saw Deva.

In the round Earth, surrounded by the sky like ether, Viśvakarmā at first let flow the sweet flow of honey with divine beauty. In there, Tvaṣṭā gave his beautiful formations. Due to these actions and at the very beginning of Time the Earth entered into immortality and achieved her divine status.

वेदाहमेतं पुरुषं महान्तमादित्यवर्णं तमसः परस्तात् ।
तमेव विदित्वाऽतिमृत्युमेति नान्यः पन्था विद्यतेऽयनाय ॥

Yaj.XXXI.18

Vedāhametaṁ puruṣaṁ mahāntamādityavarṇaṁ tamasaḥ parastāt I
Tameva viditva'timṛtyumeti nānyaḥ panthā vidyate' yanāya II

Thus, I came to know about the Supramental Being, the Deva, who is above all darkness and is resplendent and glorious like the great Sun. By knowing the Supreme Being, Deva the Truth, we conquered old age and death. There is no other way to conquer death and to become immortal in the cyclic movement of time, ayana. (In this our journey must be towards Deva, then only can we conquer death and attain immortality. There is no other way in this cyclic movement except through the Devāyaṇa.)

हिरण्मयेन पात्रेण सत्यस्यापिहितं मुखम् ।
योऽसवादित्ये पुरुषः सोऽसावहम् ।
ॐ खं ब्रह्म ॥

Yaj.XL.17

Hiraṇmayena pātreṇa satyasyāpihitaṁ mukham I
Yo'asavāditye puruṣaḥ so'asāvahaṁ I
OM, khaṁ brahma II

The face of Truth remains covered with a golden disc. He is the Deva, who exists in the Sun and is eternal. He is in eternal sound, the OM. He is the Truth, He is the Brahman.

Whenever we spoke about the Truth, it remained incomplete because no one can speak fully about the Truth. Words cannot express Him fully. Words, themselves, express Him with force due to His own power. One has to realise the Truth with one's own heart. So we speak here about his manifestation upon the Earth through Yajña, which is sacrifice from the heart. The sacrificial fire lit in the heart of Bengal is reaching up to touch the Heaven and is calling for the Deva. That is Yajña, the sacrificial fire. In other words, Yajña is the fervent psychic aspiration, the ardent desire for identification with the Deva with a total dedication and a complete surrender to the Truth. By this, the egoistic "I", the one enjoying vital foods and material wealth, will dissolve in the *ānanda* of Truth. The Truth itself will replace the "I" and enjoy immortality. Then individuals will feel that they are immortal, and that they will not have to experience diseases, death, pain or sufferings. They will remain ever young and joyful. This is Yajña.

We, the Ṛṣis, kindle this Yajña in the Earthly consciousness at the beginning of the Golden Age to realise the Truth. This Yajña opens the secret path of Deva and the Devāyaṇa stands revealed. Through this golden path, the Deva comes down on this Earth, because he is the Lord of the Yajña. He comes to the Yajña – as Yajurveda says:

यज्ञ यज्ञं गच्छ यज्ञपतिं गच्छ स्वां योनिं गच्छ स्वाहा ।
एष ते यज्ञो यज्ञपते सहसूक्तवाकः सर्ववीरस्तं जुषस्व स्वाहा ॥

Yaj.VIII.22

Yajña yajñaṁ gaccha yajñapatiṁ gaccha svāṁ
yoniṁ gaccha svāhā /
Eṣa te yajño yajñapate sahasūktavākaḥ sarvavīrastaṁ
juṣasva svāhā //

O Yajña! Take your seat here to call the Deva and become united with your Lord Satyadeva. Take your seat on the root of the creation of the word. Be seated on the tongue of Bengal, with the word svāha (Vaṅga-vaka svāha). We offer thus our sacrificial rite. In this way, O Yajña! Be unified with your Lord by the light, power and consciousness of Truth. With the expression of Truth, appear powerfully. Like an all-powerful hero, hold the true words to conquer falsehood.

दिवि धाऽ इमं यज्ञमिमं यज्ञं दिवि धाः ।
स्वाहग्नये यज्ञीयाय शं यजुर्भ्यः ॥

Yaj.XXXVIII.11

Divi dhā' emam yajñamimaṁ yajñaṁ divi dhāḥ /
Svāhagnaye yagñiyāya śaṁ yajurbhyaḥ //

To be identified with this divine Yajña, which was established in Heaven, offer your sacrificial rite in the fire with the word "Svāha". Let the Earth be peaceful and happy with the identification of Yajña with Heaven. This is the voice of Yaju for the peace of the Earth.

देवा यज्ञमतन्वत भेषजं भिषजाऽश्विना ।
वाचा सरस्वती भिषगिन्द्रायेन्द्रियाणि दधतः ॥

Yaj.XIX.12

Devā yajñamatanvata bheṣajaṁ bhiṣajā'śvinā /
Vācā sarasvatī bhiṣagindrāyendriyāni dadhataḥ //

The Deva holds the bheṣajā (medicine for immunity) which has emerged from the Yajña. With this bheṣajā, the Aśvinīs became the divine physicians to cure diseases and to remove infirmity and old age. Sarasvatī establishes the bheṣajā, the power of immunity, in the physical senses with words. Through the tongue, she influences the other senses of the body.

देवहूर्यज्ञ ऽ आ च वक्षत् सुम्नहूर्यज्ञ ऽ आ च वक्षत् ।
यक्षदग्निर्देवो देवां आ च वक्षत् ॥

Yaj. XVII.62

Devahūryajña'ā ca vakṣat sumnahūryajña' ā ca vakṣat /
Yakṣadagnirdevo devaṁ ā ca vakṣat //

In the sacrificial flame of Truth, the aspiration for Truth is rising up from the fire. That aspiration is pulling down the Truth, the Deva, to the sacrificial shrine. Agni, the Lord of Fire, while pulling down forcefully the self manifested Deva, says the following sweet words.

सा मे सत्यशीर्देवान् गम्याज्जुष्टाज्जुष्टतरा पन्थात् ।
पन्थतराहेऽता मनसा देवान् गच्छ यो देवयानः पन्थास्तेन ।
देवान् गच्छ यज्ञो देवान् गच्छतु यज्ञो देवान् ।
गम्याददो मा गच्छतु ॥

Kāṭhaka Saṁhitā 5.12

Sā me satyaṣīradevān gamyājjuṣṭājjuṣṭatarā panthāt /
Panthatarāhe' tā manasā devān gaccha yo
devayānaḥ panthāstena /
Devān gaccha yajño devān gacchatu yajño devān /
Gamyādado mā gacchatu //

These are the blessings for Truth, when Deva moves towards us through the royal path. We meditate on the path, the Devayāna, on which the Deva moves towards the Earth. We meditate on the Devayāna, as the Deva moves towards the Yajña where he manifests himself. When the Devayāna opens with the Yajña; the Deva approaches us to bless us with his purity, light and beauty to make us divinised and transformed.

ये देवा यज्ञहनो यज्ञ मुषः पृथिव्यामध्यासते ।
अग्निर्मा तेभ्यो रक्षतु गच्छेम सुकृतो वयम् ॥

Kathaka Samhita

Ye devā yajñahano yajña muṣaḥ pṛthivyāmadhyāsate /
Agnirmā tebhyo rakṣatu gachhema sukṛto vayam //

The Deva, who holds the Yajña, appears through it when He manifests on this Earth. Agni, the Lord of the Fire, protects us from all opponents and leads us to purity to perform the work of Truth.

When this sacrificial fire is rising high to touch the Heaven, the other Ṛṣis start chanting the Hymns to the Truth. As Agastaya said:

O Satyadeva! You are blazing powerfully like the Sun and shining beautifully like the Moon. Protect us and your eternal home Bengal. O Deva! You are the giver of immortality as Somadevata. You are both the destroyer of Darkness and the manifestor of the Dawn. We worship you, O Deva! Increase the divine beauty and riches in us, release us from the vital bondage that holds us in thrall and awaken in us the new consciousness with the word "svāha".

Our past memories have not come back. We have even forgotton that realising You was our only goal and in future this has to be achieved. That is the reason, O Satyadeva, that we adore only you. O Vanaspati! For the adoration of the Deva, please help us arrange the items you require. So that we attain Lord Viṣṇu together with the Deva. And, O Plant (Bheṣajā)! Save us from the attacks of our enemies particularly those who want to destroy our body.

Then the Son of Kaṇva, Praskaṇva said:

O Vācaspati, the Lord of Words, give us purity in words and Lord Viṣṇu guide our works so that they attain the acceptance of the divine. There, O Satyadeva! Quickly acquire our purified and divinised parts from the Gods.

O Satyadeva! In your feast, the Jātaveda, Fire, himself comes before you with his power "svāha" and by unifying with the Sun discloses the scenes of the world. This itself manifests your glory.

The son of Atharvaṇ, Dadhyaṅga added:

O Lord of the World! O Lord of the Mind! O Lord of the Word! O Lord of the Word of all Worlds! Regain for us the ability to hear the Truth, to establish Truth in our lives and by attaining Truth enter into immortality. Offer the feast to the Deva, let the food and drink become divine. Enter into the

Vitihotra and be unified with the Deva. To attain immortality, drink the divine sweetness and let the sweetness of the divine honey flow over the entire Earth.

O Fire! Disclose to us the new path of Truth which is decorated by divine riches. By that the intellectuals of the world can be fulfilled by attaining a wide education and the Truth knowledge. The heroes and the warriors can attain or establish themselves in the power and immensity of Truth. For the fulfilment of these words of the Creator, I prostrate before you.

A golden disc remains in front of the Truth, covering his face. The Immortal Being exists in the Sun. He exists there eternally. He is the Truth, who remains in the word "OM". He is the Brahman.

At the beginning of this creation, the Seers of Truth worshipped the eternally shining Truth to increase the purity of the Earth. They drank the pure, supreme joy like a shower of water as if the Earth was drinking the rain from the clouds.

Then, the Son of Āptya, Tritā said:

O Abhi, the Light exists in the centre of the Heaven and shines on all the creations. Is He the Truth? Is He the Immortality? Is He the Eternal? The Lord of All. If yes, then disclose to us what we could offer to Him as our adoration.

The Son of Gautama, Vāmadeva said further:

ऋचं साम यजामहे याभ्यां कर्माणि कृण्वते ।
विते सदसि राजतो यज्ञं देवेषु वक्षतः ॥

Sām.369, Ath.VII.56.1

Ṛcaṁ sāma yajāmahe yābhyāṁ karmāṇi kṛṇvate I
Vite sadasi rājato yajñam deveṣu vakṣataḥ II

For whom we recite the mantras of the Ṛgveda and the mantras of Sāmaveda and by whom all the works are accomplished. He is the Truth, who is standing inside the sacrificial flame for the Supreme. He was called Deva, the name given to Him by the Ṛṣis.

Parucchepa said:

We meditate constantly on the all-beautiful and famous Agni devata, the Lord of the Fire. We meditate constantly and increase it gradually. Above the Fire, the divine Indra and the Vāyudevata, the Lord of the Winds rule. Let them guide us by their divine voices. In between these two, there is the Sun-Vivasvat shining brightly. With his power he gives us new ideas. With the excitement of these divine ideas, a supreme meditation forms. He is the Deva, whom we desire eternally and for whom we meditate through the divine ideas given by the Sun.

And Nakula said:

O Deva, Son of Abhi! The poets are giving You the same homage that they give to the Sun. I say that you are the Supreme Truth, the root of all creations. You hold all the riches and Your actions are of the highest, crowned with an elegant beauty. On Your Head glitters a powerful crown of light. That shining light scatters its rays all around. O Son of Abhi, with the golden hands! Giver of divine fruits of Yajña, shower your Grace on me and make me free from the bondage of birth and works.

Gritsmada added:

There is a triangular room above the top of this Earth. Beauty, peace and joy reign there. In that fully-enlightened all-powerful pure home, Lord Viṣṇu drinks the nectar (soma). Whatever we do here on this Earth goes to the supreme palace. There the Deva resides, who is the Truth and Consciousness Himself. He is existing, O Indu! We call him Satyadeva or the Lord of Truth. O Indra, He is the Supreme Truth.

The Deva took birth from the sacrificial fire with the powerfully enlightened words of Truth. He grew up with an all-conquering indomitable power and heroism. He has a beautiful appearance. He gives us all we need when we offer Him our worship, homage and desires. He guides the Vasus to give us divine riches. He is the Truth and Consciousness. O Indu, He appeared in front of us with his indomitable heroism. He was called Deva-Satya or Satyadeva. O Indra! See, He is the Supreme Truth.

In this lower consciousness and the inconscient field, He gives us power to rise up and makes us conscious of the divinity. He guides us by conquering all oppositions with the all-powerful heroism and raises us to the supreme status. In the lower vital plane, where the needs of hunger and thirst are ever-present, he appears in the form of love and makes us surrender to the Divine. He is the Deva, who is Truth and Consciousness himself. O Indu! He raises us from the lower inconscient to the supreme consciousness. He was called Deva-Satya or Satyadeva; O Indra! He is the Supreme Truth.

Finally, other Ṛṣis said:

Have you heard, O Earth! The Supreme Will, Satyadeva, sent the message through the mouth of Agni, the Lord of the Fire, that He himself will manifest in the course of time to increase your purity and prosperity.

O Abhi! By your power of tapasya and influence, let our life-water be as sweet as honey and let it be free from bitterness and ignorance. Then Satyadeva might disclose a new Golden Age where the Godheads will have full play.

In the beginning of the new Golden Age, there are astonishing descriptions of the different Godheads and all events of the world to purify the words and the letters so that one could enter into the Truth by the showering of the stream of *soma* with all sweetness and beauty. This is the divine epic, Devāyaṇa, which narrates the secrets of the eternal truths.

Among the poets, he is the best as he has described the union of Deva with Gauribiti, the truth aspirant power. This epic describes the secret knowledge of the Deva-Biti union, narrates all the important happenings of the world even of that period which is protected by Abhivarta. Together with the narration of all the events in the past, it also describes how to enter into the glorious future.

Satyadeva provides us with absolute purity by removing all sorts of impurities. It is He who established all the Godheads in purity. He establishes purity on this Earth with the Vasus and other Godheads so that the people of the world are able to beome immortal.

In this world, life becomes like a new-born child. Gradually, day-by-day, it enters into the immunity or the infirmity. See, the ray of truth is glimmering. O Dvitā! Clasp this world and protect the declining truth in life.

For bringing about the manifestation of the divine Epic and to attain the truth and immortality, the Ṛṣis paid homage to the Truth and Immortality as in the former Golden Age. Amongst them Abhivarta-Aṅgirāsa and Sauciki-Agñeya were the main Ṛṣis. Abhivarta started this work by kindling the sacrificial fire to attain Deva. Then, Sauciki performed the sacrificial rite to manifest the Truth. This has been narrated in the Devāyaṇa by Piṅgala Maheśvara. However to provide you with more proof, we had worshipped the Immortality in former Ages through the Deva Yajña. This we disclose here once again.

15

PROPHET OF IMMORTALITY

For the completion of the yogic sacrifice and for Abhivarta's yajna to realise the Deva and to attain immortality, we offer our homage today again, as we did in the past. Listen, O Child of Earth! These were the mantras that we chanted for immortality.

Let Somadevata, the Lord of Nectar, bring to a close the work of destructive death and lead us into immortality. Whenever we drink the elixir of Truth, let us become liberated from the clutches of blind ignorant forces. Then our purified senses should feel the presence of Truth. Let Indra fill up our active senses with his unique power and heroism; so that we enter into the sweet divine life that is immortal and immune.

In this vast creation, whenever there is a flow of the nectar then life drinks this elixir and enters into the pure divine consciousness. Whenever we drink the elixir of Truth, we are liberated from the clutches of blind ignorant forces. Then our purified senses feel the presence of truth; and Indra fills up our active senses with his unique power and heroism; and we enter into the sweet divine life of the immortal and the immune.

Throughout the creation, with a sweet divine rhythm, the river of nectar is constantly flowing. Life is like a swan that swims in that stream and attains its purity. Whenever we drink the elixir of Truth, we are liberated from the clutches of blind ignorant forces. Then our purified senses feel the presence of Truth; and Indra fills up our active senses with his unique power and heroism. We enter then into the sweet divine life of the immortal and the immune.

The distilled rice juice (wine) is an energetic drink for the Kṣatria (fighters) to give them more energy but the Soma gives them purity. The divine wine is a drink for the Vipras (wise men). It broadens their knowledge as decided by Prajāpati. Whenever we drink the elixir of Truth, we are liberated from the clutches of blind ignorant forces. Then our purified senses feel the presence of Truth; and Indra fills up our active senses with his unique power and heroism; and we enter into the sweet divine life of the immortal and the immune.

In the womb of women, the semen enters like a liquid. Day by day it takes the formation of a child. When the baby is fully developed, then it takes birth and leaves the womb. This is the reason for the earthly birth. Know this and be free from the bondage of mortal birth. Whenever we drink the elixir of Truth, we are liberated from the clutches of blind ignorant forces. Then our purified senses feel the presence of Truth; and Indra fills up our active senses with his unique power and heroism; and we enter into the sweet divine life of the immortal and the immune.

In this creation, we see two kinds of formations. One is the truth formation that is divine and the other is false, which is undivine. Thus Prajāpati decided faithfulness for the divine and unfaithfulness for the undivine. This is the reason that we remain faithful to the divine and we pay no attention to the undivine. Whenever we drink the elixir of Truth, we are liberated from the clutches of blind ignorant forces. Then our purified senses feel the presence of Truth; and Indra fills up our active senses with his unique power and heroism; and we enter into the sweet divine life of the immortal and the immune.

The sons and daughters of the Creator Prajāpati are there throughout the four Vedas. By obtaining knowledge of His formations we attain a height above the creations. In other words, we pass over the cycle of birth and death. Whenever we drink the elixir of Truth, we are liberated from the clutches of blind ignorant forces. Then our purified senses feel the presence of Truth; and Indra fills up our active senses with his unique power and heroism; and we enter into the sweet divine life of the immortal and the immune.

There are three kinds of drinks provided by the Prajāpati. One is highly energetic, the distilled rice-juice (the wine) meant for the fighters (the Kṣatrias), the second is for quenching the thirst of common people and that is water and the third is to increase the knowledge and improve the purity of the Vipras (the wise persons) and that is Soma (the divine wine). Drink the Soma and become spiritually advanced. Whenever we drink the elixir of Truth, we are liberated from the clutches of blind ignorant forces. Then our purified senses feel the presence of Truth; and Indra fills up our active senses with his unique power and heroism; and we enter into the sweet divine life of the immortal and the immune.

16

ABHIVARTA: FROM MIND TO SUPERMIND

Abhivarta is the mediator between the Transcendent Truth and the material Earth, mortality and immortality, mind and the superman. He takes our earthly prayers and hymns and offers them to the Supreme Truth. He clasps the Supreme Truth, the Deva as his son and brings him down so that the Earth can become transformed and divinised by his activities.

Long ago, Abhivarta performed a great tapasya for the manifestation of the Truth and he realised the Deva as his son. By his presence in Heaven, the Heaven became pure, peaceful, highly enlightened and immortal. Then he brought his son down to the Earth. With the influence of Satyadeva, the human beings entered into divinity. Through the work of all Godheads on the Earth, he literally made the heavenly stream of *soma* fall down on the Earth. With this the Earth entered into divine purity and peace. For this reason, we here on Earth consider that by worshipping *soma*, the divine wine, human beings can enter into the divine purity and joy of Truth. Satyadeva conveyed the prayer of the Earth and moved towards the greater Heaven, to re-open the new Golden Age for the fulfilment of Yajña. For his attainments, we adored Abhivarta, the King of the Ṛṣis. Listen to the hymns to Abhivarta.

By Abhivarta's tapasya through his sacrificial fire, the Deva manifested. The Divine Emperor, Indra opened the way for Abhivarta, by making a connecting link between Heaven and

Earth. O Brahmanspati! Help Deva, to manifest here on the Earth. Let the suzerainty of Abhi, the truth-influenced kingdom be established here on the Earth in course of time. O Siddhidata, Giver of Accomplishment, bring this triumph to the Earth.

On this Earth, there are many divisions and diversities. On that basis, we have now several states, nations, languages, religions and castes etc. Through the influence of Abhivarta and with the advent of Truth, let those enemies, who are destroying the peace and unity of Earth, be conquered. Let us enter into the kingdom of Abhi, the peaceful united divine kingdom, where we shall enjoy the constant presence of Truth.

अभि त्वा देवः सविताभि सोमो अवीवृतत् ।
अभि त्वा विश्वा भूतान्यभीवर्तो यथाससि ॥

Ṛg. X.174.3

Abhi tvā devaḥ savitābhi somo avīvṛtdt I
Abhi tvā viśvā bhūtānyabhīvarto yathāsasi II

O Abhi! Please guide this universe like the Sun and the Moon God. Also become part of the entire humanity and become active in them to realise Deva. O Lord of Ṛṣis! We feel that we lack in receptivity.

अभिवर्तो अभिभवः सपत्नक्षयणो मणिः ।
राष्ट्राय मह्यं बध्यतां सपत्नेभ्यः पराभुवे ॥

Ath.I.29.4

Abhivarto abhibhavaḥ sapatnakṣayaṇo maṇiḥ I
Rāṣṭrāya mahyaṁ badhyatāṁ sapatnebhyaḥ parābhuve II

O Abhivarta! Influence the whole universe with the power, light and purity of Satyadeva. Eliminate the existing divisions among the many states in the world. Let us all remain in the one united divine world influenced by Truth. Let us enjoy the pure state of Truth throughout the Earth by conquering the enemies of unity and by removing the myriad diversities in the one united world.

The sacrificial flame was kindled in the palace of Abhivarta to invoke the Truth, Deva as his son in the presence of all the Ṛṣis and the Godheads. This event was narrated in great detail by Piṅgala Maheśvara in the great Epic Devāyaṇa. The Sāmaveda says:

अभि वायुं वीत्यर्षा गृणानोऽभि मित्रावरुणा पूयमानः ।
अभी नरं धीजवनं रथेष्ठामभीन्द्रं वृषणं वज्रबाहुम् ॥

Sām.1426

Abhi vāyuṁ vītyarṣā gṛṇāno' bhi mitrāvaruṇā pūyamānāḥ I
Abhi naraṁ dhījavanaṁ ratheṣṭhāmabhīndraṁ vṛṣaṇam vajrabāhum II

To establish *Vitihotra*, the aspirant power of the Truth, in the home of Abhivarta, Vāyu, the Lord of the Wind, became the announcer and Mitra-Varuṇa, the organiser of the ceremony for the union of Satyadeva with Gauribiti. Nara, the brother of Abhivarta, became active as a host to receive the divine guests, comprising of Gods and the Ṛṣis. And the all powerful Vajrabāhu, Indra, acted as the adminstrator.

अभि वस्त्रा सुवसनान्यर्षाभि धेनुः सुदुघाः पूयमानः ।
अभि चन्द्रा भर्तवे नो हिरण्याभ्यश्वान्रथिनो देव सोम ॥

Ṛg.IX.97.50

Abhi vastrā suvasanānyarṣābhi dhenūḥ sudughāḥ pūyamāṇaḥ I
Abhi candrā bhartave no hiraṇyābhyaśvānrathino deva soma II

Abhivarta gave the divine clothes and garments to Gauribiti for her purification and also gave her divine milk to drink by milking the Heaven-Cow. Then Candra, the Moon God, gave her purity – he gave the golden colour to her body. At the moment of the union of Deva with Gauribiti, he gave a golden pot of nectar to her filled with the heavenly *soma*.

अभि नो अर्ष दिव्या वसून्यभि विश्वा पार्थिवा पूयमानः ।
अभि येन द्रविणमश्नवामाभ्यार्षेयं जमदग्निवन्नः ॥

Sām.1428

Abhi no arṣa divyā vasūnyabhi viśvā pārthivā pūyamānaḥ /
Abhi yena draviṇamaśnavāmābhyārṣeyaṁ jamadagnivannaḥ //

Then Abhivarta filled the whole universe as well as the Earth with divine riches through the eight Vasus. At that moment, Abhivarta appeared as the giver of all riches through his worship of Satyadeva. Jāmadagni, son of Bhṛgu, circulated these activities among the people of the Earth so that they could join with him.

अभि ते मधुना पयोऽथर्वाणो अशिश्रयुः ।
देवं देवाय देवयु ॥

Rg.IX.11.2

Abhi te madhunā payo'tharvāṇo aśiśrayuḥ /
Devaṁ devāya devayu //

O Abhivarta! Let this life giving water be as sweet as honey with your influence. Let bitterness and ignorance be removed, so that Satyadeva together with the other Godheads can manifest in the Golden Age.

अभि व्रतानि पवते पुनानो देवो देवान्त्स्वेन रसेन पृञ्चन् ।
इन्दुर्धर्माण्यृतुथा वसानो दश क्षिपो अव्यत सानो अव्ये ॥

Sām.1021

Abhi vratāni pavate punāno devo devāntsvena rasena pṛñcan /
Indurdharmāṇyṛtuthā vasāno dasha kṣipo avyata sāno avye //

Abhivarta did a tapasya for the manifestation of Truth. With the influence of Satyadeva, he brought about the purity of this

Earth. With the help of the other Godheads, he brought divine sweetness and purest joy in life. He did a tapasya of *Soma* devata, the Lord of Nectar. His aim was to bring purity to this Earth with the power of *soma.* To do this yajña, he visited all creations to collect the materials for this sacrifice to realise the Satyadeva.

पवमाना असृक्षत सोमाः शुक्रास इन्दवः ।
अभि विश्वानि काव्या ॥

Ṛg.IX.63.25

Pavamānā asṛkṣata somāḥ śukrāsa indavaḥ I
Abhi viśvāni kāvyā II

For this reason, Indu, the Moon God brought down purity to this Earth with the stream of the golden *soma* and the Earth conscience became absorbed in Heavenly bliss, *ānanda* and the great Epic "*Abhi-Kavya*" manifested for attaining the purity, immortality and a peaceful united empire on the Earth.

When this news was circulated by Jāmadagni, at that moment, Vājasateya, a disciple of Yaju, performed a great tapasya to establish "*Abhi-Raṣtra*", the one united and divine kingdom on the Earth, that was completely peaceful. He made this link for uniting Earth with Heaven by worshipping the Lord Indra for the victory of Truth, Sāmaveda says:

विभ्राड् बृहत्सुभृतं वाजसातमं धर्मन्दिवो धरुणे सत्यमर्पितम् ।
अभित्रहा वृत्रहा दस्युहंनमं ज्योतिर्जज्ञे असुरहा सपत्नहा ॥

Ṛg.X.170.2

Vibhrāḍ bṛhatsubhṛtaṁ vājasātamaṁ dharmandivo dharuṇe satyamarpitam I
Abhitrahā vṛtrahā dasyuhaṁnamaṁ jyotirjajñe asurahā sapatnahā II

O Vājasātaya! You undertook a great penance and austerity for Indra to remove disorder and disharmony from the Earth through the unifying peaceful activities of Truth and to bring down order and harmony. Indra was worshipped by the people as follows: O Indra! Thou art the *"Abhitraha"*, killer of the opponents. Thou art the *"Vṛtraha"*, slayer of Vṛtra – the demon who brought diversity into unity. Thou art the *"Dasyuhanta"*, the killer of Dasyus, the robbers of divine riches. In the sacrifice for the Truth, Indra also became the *"Asuraha"*, killer of Asuras, opponents of the divine empire and *"Saptanaha"*, the destroyer of dualities.

After the tapasya of Vājasātaya, the Earth was going to become peacefully united with the kingdom of Heaven. At that time, the other Ṛṣis chanted thus:

We have come to this life. Existing in this body, we are following the wrong path by wishing for material prosperity and for vital enjoyment. Always, we eagerly desire food, wealth and fame. We should however be taking the right steps to attain the Supreme. To achieve immortality we are not meditating on the Satyadeva, even for a moment. It is He who conquers darkness and suffering, gives us light and consciousness and leads us into purity and peace.

सुविज्ञानं चिकितुषे जनाय सच्चासच्च वचसी पस्पृधाते ।
तयोर्यत्सत्यं यतरदृजीयस्तदित्सोमोऽवति हन्त्यासत् ॥

Ṛg. VII.104.12

Suvijañāṁ cikituṣe janāya saccāsacca vacasī paspṛdhāte /
Tayoryatsatyaṁ yataradṛjīyastaditsomo' vati hantyāsat //

In the supramental light, Truth is shining and scattering rays over these people. In words, there is both Truth and Falsehood; let the words of Truth become enlightened and powerful with the union of the eternal *ānanda* of Truth. Let them enter into the immortality.

उत स्वराजे अदितिः सोममिन्द्राय जीजनत् ।
पुरुप्रशस्तमूतय ऋतस्य यत् ॥

Ṛg. VIII.12.14

Uta svarāje aditiḥ somamindrāya jījanat ।
Purupraśastamūtaya ṛtasya yat ॥

O Divine Mother Aditi! Come back to be established in your own divine empire upon the Earth. The most intense adoration goes to You from the entire divine kingdom. Out of these, the best offering received by Indra, which opens the path of Truth again, is the Devāyaṇa.

अभि वह्नय ऊतयेऽनूषत प्रशस्तये ।
न देव विव्रता हरी ऋतस्य यत् ॥

Ṛg.VIII.12.15

Abhi vahnaya ūtaye'nūṣata praśastaye ।
Na deva vivratā harī ṛtasya yat ॥

The sacrificial fire of Abhi has been kindled and established upon the Earth, by which the path of Truth has been completely opened. Our Satyadeva remains identically one with the all powerful Hari; let Hari manifest with Deva, here upon the Earth.

अभि प्रेहि माप वेन उग्रश्चेत्ता सपत्नहा ।
आ तिष्ठ मित्रवर्धन तुभ्यं देवा अधि ब्रवन् ॥

Ath.IV.8.2

Abhi prehi māpa vena ugraścettā sapatnahā ।
Ā tiṣṭha mitravardhana tubhyaṁ devā adhi bravan ॥

King Vena on the Earth did an arduous tapasya and was able to establish the "Abhi-Samrājya", the one united peaceful kingdom of Heaven upon the Earth; therein Mitra, Lord of Life, added harmony and friendship by which the identification of Heaven with Earth was strengthened. Through that love and unity, Satyadeva the Truth, manifested upon the Earth.

17

VIŚVAKARMĀ, THE WORK OF TRANSFORMATION

The King among the Ṛṣis, Abhivarta received Satyadeva, the Truth, as his son after the completion of his sacrificial adoration. At that moment, through the virtues and purity of the Deva, Heaven became highly enlightened and entered into immortality. Viśvakarmā, son of Bhuvana, observed with joy the glorious immortality of Heaven. He is the artist who gave all shapes and formations in this world. He aspired to bring the divine beauty of the immortal Heaven in this earthly creation. For this he meditated on Heaven and chanted hymns to the Deva.

The question arises – who is our father, our mother and creator, who knew the place of our shelter in the whole universe. Among the Gods, the Deva is the Lord of All. With his knowledge, He is the solution to all the queries and problems of this world. As he is the Truth, He has manifested.

Above there is the superior enlightened Heaven and down here the inferior dark Earth. At the beginning of creation, Devas and Asuras, Gods and the Demons, all remained in Heaven like brothers, but then there commenced a dispute. The question arose about who would have supremacy in the Heaven, the Devas or the Asuras. To seize authority, the Asuras used their own power, while the Gods worshipped the Truth. From the transcendental plane, Deva the Truth descended on Heaven with his all-powerful pure light. On receiving the adoration of the Gods, he entered into them.

With the manifestation of Truth, the Gods were victorious. On seeing the Truth enlightened Heaven, the Earth offered her adoration to Heaven and achieved the Truth with the Gods.

When the Earth worshipped the Heaven, Deva, together with all Godheads came down. With the embrace of Heaven, the Earth was transformed and became divine. She appeared heavenly, enlightened, beautiful and immortal.

At that moment, Viśvakarmā through his tapasya for the Truth and to please the Godheads, painted the picture of the Earth as Heaven. Then the Earth appeared like Heaven and human beings here were called Supermen. When Viśvakarmā filled the Earth with divine beauty, the Gandharvas, the celestial musicians, provided divine rhythms and music. They also gave the divine movement to mankind in their limbs so that human beings could dance and sing divinely. Finally, the Earth received Heaven's sweet juice in the plant "Apamgarva" by which men could have their divine life, away from infirmity, disease and death.

बलविज्ञाय स्थविरः प्रवीरः सहस्वान्वाजी सहमान उग्रः ।
अभिवीरो अभिसत्वा सहोजा जैतमिन्द्र रथमा तिष्ठ गोवित् ॥

Ṛg.X.103.5

Balavijñāya sthavirah pravīrah sahasvānvājī sahamāna ugrah |
Abhivīro abhisatvā sahojā jaitamindra rathamā tiṣṭha govit ||

We came to know the eternal powerful hero riding on a horse, with an open sword. He appeared in the family of Abhivarta and was called Abhi-Vira, the Satyadeva, who was scattering pure light from his body. With his simple sweet smiling face, he gave hope to mankind, he came on the Earth in the chariot of Indra to conquer all opposition and establish his perfect victory on the Earth.

अभि गोत्राणि सहसा गाहमानोऽदाय उग्रः शतमन्युरिन्द्रः ।
दुश्च्यवनः पृतनाषाड्योध्योऽस्माकं सेना अवतु प्रयुत्सु ॥

Ath. 19.13.7

Abhi gotrāṇi sahasā gāhamāno' dāya ugraḥ śatamanyurindraḥ /
Duścyavanaḥ pṛtanāṣāḍayodhyo' smākaṁ senā avatu prayutsu //

There is a sudden advent of Satyadeva, born in the family of Abhivarta. He is coming. The all conquering-hero, ten thousand times more powerful than Indra, is imminent. By his worship, Cyavana conquered his infirmity and became like a young boy of sixteen years. He is coming to conquer our infirmity and give us immunity with eternal youth. O Earth! Adore the advent of Truth and meditate on Him.

इन्द्र आसां नेता बृहस्पतिर्दक्षिणा यज्ञः पुर एतु सोमः ।
देवसेनानामभिभञ्जतीनां जयन्तीनां मरुतो यन्त्वग्रम् ॥

Ṛg.X.103.8

Indra āsāṁ netā bṛhaspatirdakṣiṇā yajñaḥ pura etu somaḥ /
Devasenānāmabhibhañjatīnāṁ jayantīnāṁ maruto yantvagram //

Marut, the divine military commander, ordered his forces to advance towards the Earth by gaining supreme power. He assumed the complete leadership by drinking *soma*, the divine elixir, during the Yajña offered by Bṛhaspati and Dakṣina, told his armies to conquer the anti-divine powers and establish the divine victory and the United Empire of Indra.

इन्द्रस्य वृष्णो वरुणस्य राज्ञ आदित्यानां मरुतां शर्ध उग्रम् ।
महामनसां भुवनच्यवानाघोषो देवानां जयतामुदस्थात् ॥

Ṛg.X.103.9

Indrasya vṛṣṇo varuṇasya rājña ādityānāṁ marutāṁ śardha ugram /
Mahāmanasāṁ bhuvanacyavānāṁ ghoṣo devānāṁ jayatāmudasthāt //

The victorious power and order of Indra, the peaceful and harmonious United Empire of Varuṇa, the all-conquering heroism of Aditya and Marut were all commanded to march towards the Earth from the Supramental plane. Cyavana, the son of Bhṛgu, announced the news of the Victory of Truth, throughout the world with the secret information concerning the defeat of infirmity, diseases and death and how to regain eternal youth.

अस्माकमिन्द्रः समृतेषु ध्वजेष्वस्माकं या इषवस्ता जयन्तु ।
अस्माकं वीरा उत्तरे भवन्त्वस्मां उ देवा अवता हवेषु ॥

Ṛg.X.103.11

Asmākamindraḥ samṛteṣu dhvajeṣvasmākaṁ yā iṣavastā jayantu /
Asmākaṁ vīrā uttare bhavantvasmān u devā avatā haveṣu //

Although, Indra, the ruler of the divine empire exists with his divine nectar, *amṛta,* above us. Still we suffer from tribulations through the anti-divine forces such as diseases, infirmity and death etc. We wish to be liberated from the influence of these hostile forces and become immortal. We look towards the north of Indradevata, there exists our victorious hero Satyadeva. We offer our sacrifice to the Deva with the ardent wish – let the divine kingdom be established on the Earth.

मर्माणि ते वर्मणा छादयामि सोमस्त्वा राजामृतेनानु वस्ताम् ।
उरोर्वरीयो वरुणस्ते कृणोतु जयन्तं त्वानु देवा मदन्तु ॥

Ṛg.VI.75.18

Marmāṇi te varmaṇā chādayāmi somastvā rājāmṛtenānu vastām /

Urorvarīyo varuṇaste kṛṇotu jayantaṁ tvānu devā madantu //

With your divine protection, O Lord of Nectar! Protect us from our internal foes. O Soma devata! You are the saviour of the pot of nectar. O Varuṇa! With your heroism, conquer diversity and replace it with your love, unity and harmony on the Earth. To bring joy to the Gods, bring about the victory of Truth.

यस्य कुर्मो गृहे हविस्तमग्ने वर्धया त्वम् ।
तस्मै देवाऽअधि ब्रुवन्नयं च ब्रह्मणस्पतिः ॥

Yaj.XVII.52

Yasya kurmo gṛhe havistamagne vardhayā tvam /
Tasmai devā' adhi bruvannayaṁ ca brahmaṇaspatiḥ //

In whose hidden home (in the innermost cavern of the heart), where the Fire is strong enough to receive the offering the "havi", clarified butter; through which Satyadeva and Brahmaṇaspati (giver of accomplishment) appear to speak to that being in their sweet divine voices.

उदु त्वा विश्वे देवाऽअग्ने भरन्तु चित्तिभिः ।
स नो भव शिवस्त्वं सुप्रतीको विभावसुः ॥

Yaj.XVII.53

Udu tvā viśve devā' agne bharantu cittibhiḥ /
Sa no bhava śivastavaṁ supratīko vibhāvasuḥ //

In the ages past, O Fire, you invited and brought down Satyadeva here in this universe. You filled up all our hearts with peace and purity. For this reason, O Vibhāvasuḥ! You appeared as the beautiful symbol of Śiva in our mortal home.

समिद्धे अग्नावधि मामहानऽउक्थपत्रऽईड्यो गृभीतः ।
तप्तंघर्मं परिगृह्यायजन्तोर्जा यद्यज्ञमयजन्त देवाः ॥

Yaj.XVII.55

Samidhe agnāvadhi māmahāna' ukthapatra' īḍyo gṛbhītaḥ /

Taptaṁ gharmaṁ parigṛhyājantorjā
yadyajñamayajanta devāḥ ॥

Near the blazing fire, the mantras are being chanted with a great humility that is sweet and rhythmical. It appears as if it is the enlightened divine self that unites with the Truth. Only those who sacrifice themselves for the Truth, receive the manifestation of Truth as the pure divine life.

दैव्याय धर्त्रे जोष्ट्रे देवश्रीः श्रीमनाः शतपयाः ।
परिगृह्य देवा यज्ञमायन् देवा देवेभ्यो अध्वर्यन्तो अस्थु ॥

Yaj.XVII.56

Daivyāya dhartre joṣṭre devaśrīḥ śrīmanāḥ śatapayāḥ ।
Parigṛhya devā yajñamāyan devā devebhyo
adhvaryanto asthuḥ ॥

The Deva reserves for us high honour, divine beauty, prosperity and good fortune. Deva is the Lord of Sacrifice who accepts all sacrificial offerings, offered to any God and he gives them further to all Gods for their nourishment.

वीतं हविः शमितं शमिता यजध्यै तुरीयो यज्ञो यत्र हव्यमेति ।
ततो वाकाऽ आशिषो नो जुषन्ताम् ॥

Yaj.XVII.57

Vītaṁ haviḥ śamitaṁ śamitā yajadhyai turīyo yajño
yatra havyameti ।
Tato vākā' āśiṣo no juṣantām ॥

To obtain the fulfilment of Yajña and to achieve the desirable Truth, we offer our sacrifice in the true spirit. When we offer our sacrificial offering in the transcendental sacrifice, the "havi" reaches its goal and from there we hear the resounding blessings of the Truth, to be purified and fulfilled.

देवहुर्यज्ञ ऽ आ च वक्षत्सुम्नहूर्यज्ञ ऽ आ च वक्षत् ।
यक्षदग्निर्देवो देवान् आ च वक्षत् ॥

Yaj.XVII.62

Devahūryajña' ā ca vakṣat sumnahūryajña' ā ca vakṣat I
Yakṣadagnirdevo devān ā ca vakṣat II

Through the call of "Agni", the Lord of Fire, Truth itself is descending in the divine sacrificial flame. Agni pulls down the Truth with his own power and talks in an amicable manner with the self-manifested Deva.

उद्ग्राभं च निग्राभं च ब्रह्म देवाऽअवीवृधन् ।
अधा सपत्नानिन्द्राग्नि मे विषूचीनान्व्यस्यताम् ॥

Yaj.XVII.64

Udgrābhaṁ ca nigrābhaṁ ca brahma devā avīvṛdhan I
Adhā sapatnānindrāgnī me viṣūcīnānvyasyatām II

Before the creation came into existence by the words of Brahman, we learnt that the violence and the quietude, both remained in action and nature of the Deva. That is the reason why in all creations, and even in the lower nature, diversities and quarrels are so widely prevalent. Let them all be removed by the power of Truth and let there be established, a united, peaceful divine empire of Indra upon this Earth, through the medium of Agni devata. Today, we meditate on the words of Brahman.

Who is the Truth, the Satyadeva is the Truth. Who is eternal, it is the Deva who is existing eternally. Who holds the creation, it is always the Deva. Finally, who rules over the creation, He is the Eternal Ruler.

Who has entered into the Truth is called Satyajit, who is established in the Truth is called Senajit or Suśena. In the transformed condition here upon the Earth, he becomes Suśena. By entering and by establishing himself in the Truth, he enjoys the divine life and beautiful health. In this society of innumerable men, he is neither attached to friends nor detached from enemies. He has neither friends nor enemies.

18

HYMNS FOR THE AGE OF TRUTH

After his meditation on Truth, Viśvakarmā, the son of Bhuvana, touched his divine artistic brush upon the inner subtle forms of nature. At that time, the light, purity and beauty of Truth focussed and surcharged his works of divine art. With that action, transformation came in a subtle form to all beings on the vital plane. By seeing the divinisation of the subtle vital consciousness, the physical consciousness on the Earth became eager to attain the light, purity and *ānanda* to enter into immortality and bliss. She sang Hymns to the Truth for her transformation. The Ṛṣis chanted the *mantras* for the Earth to become like Heaven. Today, again, we intone the same mantras for the divinisation of the Earth and the manifestation of Truth in the Golden Age.

The Earth is our mother and the Heaven our father. We are their immortal children. When the Mother Earth unites with the Father Heaven and they clasp each other, then there manifests divine love, peace, harmony and *ānanda* in us. We feel we are the children of immortality. We sing the songs of immortality with great joy. As the Ṛg and Sāmaveda both said:

युजे वां ब्रह्म पूर्व्यं नमोभिर्वि श्लोक ऽ एतु पथ्येव सूरेः ।
श्रुण्वन्तु विश्वे अमृतस्य पुत्रा ऽ आ ये धामानि दिव्यानि तस्थुः ॥

Ṛg. X.13.1,Yaj.XI.5

Yuje vām brahma pūrvyaṁ namobhirvi śloka' etu pathyeva sūreḥ I
Śruṇvantu viṣve amṛtasya putrā' ā ye dhāmāni divyāni tasthuḥ II

In former ages, Prajāpati Brahma chanted this *mantra* for the Earth to make it one with the Heavens. This mantra opens the divine path which is the Devāyaṇa. Listen, O people of Earth! You are the sons of Immortality. There is a divine home for you, realise it here.

The power of Nakta created the separation between Earth and Heaven. He was always covetous of the riches of Heaven and he invaded Mother Earth with the sombre powers of Kali (Leader of the Iron Age) to take his revenge against his Father, the Heaven. His attack created pain and suffering among the children of the Earth. By the influence of the hostile and negative forces, we became separated from our affectionate Father Heaven. As we are mourning in sorrow with our Mother Earth, we lose our consciousness of immortality, our brotherhood amongst ourselves and also our faith and our relationship with Heaven. We do not believe in the existence of Heaven. We suffer, quarrel and fight amongst each other, being totally under the influence of diversity. Thus, we have no peace, unity, or repose in our life until we die.

After intense suffering lasting for ages, the time has come to regain our immortality, peace and unity through the union of Earth and Heaven. As the Ṛgveda said,

O our divine Earth! O Pṛthivi! O Mother! Humanity is under the unremitting onslaught of diseases, infirmity and death. Guide them like Deva before to take this humanity into divinity. Undertake those activities by which Satyadeva may manifest throughout this world. On the Earth, Viṣṇu holds his divine *cakra*, with his unique heroic power and destroys all anti-divine forces present here to prepare a heavenly home, divided in seven, for Truth to dwell throughout the land.

Lord Viṣṇu is the holder of the *cakra*, the weapon shaped like a disc. After destroying the inimical forces, O Earth! He gave you three supporting paths (religion, works and yajña or sacrifice) by which you entered into divine bliss.

That is why, O Earth! You were called the three-footed Cow of the all-powerful Lord Viṣṇu. Through Him you maintain the sacrifice, religion and works.

O Earth! Always remember Lord Viṣṇu, the indefatigable worker. Do your sadhana with a quiet and controlled mind for Lord Viṣṇu. Surrender yourself to Him, who is the eternal friend of Indra. For attaining your best fortune, let the twin Godheads, Indra and Viṣṇu, jointly manifest in you.

O Earth! Always meditate at the Lotus Feet of Lord Viṣṇu. Observe that the Gods and Ṛṣis, with their wide far-seeing eyes, are observing and meditating always at His Enlightened Feet. These Feet were seen always in trance by all Seers. They remove our problems in life and take us to the divine consciousness, to immortality. O Earth! Meditate always on the Supreme Feet of Lord Viṣṇu.

O Fire! You know what is best for us. We pray to you, please grant us a long life that is always turned towards the Truth. We also pray to the Godhead Mitra-Varuṇa, to remove our ignorance and self-egoism as well as the sense of alienation. O all-powerful Mitra-Varuṇa, take us into the vastness of the infinite and unite Earth with Heaven.

The sacrificial offering, made to Heaven, was increased by Satyadeva. Praceta understood the Hymns of Mahī and he increased the Earth's power of meditation to attain the son of Deva, Puṣā. Puṣā conquers and removes all darkness while Uṣā, the Divine Dawn, manifests to make the Earth conscious for it to enter into divinity.

Awake, O Mother Earth! Be conscious and love Father Heaven and be united with Him. Let all the dissensions be dissolved and love each other to cling to the Truth. The Power of Truth remains in the Father Heaven. O Mother Land! Pull down the Power of Truth from the Heaven. This will be the divine sacrifice for the divine birth and you will receive immortal children. Through them, Deva, who is honoured in the whole universe will manifest in you.

O Mother Mahī! Remember your past, through the sacrificial fire, when your children were enjoying a beautiful divine health, without infirmity and death, without divisions and antidivine activities. All was quiet and peaceful. They were well-established in the Truth and were active and religious-minded. Their path was wide open to enter into the transcendental Truth.

O Pṛthivi (Earth)! You are imprisoned in ignorance, through the influence of the power of attachment, the *mahāmāyā*. Throw away this sombre ignorance and the thought of alienation and embrace the ever-enlightened united peaceful Heaven by spreading your arms. With the influence of heavenly thoughts and by the creative power of the Deva let the divine creation be manifested. In other words, allow new divine bodies to appear in you like eddies in the ocean to develop your fortune and prosperity.

O Pṛthivi! For this reason, adore the Savitṛ Deva. Meditate on his divine birth by which we shall enter into divinity. We are conscious that the Mother Earth and the Father Heaven are embracing each other and are becoming one. Look, the Earth with the manifested divine consciousness and the Heaven are uniting into one. O Earth! You will become rich and full of riches and gems day by day and will be called Vasumati. You will remain with that heavenly ornamented appearance for at least ten thousand years. (The Ṛṣis estimate that in the cyclic movement of time, *ayana*, the Age of Truth - the Golden Age - remains upon this Earth for at least ten thousand years). This is mentioned in the following mantra from the Ṛgveda,

शतमिन्नु शरदो अन्ति देवा यत्रा नश्चक्रा जरसं तनूनाम ।
पुत्रासो यत्र पितरो भवन्ति मा नो मध्या रीरिषतायुर्गन्तोः ॥

Ṛg.I.89.9, Yaj.XXV.22

Śatminnu śarado anti devā yatrā naścakrā jarasaṁ tanūmān |
Putrāso yatra pitaro bhavanti mā no madhyā iriṣatāyurgantoḥ ||

This means that the Deva will exist in this earthly creation for one hundred times hundred autumns, that is ten thousand years. During this period there will be no diseases. As old age will not torture the body, it will remain ever young.

With the union of Heaven and Earth, the consciousness, power and activities of the Lord of Truth, Satyadeva, the Visvedevas* will manifest in the world. Let the divine birth again come down to the Earth with purity and power in the human form to act like Gods and Goddesses.

O Mother Earth! Call Father Heaven with your dear sweet voice to save mankind that was created by both of you. When both of you become one, when the separate names of Earth and Heaven disappear, then your name is Rodasi. Become joyful with the Truth. Let the eternal father Heaven descend to stay within the boundary of your individual formation. Let Heaven be manifested here.

With the pure creative power of Father Heaven, the children take birth in the womb of Mother Earth, Mahī. They are called Manava – human beings. Let them be released from their ignorance and folly. By becoming conscious of their divine birth, they should enter into the purity, knowledge of Truth and become aware of their true self.

From the body of Satyadeva, power and peace is flowing out to purify the impurities and contaminations caused by the dark hostile forces. With the identification of Earth and Heaven, a truthful world would manifest. In this divine world brought about through the sacrificial offering and divine works: let the human beings be enlightened, immortal and immune. Then the Earth will appear like Heaven.

O Mahī (Earth)! Be free of all attachment, ignorance and folly and appear like the enlightened Heaven. Through your

---

** The word Viśva means the world and the Devas means the Gods. Thus Viśvadevas means the Gods born in this world, on this earth. The divine birth in place of the human birth means the birth of the Superman or the supramental beings, higher than men. This is the birth of power and consciousness of truth. The Viśvadevas were pure, powerful and truly religious in their activities upon the earth. In this way, the Gods and the Goddesses took human form on the earth. They were also called "Sūrya-Śuci" purified by the sunlight, i.e. the pure divine birth, divine race or supramental race upon the earth.*

divinisation, O Earth! Your children will become wise like seers, heroic like gods on your wide breast and they will appear divine. Let this world enter into the divine civilization and adopt the divine culture. By worshipping the divine civilization, let this Earth be fully united with Heaven.

These are innumerable words, which came from the wise poets; we cannot estimate how many came before and how many afterwards, as there is no end of ideas. In the mental world, there are many ideas and each idea takes a different shape and name. *Uṣā*, the Divine Dawn, with her encircling adventure over the Earth, has continuously created new ideas. There is no end to them.

For the word idea, we have the Vedic word, called *bhāva*. From the *bhāva*, we develop *bhāvanas*, thoughts. *Bhāva* is the mother of *bhāvanas*, then the equivalent word for *bhāva* might be ideas, opinions, inclination or disposition of mind. These are the source of thoughts. The Veda says that the *bhāvas* are always descending from the Heaven down to the Earth. Although descending from Heaven, and coming in contact with the individual ego, these come under the influence of the dark forces. As a result, they take a darker hue. In actual fact, the dark forces are separating us from the enlightened *bhāvas* of Heaven. The cause for the separation between Earth and Heaven lies here. Ṛgveda has said the following about *bhāvas* in the subsequent mantras for the identification between Earth and Heaven.

भूरिं द्वे अचरन्ती चरन्तं पद्वन्तं गर्भमपदी दधाते ।
नित्यं न सूनुं पित्रोरुपस्थे द्यावा रक्षतं पृथिवी नो अभ्वात् ॥

Ṛg.I.185.2

Bhūriṁ dve acarantī carantaṁ padvantaṁ garbhamapadī dadhāte /
Nityaṁ na sūnuṁ pitrorupasthe dyāvā rakṣataṁ pṛthivī no abhvāt //

Ideas are of two categories, one active and the other inactive. Those which are active, call for action and those which are inactive, lead to inaction. From the active thoughts, we get our children and from the children appear their fathers.

अनेहो दात्रमदितेरनर्वं हुवे स्वर्वदवधं नमस्वत् ।
तद्रोदसी जनयतं जरित्रे द्यावा रक्षतं पृथिवी नो अभ्वात् ॥

Ṛg.I.185.3

Anebo dātramaditeranarvaṁ buve svarvadavadbaṁ namasvat |
Tadrodasī janayataṁ jaritre dyāvā rakṣataṁ pṛtbivī no abbvāt ||

It is the divine Mother Aditi, who unifies all and establishes herself in the transcendental eternity. Her manifested creations are divine, ever adorable, immortalised figures of divine ideas and we worship them all. Let the Earth, with all the creations, be full and overflow with the divine figurative ideas from Heaven. With the enlightened world of ideas, the Heaven is protecting this Earth with her children.

अतप्यमाने अवसावन्ती अनुष्याम रोदसी देवपुत्रे ।
उभे देवानामुभयेभिरह्नां द्यावा रक्षतं पृथिवी नो अभ्वात् ॥

Ṛg.1.185.4

Atapyamāne avasāvantī anuṣyāma rodasī devaputre |
Ubbe devānāmubbayebbirabnāṁ dyāvā rakṣataṁ pṛtbivī no abbvāt ||

Heaven is manifesting on this Earth with divine ideas and works, replacing those that are powerful but steeped in dumb ignorance. For this reason there is a similarity between the mortal and immortal figures. With the enlightened world of ideas, the Heaven is protecting this Earth with her children.

सङ्गच्छमाने युवती समन्ते स्वसारा जामी पित्रोरुपस्थे ।
अभिजिघ्रन्ती भुवनस्य नाभिं द्यावा रक्षतं पृथिवी नो अभ्वात् ॥

Ṛg.I.185.5

Saṅgacchamāne yuvatī samante svasārā jāmī pitrorupasthe ।
Abhijighrantī bhuvanasya nābhiṁ dyāvā rakṣataṁ pṛthivī no abhvāt ॥

On seeing a beautiful girl, when a man feels a desire to touch her, to love her, this is then the beginning of the process of becoming a father. That power arises from the navel centre of this world for the manifestation of creation. With the enlightened world of ideas, the Heaven is protecting this Earth with her children.

उर्वी सद्मनी बृहती ऋतेन हुवे देवानामवसा जनित्री ।
दधाते ये अमृतं सुप्रतीके द्यावा रक्षतं पृथिवी नो अभ्वात् ॥

Ṛg.1.185.6

Urvī sadmanī bṛhatī ṛtena huve devānāmavasā janitrī ।
Dadhāte ye amṛtaṁ supratīke dyāva rakṣataṁ pṛthivī no abhvāt ॥

O Earth! Become conscious of the reality that you are the home of Truth and Eternity. The Divine Mother, the Supreme Goddess Aditi will establish Truth in you and give you immortality. With the enlightened world of ideas, the Heaven is protecting this Earth with her children.

उर्वी पृथ्वी बहुले दूरे अन्ते उप ब्रुवे नमसा यज्ञे अस्मिन् ।
दधाते ये सुभगे सुप्रतूर्ती द्यावा रक्षतं पृथिवी नो अभ्वात् ॥

Ṛg.I.185.7

Urvī pṛthivī bahule dūre ante upa bruve namasā yajñe asmin ।
Dadhāte ye subhage supratūrtī dyāvā rakṣataṁ pṛthivī no abhvāt ॥

O Earth! Become conscious of yourself in the immensity and amongst the innumerable Ideas of the eternal wide world. There by your self-sacrifice, offer yourself and prostrate before Heaven. That will increase your prosperity and you will conceive divine creations. With the enlightened world of ideas, the Heaven is protecting this Earth with her children.

देवान्वा यच्चकृमा कच्चिदागः सखायं वा सदमिज्जास्पतिं वा ।
इयं धीर्भूया अवयानमेषां द्यावा रक्षतं पृथिवी नो अभ्वात् ॥

Ṛg.1.185.8

Devānvā yaccakṛmā kaccidāgaḥ sakhāyaṁ vā sadamijjāspatiṁ vā |
Iyaṁ dhīrbhūya avayānameṣāṁ dyāvā rakṣataṁ pṛthivī no abhvāt ||

Satyadeva, as a sign of his presence, is always pulling at the life breath. He exists in the body as the soul, the friend of all. He was called Amijaspati. Keeping this idea in your mind, meditate and enter into the eternal *ānanda* and you will remain always truthful.

The above mantras of Agastya Ṛṣi have disclosed to us the world of enlightened ideas. They tell us how Heaven and Earth could become one and Earth could have divine beings as her children. Following these, the Ṛṣi gave further mantras through which the people of the Earth could become divinised and described the process of transformation.

With the union of Heaven and Earth, a wonderful creation manifests. Both the Heaven and Earth compliment each other. When the Earth conceives the soul of divine ideas, Heaven enters into the Earth, thus manifesting divine shape and beauty, which is ever young and luminous. Attaining the eternal consciousness and immense variety in ideas brings an end to the undivine forces such as diseases, frailty and death. Then dawns the divine life upon the Earth.

In the coming days of Truth, in the Golden Age, O Earth! Listen to the eternal voices giving you the Truth-ideas that exist by influencing all creations. Look at these ever-existent ideas with your far-sighted gaze and recognise who is your father and who your mother. Then you will always be protected. In other words, O Earth! Be conscious about your birth. Your father is the Deva and your Mother Suhavā. You are their immortal daughter. They bestowed you to Heaven. You have conceived your children from Heaven and they are *amṛtasya putrāḥ*, the children of immortality.

There is the Father Heaven and here the Mother Earth. By their union let the Truth be manifested. Although our father and mother created us with beauty, but still without Satyadeva, they are not able to bear and protect their creations. Heaven alone is incapable of maintaining the Gods and the Earth is unable to bear the pressure of human beings. Without the Deva, the creations of both Heaven and Earth are on the verge of destruction. To know the Deva is to attain all satisfaction and complete fulfilment. This knowledge is given to us by the Veda. With this knowledge conquer infirmity, enter into immunity and become joyful through the divine play in life.

Our Earth is here and above us is the Heaven. By their identification, let them be established in the Truth. O people of the Earth, become conscious. Always repeat the words – Let the Earth and Heaven become one and be established in Truth. By repetition, you will attain longevity and immunity. On this Earth, the eighth Vasu, Vasuyuva, worshipped in this manner. O Pṛthivi! Be supramentalised by receiving *Mahas*, the Supramental world.

Let the united Earth and Heaven, cling immediately to the Truth. Let them give their sacrificial offering to the Satyadeva for their unity to attain their desirable aims.

With the union of the Earth and Heaven, the Earth will have her divine children, a new race will manifest which will be the supramental beings. In that race, we will see the divine civilization. Ṛgveda gave us the following mantras:

मही द्यावापृथिवी इह ज्येष्ठे रुचा भवतां शुचयद्भिरर्कैः ।
यत्सीं वरिष्ठे बृहती विमिन्वन्नुवद्धोक्षा पप्रथानेभिरेवैः ॥

Ṛg.IV.56.1

Mahī dyāvā pṛthivī iha jyeṣṭhe rucā bhavatām
śucayadbhirarkaiḥ /

Yatsīṁ variṣṭhe bṛhatī viminvanruvadhokṣā paprathānebhirevaiḥ //

O Mahī! The union of the Earth and Heaven gives birth to a pure divine civilization, cleansed by sunlight. This was adored and worshipped by the whole universe and was welcomed by all. Freedom spread everywhere, with a peaceful rule and order and all became absorbed in the divine *ānanda*.

देवी देवेभिर्यजते यजत्रैरमिनती तस्थतुरुक्षमाणे ।
ऋतावरी अद्रुहा देवपुत्रे यज्ञस्य नेत्री शुचयद्भिरर्कैः ॥

Ṛg.IV.56.2

Devī devebhiryajate yajatrairaminatī tasthaturukṣamāṇe /
Ṛitāvarī adruhā devaputre yajñasya netrī śucayadbhirarkaiḥ //

O Earth! The Gods are worshipping the Devi Suhavā in their pure divine civilization. With that adoration, there manifests a supremely beautiful creation, in which the divine children under the leadership of Devi Ṛtavari (the Power of Truth) sacrifice for the Truth to attain a purity radiant with the luminosity of the Sun. It seems as if the Gods and Goddesses on the Earth are worshipping the Gods and Goddesses in Heaven. Gods are meditating on Gods, that is the manifested Truth as we know.

This is the divine civilization and the manifested Age of Truth, the Golden Age. Then the Gods move, play and enjoy their divine life on the Earth under the guidance of the Godheads of Heaven. They communicate with each other with love and affection. In that divine civilization, the Earth attains her divine status. This has been mentioned in the Ṛgveda in the following words:

As a result of the divine thoughts attained by this world, Earth and Heaven became united into one. Consequently, the pure ideas of unity, existing in the inner immensity of this creation, spread throughout the whole creation as self-knowledge, divine purity, unalloyed peace and bliss.

Through the union of Earth and Heaven, a greater Heaven was established called Rodasi. As the wife settles down in the home of her husband, he becomes full of joy to be with his wife. Similarly, the Earth makes a home in Heaven and Heaven manifests the divine love and joy to be unified with the Earth. O People of the Earth! Put the sacrifice for Truth in place of your ego or individuality and enjoy Earth like the Heaven. That is your life divine.

O Earth! Establish yourself in Heaven, get your divine fulfilment, attain purity with peace and be in your best form. O Mahī (Earth)! With the help of Mitra devata, overcome the separation from Heaven with your effort and sadhana. Become one with Truth and be self-satisfied. Let all opposition to your self sacrifice be dissolved by Mitra devata.

The Heaven becomes enlightened due to its activities and the Earth also appears as it is due to its works. They suffer and enjoy according to their actions. Nothing takes place without any reason.

O Pṛthivi! Offer your sacrifice to Heaven and prostrate before it. To become a part of the eternal Truth, worship Ilādevi and appeal to her with the following words – O Ilā! Whatever wealth of consciousness I have attained, has been through the efforts of the Seers and the Poets. At that moment you blessed me by saying – O Mahī! You had divine children when you established yourself in divinity. You will be again surrounded by your divine children and achieve your immortality.

In former times, these supramental beings were born here. Let them return with a new luminous body and help us in gaining access to the home of Truth. With the union of Earth and Heaven and in the presence of all Gods, let mankind give birth to divine children like their ancestors.

19

SUHAVĀ, POWER OF TRUTH FOR THE IMMORTALITY

Three great powers are working towards the immortality of the Earth, to bring about the union of Earth and Heaven and to have a united divine empire on the Earth.

1. Yahvī, the Mother of Truth; who brings about the union between Earth and Heaven.
2. Queen Suhavā, the Power of Truth, who brings down the Truth with her for manifestation on the Earth.
3. Aditi, the Divine Mother of Gods, who comes on the Earth to realise her divine children here.

The power who brings about the identification or union of Earth and Heaven by removing dissensions, who conquers the power of conflicts and who unifies by removing the dark forces is Yahvī, the Mother of Truth.

The Ṛgveda says:

शं रोदसी सुबन्धवे यह्वी ऋतस्य मातरा ।

Ṛg.X.59.8

Śaṁ rodasī subandhave yahvī ṛtasya mātarā .

Who brings about the much sought after identification of Earth with Heaven? She is Yahvī, the Mother of Truth.

अपां नपादा ह्यस्थादुपस्थं जिह्मानामूर्ध्वो विद्युतं् वसानः ।
तस्य ज्येष्ठं महिमानं वहन्तीर्हिरण्यवर्णाः परि यान्ति यह्वीः ॥

Ṛg.II.35.9

Apāṁ napādā hyasthādupasthaṁ jihmānāmūrdhvo vidyutaṁ vasānaḥ |
Tasya jyeṣṭhaṁ mahimānaṁ vahantīrhiraṇyavarṇāḥ pari yanti yahvīḥ ||

At the base of this creation, there is a powerful sweet flow of juice. O Apānapāt! Pull the place just above the tongue, where you see the most glorious sight with rays of light glittering all around. There exists the golden colour Yahvī, the Mother of Truth. Present her this earthly offering, through which we shall attain immortality.

हिरण्यरूपः स हिरण्यसन्दृगपां नपात्सेदु हिरण्यवर्णः ।
हिरण्ययात्परि योनेर्निषद्या हिरण्यदा ददत्यन्नमस्मै ॥

Ṛg.II.35.10

Hiraṇyarūpaḥ sa hiraṇyasandṛgapāṁ napātsedu hiraṇyavarṇaḥ |
Hiraṇyayātpari yonerniṣadyā hiraṇyadā dadatyannamasmai ||

O Apānapāt! Look at the supreme beauty, the Golden Figure. The golden rays are scattering from that figure and the golden light is glittering in the golden home. She is wearing golden ornaments embedded with precious stones all over her shining body. She is the main power behind all powers. She is the Mother of Truth and of Immortality. She is the giver of gold and she fills up all the creations with the wealth of gold. Hers is the power which has come out from unmanifested eternity for the manifestation of creations.

तदस्यानीकमुत चारु नामापीच्यं वर्धते नप्तुरपाम् ।
यमिन्धते युवतयः समित्था हिरण्यवर्णं घृतमन्नमस्य ॥

Ṛg.II.35.11

Tadasyānīkamuta cāru nāmāpīcyaṁ vardhate napturapām |
Yamindhate yuvatayaḥ samitthā hiraṇyavarṇaṁ ghṛtamannamasya ||

From her pure and beautiful navel has appeared the all powerful manifestor of the entire creation and provider of all nourishment with milk and honey. He is also the giver of immunity and ever-lasting youth. His body is golden in colour and he is the personification of beauty. He is the immortal Puruṣa, the divine luminous being. The Ṛṣis called him Satyadeva. The Power of Immortality has come into existence from the navel of this Immortal Being, the Lord of Truth. This power was named Amṛtasya Patni, the power of immortality or Deva Patni, the power of Deva; the Goddess Uṣati or Devi Suhavā.

The Goddess or Devi that came into existence from the Deva was called Suhavā, the Power of Truth. This power is at the root of all powers. In other words, She exists in all powers throughout the Heaven. All the Goddesses are glorified with the name of Devi, which is her name. For example, there is the Devi Aditi, the Devi Ilā, the Devi Bharati, the Devi Sarasvatī etc.

She is the only one who can provide immortality to beings throughout the many creations according to their needs or demands. She can grant immortality to all Godheads and Goddesses in Heaven according to their tapasya, their yogic effort. But she never comes near the Asuras. She hates them for their egoistic pride even though they undergo a tremendous penance for achieving their all encompassing desires. The Devi Suhavā is always kind and compassionate to those who have no ego or desires and who have surrendered themselves to Truth in all their actions. Even when they wish to conquer their enemies, attain high positions or become famous and honourable, first they have to surrender to Truth. Then the power of Truth gives them what they desire, it could be victory, honour or position. They are Gods in Heaven. She is the Power of Truth, who brings victory to the Gods, by conquering the Asuras. She gave nectar to the Gods for their immortality.

The Deva also exists in all Godheads.

य एतं देवमेकवृतं वेद

Ath.XIII.4.22

Ya etam devameka vritam veda,

Although there are many Gods in the Vedas, there is only one Deva who is present in all Godheads. With his presence in the Gods, they are known as Deva Brahmā, Deva Viṣṇu, Deva Hari, Deva Śiva, Deva Rudra as well as Deva Indra, Deva Candra, Deva Sūrya, Deva Vāyu, Deva Agni etc.

Similarly, the Devi is always identified with the powers of all Godheads. Thus the powers of the Godheads, the Devis are known as Devi Brahmaṇi, Devi Vaiśṇavi, Devi Rudra, Devi Śiva as well as Devi Indra, Devi Sūrya, Devi Candra, Devi Agñeya, Devi Vāyavi etc.

At one time, she left the Godheads to defeat the Asuras. At that time she was called the Devi Candika. She also appeared in front of the Godheads to give them her boon, as was disclosed by the Sage Markandeya. Then she was called Devi Ambika. Whatever has been disclosed about her activities demonstrates that her work is always for the victory and immortality of Heaven. The Ṛṣikā Vāghambhrinī came to know more about the Devi Suhavā when she attained the self-realisation of her soul. (The Ṛṣis had meditated on the Deva as the supreme soul, Paramatma. Similarly, the Devi was realised by Vāghambhrinī as her soul. This is elaborated in the famous Devi Sūkta of the Ṛgveda.) Through Vāghambhrinī, the Devi declared – I am Rudra, I am Vasu, I am Aditya, I am Viśvedeva, I am Mitra-Varuṇa, I am Indra, I am Aśvinīs, I am *Soma*, Tvaṣṭā, Pūṣā and Bhaga. I give whatever sacrificial offering is offered by them to the Supreme Truth and I bring to them His Compassion.

Ahaṁ dadhami dravinan havishmate supravye yajamanaya sunwate.

Then she said the following regarding her activities on the Earth:

अहं रुद्राय धनुरा तनोमि ब्रह्मद्विषे शरवे हन्तवा उ ।
अहं जनाय समदं कृणोम्यहं द्यावापृथिवी आ विवेश ॥

Ṛg.X.125.6

Ahaṁ rudrāya dhanurā tanomi brahmadviṣe śarave hantavā u /
Ahaṁ janāya samadaṁ kṛṇomyahaṁ dyāvāpṛthivī ā viveśa //

I hold the body of Rudra as an arc, to destroy the anti-divine with the arrow of Truth. I also bring equanimity and peace to the people of the Earth and unite Earth and Heaven.

When she works for the Earth, she identifies herself with Kāla (Time). At that time, Kāla – the Time becomes Mahākāla – the Great Time. When Kāla identified with the Deva, he became Mahākāla or Mahādeva. When the power of the Kāla Puruṣa identified with the Devi, she was called Mahākāli or Mahādevi. As mentioned in the Yajurveda,

Udagrabham cha nigrabham cha brahmā deva avivridhan.

In the beginning of the Creation, the Creator Brahmā said, both the violent and the quiet and peaceful appearances are remaining in the Deva.

To bring down immortality to the Earth, the Deva identifies himself with the Kāla (Time). At that time, Kāla becomes Mahākāla Maheśvara. When the Deva is in a vehement mood to destroy the anti-divine forces and to remove the impurities found on the Earth, Time takes the form of Mahākāla Rudra Maheśvara. When the Deva is in a peaceful quiet mood for bringing in the new divine creation, as well as purity and immortality down to the Earth, Time takes the form of Mahākāla Piṅgala Maheśvara. As the time cycle revolves on continuously, then appears Kali, the Lord of Falsehood which is an unfortunate moment.

At present, we are at that moment of the time cycle when efforts are being made to get rid of Kali and invoke Deva for the immortality for the Earth. This effort is called Devāyaṇa. To realise truth and immortality, Devi Suhavā is the power that acts on the Earth through the Vitihotra, the aspirant fire of the Earth for the Truth. This had been established by the yogic efforts of Gauribiti to invoke the Deva, who had disappeared for a long time from the Earth. The cause of the disappearance was the desire of the Earth for vital enjoyment. By the sacrificial offering and adoration, Vitihotra replaced the Truth. On one side, the Goddess Suhavā touched the Vitihotra on the Earth, on the other side she touched the Deva in Heaven and thus made a union between Deva and Vitihotra.

For the manifestation of Truth on the Earth, Devi Suhavā is the Power who brings down the Truth to the Earth through the Vitihotra. She works through Gauribiti to remove the impurities of the Earth and to create the pure Truth creation. Through the power of Truth, she manifests beautiful creations for the Earth, they are Ūṣā and Pūṣā. Ūṣā, the Dawṇ, manifests the Light of Truth and Pūṣā, the Power of Truth to conquer the dark forces, remove them and enlighten the Earth with the Light of Truth. Although Ūṣā and Pūṣā were the children of Truth, still they had to confront impurities, conquer the dark forces and remove them from the Earth. To this end, Devi Suhavā takes a shade of the pure ardent penance of the Earth for a new creation of truth. That is the reason why Gauribiti becomes the heroine of the great Epic Devāyaṇa in the place of Devi Suhavā. Once the antidivine forces, impurities and the deep ignorance is conquered by Uṣā and Pūṣā, then the work of Gauribiti comes to an end. Till the Deva manifests on the Earth, the Devi Suhavā acts through the power of tapasya of the Earth, which is Gauribiti. After the manifestation of Deva, the Devi Suhavā acts directly for the immortality of the Earth. The Atharvaveda says:

देवानां पत्नीरुशतीरवन्तु नः प्रावन्तु नस्तुजये वाजसातये ।
याः पार्थिवासो या अपामपि व्रते ता नो देवीः सुहवाः शर्म यच्छत ॥

Ṛg.V.46.7

Devānāṁ patnīruśatīravantu naḥ prāvantu nastujaye vājasātaye ।

Yāḥ pārthivāso yā apāmapi vrate tā no devīḥ suhavāḥ śarma yacchata //

The Deva-patni, power of Truth was called Uṣatī. She is wealthy with all the divine riches and has appeared from the transcendental eternity. She has come to conquer the sombre ignorance of the Earth. She stands between Earth and eternity to work for the Truth. She is Uṣatī, who opens the veil between Earth and the Truth and brings about a direct contact between Earth and Heaven. O Devi Uṣatī! Take our offering and give it to Satyadeva. For this we call you Suhavā as you are the one who takes the sacrificial offering to Deva.

उत ग्ना व्यन्तु देवपत्नीरिन्द्राण्यऽग्नाय्यश्विनी राट् ।
आ रोदसी वरुणानी शृणोतु व्यन्तु देवीर्य ऋतुर्जनीनाम् ॥

Ṛg.V.46.8

Uta gnā vyantu devapatnīrindrānya' gnayyaśvinī rāṭ /
Āa rodasī varuṇānī śṛṇotu vyantu devīrya ṛturjanīnām //

Appear in this universe through the fire, O Devapatni, the Power of Truth. Complete the divine empire of Indra, the activities of Agni and the Aśvinīs by defeating the forces of dissension, infirmity and death. Let Earth and Heaven become united in a harmonious way through the power of Varuṇa. Listen, O Ṛtus! The Devi has appeared, perform your divine ceremony.

देवोदेवः सुहवो भूतु मह्यं मा नो माता पृथिवी दुर्मतौ धात् ।

Ṛg.V.43.15

Devodevaḥ suhavo bhūtu mahyaṁ mā no mātā pṛthivī durmatau dhāt /

O Deva! The Father, O Devi! The Mother Suhavā of the Earth, let our souls be liberated from all bondages, let the misfortune of the Earth be removed. Descend, O Deva! Come and manifest on this Earth without hesitation so that the Earth becomes filled with Truth.

देवानां भद्रा सुमतिर्ऋजूयतां देवानां रातिरभि नो नि वर्तताम् ।
देवानां सख्यमुप सेदिमा वयं देवा न आयुः प्र तिरन्तु जीवसे ॥

Ṛg.I.89.2

Devānāṁ bhadrā sumatirṛjūyatām devānāṁ rātirabhi no ni vartatām /
Devānāṁ sakhyamupa sedimā vayaṁ devā na āyuḥ pra tirantu jīvase //

O Bhadrā! Beloved of the Deva, who provides us with the Truth-concept. O Suhavā! Remove our obstinacy and give us sincerity and simplicity. Manifest the Light of Truth in us and let the obscure Night vanish. Establish us in the home of Truth with the affection of Deva. Let Satyadeva increase our longevity and protect us from the attack of the anti-divine forces in every life.

भद्रं कर्णेभिः शृणुयाम देवा भद्रं पश्येमाक्षभिर्यजत्राः ।
स्थिरैरङ्गैस्तुष्टुवांसस्तनूभिर्व्यशेम देवहितं यदायुः ॥

Ṛg.I.89.8

Bhadraṁ karṇobhiḥ śṛṇuyāma devā bhadraṁ paśyemākṣabhiryajatrāḥ /
Sthirairaṅgaistuṣṭuvāṅsastanūbhirvyaśema devahitaṁ yadāyuḥ //

Let our ears become gentle (bhadra) and quiet to hear the voice of Truth with the influence and the power of Truth and our eyes to see the Truth; let our members be quiet to feel the presence of Truth and our body to work for the Truth by the influence of Bhadrā Devi.

उरौ वा ये अन्तरिक्षे मदन्ति दिवो वा ये रोचने सन्ति देवाः ।
ऊमा वा ये सुहवासो यजत्रा आयेमिरे रथ्यो अग्ने अश्वाः ॥

Ṛg.III.6.8

Urau vā ye antarikṣe madanti divo vā ye rocane santi devāḥ /
Ūmā vā ye suhavāso yajatrā āyemire rathyo agne aśvāḥ //

Descend, O Devi! From the Heaven together with Deva through the antarikṣa to enlighten the Earth with the Light of Truth. O Adorable Mother of Earth, O Suhavā! Come down directly on this Earth in a divine chariot, drawn by Fire in the shape of horses, to fulfil our sacrificial worship.

प्रैष स्तोमः पृथिवीमन्तरिक्षं वनस्पतींरोषधी राये अश्याः ।
देवोदेवः सुहवो भूतु मह्यं मा नो माता पृथिवी दुर्मतौ धात् ॥

Ṛg.V.42.16

Praiṣa stomaḥ pṛthivīmantarikṣam vanaspatīn roṣadhī rāye aśyāḥ I
Devodevaḥ suhavo bhūtu mahyaṁ mā no mātā pṛthivī durmatau dhāt II

Let the sweet hymn for the Truth be chanted from this Earth and resound in the antarikṣa, in the vital plane, in the forests, the plants, the matter, or stone. Come, O Devi Suhavā! Come with the Deva on this land and remove the misfortune of our Mother Earth.

बृहद्वयो बृहते तुभ्यमग्ने धियाजुरो मिथुनासः सचन्तः ।
देवोदेवः सुहवो भूतु मह्यं मा नो माता पृथिवी दुर्मतौ धात् ।

Ṛg.V.43.15

Bṛhadvayo bṛhate tubhyamagne dhiyājuro mithunāsaḥ sacantaḥ I
Devodevaḥ suhavo bhūtu mahyaṁ mā no mātā pṛthivī durmatau dhāt I

O Fire! Make us conscious to meditate for the Truth in this life of vital enjoyment. Let us chant songs to the Truth who is the greatest of all and is existing in the transcendental Heaven. Come, O Devi Suhavā! Remove the misfortune of our Mother Earth with Deva.

उरौ देवा अनिबाधे स्याम ।

Ṛg.V.42.17

Urau devā anibādhe syāma I

Descend, O Devi with the Deva to protect your daughter, the Earth. Let the Earth become full of Truth.

प्रथमभाजं यशसं वयोधां सुपाणिं देवं सुभगास्तिमृभ्वम् ।
होता यक्षद्यजतं पस्त्यानामाग्निस्त्वष्टारं सुहवं विभावा ॥

Ṛg.VI.49.9

Prathamabhājaṁ yaśasaṁ vayodhām supāniṁ devaṁ subhagāstimṛbhvam /
Hotā yakṣadyajataṁ pastyānāmāgnistvaṣṭāraṁ suhavaṁ vibhāvā //

He who manifested even before the whole creation, increased our fame and riches, is covered with divine wealth and is the giver of boons. He is Satyadeva, the Truth. The Fire is worshipping Him as a priest and is offering the sacrificial rites. At that time Tvaṣṭā is arranging and collecting the materials of sacrifice and linking with Devi Suhavā so that She may manifest with the Deva, together with Truth and the riches.

शं रोदसी बृहती शं नो अद्रिः शं नो देवानां सुहवानि सन्तु ।

Ṛg.VII.35.3

Śam rodasī bṛhatī śaṁ no adriḥ śaṁ no devānām suhavāni santu /

O Devi Suhavā! Giver of peace to the united Earth and Heaven. Establish peace throughout Rodasi, the greater Heaven. Establish a peace like an immovable mountain, with the help of Deva. In the truthful world, establish a peace without repose.

Devi Suhavā is the Mother of this Earth and Deva, is her Father. The Devi comes to relieve the agony and pain of the Earth. This is at the time when the Earth suffers greatly under the diversities, caused by the rule of Kali and by diseases, infirmity and death, which are the ruling powers of Kali. She appears with Aditi, the Divine Mother, who has the power to unite, to establish unity between Heaven and Earth and to conquer Diti, the Demon Mother, the Power of Diversity. She establishes peace and dharma, the right rule with the manifestation of divine love through light, purity and consciousness of Truth. With the activities and presence of Devi Suhavā, Earth becomes transformed and divine, a place for Truth, peace and divine love through constant identification with Heaven. Her children enjoy immortality and immunity as they enjoy a life divine.

Aditi, the Divine Mother, came on this Earth before the Devi Suhavā, to confront the power of diversity, Diti, the Demon Mother, as she is the power of unity. On observing the descent of Aditi, Diti, gained in strength and became very active in opposing Aditi. She is more powerful than the Divine Mother. The power of diversity has more strength and vigour and thus the condition of the Earth deteriorates constantly.

Completely under the influence of the sombre and dark Time, Kali, the Earth through her ignorance cannot understand the work of the Divine Mother and cannot experience her power of unity. Thus the Earth cannot turn towards Aditi, as she is full of fears and is thoroughly under the all-destroying effects of the work of Diti, the Demon Mother. She becomes so helpless that she is not able to accept and recognise the Divine Mother seated in front of her.

Aditi, the Divine Mother, saw this powerful opposition to her divine work. She meditated on the Truth and aspired to conquer the power of diversity through Truth and re-establish her united divine empire on the troubled Earth. At that moment, Devi Suhavā descended on this Earth to fulfil her mission. We, the Ṛṣis, chanted the mantras of Aditi to clear up the dark and confused ideas currently in sway on the Earth. With these, the Earth could understand the majestic presence of Aditi and her mission to bring down the divine kingdom upon the Earth. This mission will be fulfilled. As the Vedas say, we had chanted ages before the following lines,

हुवे वो देवीमदितिं नमोभिर्मृळीकाय वरुणं मित्रमग्निम् ।
अभिक्षदामर्यमणं सुशेवं त्रातृन्देवान्त्सवितारं भगं च ॥

Ṛg.VI.50.1

Huve vo devīmaditiṁ namobhirmṛḷīkāya varuṇaṁ mitramagniṁ ।
Abhikṣadāmaryamaṇaṁ suśevaṁ trātṛndevāntsavitāraṁ bhagaṁ ca ॥

We prostrate ourselves before the Devi Suhavā and Aditi, the Divine Mother. We pray to them with Mitrā Varuṇa and Agni, the Lord of Fire, to establish the United Empire of Heaven on the Earth, with the harmonious sweet divine rule and justice of Truth. These rules were passed by the divine assembly to govern the whole creation. This assembly was formed by thirty-three Gods, headed by Sūrya, Bhaga and Aryama.

भुर्जज्ञ उत्तानपदो भुव आशा अजायन्त ।
अदितेर्दक्षो अजायत दक्षाद्वदितिः परि ॥

Ṛg.X.72.4

Bhūrjajña uttānpado bhuva āśā ajāyanta ।
Aditerdakṣo ajāyata dakṣādvaditiḥ pari ॥

From the Supreme Puruṣa high above, came Yajña, the sacrifice of the Earth, *Aśā* (hope) came from the vital plane (Bhuvarloka), *Dakṣa* from the Heaven and *Aditi* from the *Mahas* (Supramental plane). In other words, Dakṣa appeared after Aditi from the supramental plane, Āśā after Dakṣa from Heaven and Yajña after Āśā from the vital plane. In short, Dakṣa was born from Aditi, Āśā from Dakṣa and Yajña from Āśā.

अदितिर्ह्यजनिष्ट दक्ष या दुहिता तव ।
तां देवा अन्वजायन्त भद्रा अमृतबन्धवः ॥

Ṛg.X.72.5

Aditirhyajaniṣṭa dakṣa yā duhitā tava ।
Tāṁ devā anvajāyanta bhadrā amṛtabandhavaḥ ॥

O Immortal Puruṣa! Your daughter power has the name Aditi. She has created the Prajāpati Dakṣa and other Godheads. She is the giver of immortality and peace to all.

अष्टौ पुत्रासो अदितेर्ये जातास्तन्वऽस्परि
देवां उप प्रैत्सप्तभिः परा मार्ताण्डमास्यत् ॥

Ṛg.X.72.8

Aṣṭau putrāso aditerye jātāstanva'spari
Devāṅ upa praitsaptabhiḥ parā mārtāṇḍamāsyat ॥

The eighth son of Aditi, born after her seven sons, became identified with Deva. He enlightened the Ocean of *Ānanda.* He was called Martanda by the Ṛṣis, when he appeared as the Truth before them.

सप्तभिः पुत्रैरदितिरुप प्रैत्पूर्व्यं युगम् ।
प्रजायै मृत्यवे त्वत्पुनर्मार्ताण्डमाभरत् ॥

Ṛg.X.72.9

Saptabhiḥ putrairaditirupa praitpūrvyaṁ yugam ।
Prajāyai mṛtyave tvatpunarmārtāṇḍamābharat ॥

The creation in the beginning, with the seven sons of Aditi, was all divine. However, in former Ages when the divine creation was covered by death, Deva, through Martanda conquered death and gave them immortality. That is why he was called Satya, the Truth, by the Ṛṣis.

उत स्वराजे अदितिः स्तोममिन्द्राय जीजनत् ।
पुरुप्रशस्तमूतय ऋतस्य यत् ॥

Ṛg.VIII.12.14

Uta svarāje aditiḥ stomamindrāya jījanat ।
Purupraśastamūtaya ṛtasya yat ॥

O Divine Mother Aditi! Be established in your own divine empire. The best offering in the whole empire has been given to you by the Divine Emperor Indra. This was the decided path for Truth by the Ṛṣis of ancient times. Let it again be like that.

अदितिर्द्यौरदितिरन्तरिक्षमदितिर्माता स पिता स पुत्रः ।
विश्वे देवा अदितिः पञ्च जना अदितिर्जातमदितिर्जनित्वम् ॥

Ṛg.I.89.10

Aditirdyauraditir antarikṣamaditirmātā sa pitā sa putraḥ /
Viśve devā aditiḥ pañca janā
aditirjātamaditirjanitvam //

Aditi is the Heaven, the antarikṣa – vital plane, the Mother, the Father and the Son. Aditi has taken these five forms in this world by identifying with the Truth. She is the creator of all and She herself has appeared in the whole creation.

That means Aditi is existing throughout her creations, from the *mahas,* the supramental plane through the Heaven and antarikṣa until the Earth, in all she is herself and this is her divine empire. She is now determined to make the whole creation into one united empire. She herself is facing the Power of Diversity and to conquer it is pulling down Deva, the Supreme Truth. At that moment through the divine sacrifice, maintained by the Divine Mother Aditi, the Power of Truth – Devi Uṣatī, the spiritual dawn, touches this Earth.

The Ṛgveda says:-

ते हि यज्ञेषु यज्ञियास ऊमाः सधस्थं विश्वे अभि सन्ति देवाः ।
तां अध्वर उशतो यक्ष्यग्ने श्रुष्टी भगं नासत्या पुरन्धिम् ॥

Ṛg.VII.39.4

Te hi yajñeṣu yajñiyāsa ūmāḥ sadhasthaṁ viśve abhi santi devāḥ /
Tān adhvara uśato yakṣyagne śruṣṭi bhagaṁ nāsatyā purandhim //

In that divine sacrifice, yajña, Devi, the Mother of the Earth, appears with the Deva and manifests herself through the Yajña in this world. There the worshipper of Deva, the Adorer of Truth, Agni, offers the sacrificial offerings to the Mother Uṣatī; by which She removes falsehood from the earthly home of Truth and cleans the home with the manifestation of the Bhaga Devata, the Joy of Truth.

श्वात्रा स्थ वृत्रतुरो राधोगूर्ताऽ अमृतस्य पत्नीः ।
ता देवीर्देवत्रेमं यज्ञं नयतोपहूताः सोमस्य पिबत ॥

Yaj.VI.34

Śvātrā stha vṛtraturo rādhogūrta' amṛtasya patnīḥ /
Tā devīrdevatremaṁ yajñaṁ nayatopahūtāḥ somasya pibataḥ //

Devi, the Power of Immortality, kills Vṛtra, the opponent of Gods, and removes the Power of Diversity, Diti. She appears with the other Godheads to manifest a New Age and a new race. The worshippers drink, *soma*, the nectar with her grace and achieve immortality.

सुत्रामाणं पृथिवीं द्यामनेहसं सुशर्माणमदितिं सुप्रणीतिम् ।
दैवीं नावं स्वरित्रामनागसमस्रीवन्तीमारुहेमा स्वस्तये ॥

Ṛg.X.63.10

Sutrāmāṇaṁ pṛthivīṁ dyamanehasaṁ suśarmāṇamaditiṁ supraṇītiṁ /
Daivīṁ nāvaṁ svaritrāmanāgasamasrīvantīmaruhemā svastaye //

The Earth and Heaven become one through identitification. At that moment, Aditi holds the Earth and Heaven together with her power of unity in the divine consciousness. There the Devi Suhavā joins the love and compassion of the Heaven with the love and self surrender of the Earth and creates a new creation that is ever beautiful, young and immortal. She declares her existence and activities to the Earth in the following words, as, we, the Ṛsis, said in the Yajurveda:

देवीमहं निर्ऋतिं बाधमानः पितेव पुत्रं दमये वचोभिः ।
या जायमानस्य जायमानस्य शिरो देवी प्रति सुरिविचष्टे ॥

Yaj.Kath. Samhita 38.149

Devīmahaṁ nirṛtiṁ bādhamānaḥ piteva putraṁ damaye vacobhiḥ /
Yā jāyamānasya jāyamanasya śiro devī prati sūrvicaṣṭe //

I am the Devi who conquers Death. The father remains the father, the son remains the son. Those who have taken birth, have been born but I will stop the birth. I am the Mother of the Earth. Through my nourishment, mankind will become free of mortality. They will appear as my immortal children, immune and beautiful.

When the Devi appeared before Prajāpati, He saw the Truth manifested by Her and She was called Uṣatī by him. The Ṛṣis called her Suhavā, when they realised that the Devi accepts all sacrificial offering which they offer to Deva. There is another secret name for her that is Kuhu. The Devas call her affectionately with that name when she serves them *soma*, the nectar. This sweet name the Seers heard from the voice of Truth.

कुहुर्देवानाममृतस्य पत्नी हव्या नो अस्य हविषा जुषेत ।
श्रृणोतु यज्ञमुशति नो अद्य रायस्पोषं चिकितुषी दधातु ॥

Ath.VII.49.2

Kuhurdevānāmamṛtasya patnī havyā no asya haviṣā juṣeta ।
Śṛṇotu yagñamuśatī no adya rāyaspoṣaṁ cikituṣī dadhātu ॥

O Devi Kuhu! Power of the Immortal Deva, take our offerings to the Deva. By the touch of Truth, let our offerings become immortal. Distribute that food with your own hands among us through which we shall enter into immortality.

And Mahāyāni, the Sister Power of Truth, gives us all the riches of Truth, by which we become truthful and enlightened by the riches of Truth. Mahāyāni! Giver of riches of Truth, let our life become smooth and easy without any problems and depressions.

सिनिवालि पृथुष्टुके या देवानामसि स्वसा ।
जुषस्व हव्यमाहुतं प्रजां देवि दिदिड्ढि नः ॥

Ath.VII.48.1

Sinīvāli pṛṭhuṣṭuke yā devānāmasi svasā /
Juṣaswa havyamāhutaṁ prajām devi dididdhi naḥ //

Another sister power of truth, Sinibali, brings a new truthful creation among the Earth. At the moment of pregnancy, when the power of the father enters into the womb of the mother; at that time she makes an offering to the Truth. This forms the children for the divine birth. At that time, O Devi! Provide that part of Truth so that immortal children can take birth upon Earth.

20

TIME FOR THE MANIFESTATION OF DEVĀYAṆA

When the Devi Uṣati influences the divine sacrifice on the Earth, the words act more powerfully with the Power and Light of Truth. They connect with Time to commence the new Age of Truth, the Golden Age. We, the Ṛṣis, continue the hymns to the Deva to enter into the Age of Truth.

विश्वे देवा वसवो रक्षतेममुतादित्या जागृत यूयमस्मिन् ।
मेमं सनाभिरुत वान्यनाभिर्मेमं प्रापत् पौरुषेयो वधो यः ॥

Ath.I.30.1

Viśve devā vasavo rakṣatemamutādityā jagṛta yūyamasmin /
Memam sanābhiruta vānyanābhirmemaṁ prāpat pauruṣeyo vadho yaḥ //

When Deva exists in the world, He influences and enlightens the Sun (who daily awakens the beings on the Earth) with His power to awaken these people into the Truth consciousness. That power acts through the Sun on the inner soul of human beings and conquers the hostile forces (those who surround the soul to make it forget its immortality and leave it defenceless to diseases, infirmity and death). His power removes the negative forces and establishes the soul into divinity. In other words, men defeat diseases, infirmities and death and achieve longevity.

ये वो देवाः पितरो ये च पुत्राः सचेतसो मे शृणुतेदमुक्तम् ।
सर्वेभ्यो वः परि ददाम्येतं स्वस्त्ये नं जरसे वहाथ ॥

Ath.I.30.2

Ye vo devāḥ pitaro ye ca putrāḥ sacetaso me śṛṇutedamuktam /
Sarvebhyo vaḥ pari dadāmyetaṁ svastye naṁ jarase vahātha //

The Deva comes to us like our father and makes us become conscious as if we were His sons. He liberates us from all bondages. We have heard this also from other Ṛṣis. Above all, with His grace and compassion we can progress far beyond mortality and achieve perfect peace with immunity.

ये देवा दिविष्ठ ये पृथिव्यां ये अन्तरिक्ष ओषधीषु पशुष्वप्स्वऽन्तः ।
ते कृणुत जरसमायुरस्मै शतमन्यान् परि वृणक्तु मृत्यून् ॥

Ath.I.30.3

Ye devā diviṣṭha ye pṛthivyām ye antarikṣa oṣadhīṣu paśuṣvapsva'ntaḥ /
Te kṛṇuta jarasamāyurasmai śatamanyān pari vṛṇaktu mṛtyūn //

The Deva exists in the transcendental Heaven. In course of time, he comes and influences this Earth and antarikṣa, the vital plane, containing plants and all life. He removes their infirmity and injuries and gives them longevity. At least for ten thousand years, death cannot enter in the earthly atmosphere.

At present, we satisfy our hunger and thirst daily in a number of ways. This is mainly by worshipping material objects for our vital enjoyment. We still have to offer our worship to the Deva, the five-fold sacrifice for attaining the Truth. We pray that it be accomplished.

Let time turn towards Deva, the Age of Truth, when Devi Suhavā comes to join Truth with Time. By accepting our divine offering, the Deva comes to control the Wheel of Time (Kālacakra) and thus starts the Age of Truth, or the Golden

Age. We chant the Hymns to the Time to effect this change. We wish to replace the Falsehood with the Truth, the undivine with the divine, by ending the Iron Age and by bringing into existence the Golden Age. We remember our past activities and wish for the future. Listen, O Earth! The mantras of Bhṛgu, as the Atharvaveda says:

कालो अश्वो वहति सप्तरश्मिः सहस्राक्षो अजरो भूरिरेताः ।
तमा रोहन्ति कवयो विपश्चितस्तस्य चक्रा भुवनानि विश्वा ॥

Ath.XIX.53.1

Kālo aśvo vahati saptaraśmiḥ sahasrākṣo ajaro bhūriretāḥ |
Tamā rohanti kavayo vipaścitastasya cakrā bhuvanāni viśvā ||

Time is carrying the seven-rayed Sun like a horse with Sahasrākṣa, the thousand-eyed Indra giving him immunity and immortality with immense power. He is rising above the dark and obscure night with an indomitable heroism. The Seers have seen that his wheel is this universe.

सप्त चक्रान् वहति काल एष सप्तास्य नाभीरमृतं न्वक्षः ।
स इमा विश्वा भुवनान्यञ्जत् कालः स ईयते प्रथमो नु देवः ॥

Ath.XIX.53.2

Sapta cakrān vahati kāla eṣa saptāsya nābhīramṛtam nvakṣaḥ |
Sa imā viśvā bhuvanānyañjat kālaḥ sa īyate prathamo nu devaḥ ||

Time is revolving on seven wheels. The seven wheels, the seven navels and the seven middles are remaining in Time and immortality is the axle. This universe is moving with Time and our Satyadeva exists in front of us.

पूर्णः कुम्भोऽधि काल आहितस्तं वै पश्यामो बहुधा नु सन्तः ।
स इमा विश्वा भुवनानि प्रत्यङ् कालं तमाहुः परमे व्योमन् ॥

Ath.XIX.53.3

Purṇaḥ kumbho'dhi kāla āhitastaṁ vai paśyāmo bahudhā nu santaḥ /
Sa imā viśvā bhuvanāni pratyan kālaṁ tamāhuḥ parame vyoman //

Time, by supporting this creation, appears as if it is a full water pot. Sometimes it appears manifold, sometimes sevenfold. Time is clasping this universe, but the one who is controlling and guiding Time is existing in the transcendental Heaven.

स एव सं भुवनान्याभरत् स एव सं भुवनानि पर्यैत् ।
पिता सन्नभवत् पुत्र एषां तस्माद् वै नान्यत् परमस्ति तेजः ॥

Ath.XIX.53.4

Sa eva saṁ bhuvanānyābharat sa eva saṁ bhuvanāni paryait /
Pitā sannabhavat putra eṣāṁ tasmād vai nānyat paramasti tejaḥ //

This is the universe, where Bharata was staying and seeing another universe. As the father maintains and nourishes his son, like that this universe is being guided and nourished by the power of the Supreme Truth.

कालोऽमूं दिवमजनयत् काल इमाः पृथिवीरुत ।
कालो ह भूतं भव्यं चेषितं ह वि तिष्ठते ॥

Ath.XIX.53.5

Kālo'mūṁ divamajanayat kāla imāḥ pṛthivīruta /
Kālo ha bhūtaṁ bhavyaṁ ceṣitaṁ ha vi tiṣṭhate //

With Time, the days manifest and with Time, the Earth becomes conscious. With Time, all beings take formations and with Time the creative sacrifice goes towards fulfilment.

कालो भूतिमसृजत काले तपति सूर्यः ।
काल ह विश्वा भूतानि काले चक्षुर्विपश्यति ॥

Ath.XIX.53.6

Kālo bhūtimasṛjata kāle tapati sūryaḥ /
Kāle ha viśvā bhūtānī kāle cakṣurvipaśyati //

Time has manifested immortality with the greater creation. The Sun shines powerfully with Time. These earthly beings appear with Time and our eyes are capable of seeing only with the power of Time.

काले मनः काले प्राणः काले नाम समाहितम् ।
कालेन सर्वा नन्दन्त्यागतेन प्रजा इमाः ॥

Ath.XIX.53.7

Kāle manaḥ kāle prāṇaḥ kāle nāma samāhitam /
Kālena sarvā nandantyāgatena prajā imāḥ //

With Time the mind thinks, life moves on and people receive their names. We obtain our new race with Time and we lose also our old race with Time only.

काले तपः काले ज्येष्ठं काले ब्रह्म समाहितम् ।
कालो ह सर्वस्येश्वरो यः पितासीत् प्रजापतेः ॥

Ath.XIX.53.8

Kāle tapaḥ kāle jyeṣṭhaṁ kāle brahma samāhitam /
Kālo ha sarvasyeśvaro yaḥ pitāsīt prajāpateḥ //

We do our yogic sacrifice with the power of Time and attain our eternal or supramental status also by Time. The creator Brahmā is fully identified with Time. It is Time that is holding all worlds with their creations. Our father, grandfather or our creator, Prajāpati, all are held by Time.

तेनेषितं तेन जातं तदु तस्मिन् प्रतिष्ठितम् ।
कालो ह ब्रह्म भूत्वा बिभर्ति परमेष्ठिनम् ॥

Ath.XIX.53.9

Teneṣitaṁ tena jātaṁ tadu tasmin pratiṣṭhitam /
Kālo ha brahma bhūtvā bibharti parameṣṭhinam //

The creations appear by Time, exist in Time and are destroyed by Time. With the help of Time, the supreme Brahman has manifested and it is Parameṣṭhi who has fashioned these creations.

कालः प्रजा असृजत कालो अग्रे प्रजापतिम् ।
स्वयम्भूः कश्यपः कालात् तपः कालादजायत ॥

Ath.XIX.53.10

Kālaḥ prajā asṛjata kālo agre prajāpatim /
Svayambhūḥ kaśyapaḥ kālāt tapaḥ kālādajāyata //

Time becomes the reason for the coming into existence of huge numbers of people. Agni and Prajāpati also appeared with Time. The Creator Svayambhū and Kaśyapa undertook a rigorous tapasya and yogic austerities for the manifestation of Time. This is the hidden reason behind the manifestation of Time.

कालादापः समभवन् कालाद् ब्रह्म तपो दिशः ।
कालेनोदेति सूर्यः काले नि विशते पुनः ॥

Ath.XIX.54.1

Kālādāpaḥ samabhavan kālād brahma tapo diśaḥ /
Kālenodeti sūryaḥ kāle ni viśate punaḥ //

Time is existing as an immense ocean. In other words, Time is the creator, tapasya and all the directions. Due to Time, the Sun rises and sets punctually.

कालेन वातः पवते कालेन पृथिवी मही ।
द्यौर्मही काल आहिता ॥

Ath.XIX.54.2

Kālena vātaḥ pavate kālena pṛthivī mahī /
Dyaurmahī kāla āhitā //

Due to Time, the pure breeze blows. This Earth with her creation has manifested due to Time and Heaven has also appeared due to Time.

कालो ह भूतं भव्यं च पुत्रौ अजनयत् पुरा ।
कालादृचः समभवन् यजुः कालादजायत ॥

Ath.XIX.54.3

Kālo ha bhuṭaṁ bhavyaṁ ca putrau ajanayat purā I
Kāladṛcaḥ samabhavam yajuḥ kālādajāyata II

Time has decided our fate, our past and future and brought into existence our children. Time will create more beings in the future. All creations are maintained by Time. For this, Time has been born.

कालो यज्ञं समैरयद्देवेभ्यो भागमक्षितम् ।
काले गन्धर्वाप्सरसः काले लोकाः प्रतिष्ठितः ॥

Ath.XIX.54.4

Kālo yajñaṁ samairayaddevebhyo bhāgamakṣitaṁ I
Kāle gandharvāpsarahsaḥ kāle lokā pratiṣṭhita II

Time has engaged all Godheads to do their own work in different ways and places. Time also guides the divine artists, the *Gandharvās*, the divine singers and the *Apsarās*, the divine dancers. The all powerful Time establishes and maintains the planes of existence in proper order.

कालोऽयमङ्गिरा देवोऽथर्वा चाधि तिष्ठतः ।
इमं च लोकं परमं च लोकं पुण्यांश्च लोकान् विधृतीश्च पुण्याः ।
सर्वांल्लोकानभिजित्य ब्रह्मणा कालः स ईयते परमो नु देवः ।

Ath.XIX.54.5

Kālo'yamangirā devo'tharvā cādhi tiṣṭhatḥ I
Imaṁ ca lokaṁ paramaṁ ca lokaṁ puṇyānṣca lokān vidhṛtisca puṇyāḥ I
Sarvāṅlokānabhijitya brahmaṅā kālaḥ sa īyate paramo nu devaḥ I

With Time, Yama, the seven Ṛṣis including Aṅgirā, Atharva etc. and the other Godheads came into existence. This earthly plane, the pure plane of Heaven and the plane containing the purity of all planes have all been influenced by Time. However, above all it is the unmanifested Parabrahaman, from whose atomic body Time has come into existence.

Time is revolving like a wheel. In front of Time, Satyadeva is standing and behind Time, Kali, the Lord of Falsehood is present. Time is influencing the three universes, the Earth with the Sun, Moon, Stars and other planets, the antarikṣa with the ancestors and the Heaven with the Gods. The years, *samvatsaras,* are existing in this universe. With the movement of the Time Wheel, the universes and the years are in constant motion. For this reason, we observe the passage from Satyayuga, the Golden Age to Kaliyuga, the Iron Age and again from Kaliyuga to Satyayuga. By this cyclic movement, *ayana,* the years are revolving and many many years have passed. One *ayana,* the complete cycle of Time, consists of twenty-six thousand years and contains the period of the Deva and that of Kali. When the Time and the Universe move towards the Deva, at that time the Devāyaṇa is disclosed. Thus Devāyaṇa appears once in every twenty-six thousand years.

In this universe, the years or the *samvatsaras* are established. With the movement of Time, they are revolving. We, the Ṛṣis, disclose here that through the mantras of the Vedas, Time is revolving in seven circles.

- In the first circle, there are the three universes and the four Ages.
- In the second circle, there are the twenty six thousand years, *samvatsaras.*
- In the third circle, there are 312,000 months, *masas* with 156,000 seasons, *ṛtus.*
- In the fourth circle, we have 9,360,000 days, *divas* with 74,880,000, three-hour periods, *praharas.*
- In the fifth circle, there are 224,640,000 hours, *pals* with 13,478,400,000 minutes or *Vipals.*
- In the sixth, there are 808,704,000,000 seconds, *anupals* with 8,087,040,000,000 *muhurtas.*
- In the seventh, there exist 16,174,080,000,000 *nimishas.* Nimisha means the twinkling of an eye.

These minute measurements exist on the eternal power of Time.

In other words, this universe is existing on the Time Wheel. In this universe, the years are existing with the Earth, the Sun, Moon, Stars and the Planets. With the movement of the Time Wheel, the years move with the universe. From the Golden Age to the Iron Age and vice versa, many years pass. When the Time Wheel has turned a full circle, this is called the *ayana*. This time cycle is completed in twenty-six thousand years.

If we observe this process from the other side, we see that it is the power of Time which is managing the time wheel by holding on to two *nimishas*. When these minute measurements of time vanish from an individual's life, then the life movement collapses. This is death. Thus the reason of death lies in the controlling power of Time. The *nimisha* is holding and guiding the whole universe. In the universe, when the individual being's connection with the *nimisha* is disconnected, his being separates from the Power of Time. As a result, his life movement comes to a sudden halt, he becomes still and all movement ceases. Thus, the Power of Time is controlling the *nimisha* and it is this only that is maintaining the motion of the Time Wheel. Thus Time is divided as follows:

- 2 *nimishas* make a *muhurtta*.
- 10 *muhurttas* make an *anupal*, a second
- 60 *anupals* make a *vipal*, a minute.
- 60 *vipals*, minutes make a *pal*, hour.
- 3 *pals*, hours make a *prahar*.
- 8 *prahars* make an *ahoratra*, day. Also 24 *pals* make an *ahoratra*, a full day and night.
- 30 *ahoratras* make a *masa*, month.
- 2 *masas*, months form a *ṛtu*, season
- 6 *ṛtus*, seasons form a *samvatsara*, year
- 3000 *samvatsaras*, years form the *Kali Yuga*, Iron Age
- 4000 *samvatsaras*, years form the *Dwitāyuga* or *Dwāpara – Yuga*, Bronze Age.
- 6000 *samvatsaras*, years make a *Tritayuga*, Silver Age.
- 13,000 *samvatsaras*, years form a *Satyayuga*, a Golden Age

- 4 Ages, *Yugas* form a *Kalpa* and each *Kalpa* starts with the Devāyaṇa.

We have made the journey from the undetectable time *nimisha* to the unimaginable *Kalpa.* The Gods are counting Time according to the Kalpas and the human beings according to the years. The reason being that this Earth is changing according to the passing of years. During a year, we have different seasons which provide wealth to the world. The passing of seasons gives an enormous amount of wealth to the Earth, like wheat, rice, cereals etc. She becomes decorated with fruits, flowers and vegetables and is full of joy and happiness. When the same seasons, *ṛtus,* are influenced by the hostile or antidivine powers then the Earth becomes poor and is unable to maintain her huge population. She becomes depressed and is full of sorrows. The food that is produced at such a time is meagre in quantity and without taste and fragrance, caused by the separation from Heaven and the Gods.

For these reasons, we, the Ṛṣis, say that the identification of Earth with Heaven is essential now to overcome the present poverty, sorrows and sufferings present on the Earth and to usher in a period full of wealth, peace and purity of Truth. With the meditation on Deva, the Earth will become filled with joy. In former Ages, when we chanted the Hymns to the Deva to establish the *Ṛtus* (the Gods of the seasons) through the meditation of Truth, the Earth became exceptionally beautiful and wealthy. She appeared as rich as Heaven with the production of rice and other cereals, fruits, flowers, gold, silver and jewels. Now, we are chanting these mantras in the same way. Listen, O People of the Earth! Be healthy, affluent, full of joy and peaceful like the Gods. As Yajurveda says:

वसन्तेन ऋतुना देवा वसवस्त्रिवृता स्तुताः ।
रथन्तरेण तेजसा हविरिन्द्रे वयो दधुः ॥

Yaj.XXI.23

Vasantena ṛtunā devā vasavastrivṛta stutāḥ /
Rathantareṇa tejasā havirindre vayo dadhuḥ //

Let the spring, the *vasanta ṛtu*, be identified with the Vasus to worship Deva with wide ranging prayers and meditations. With these the powers of the Earth would increase and they will be an offering to the Indra devata. With the fulfilment of this Yajña, worship, the divine king will give all accomplishments to the Earth.

ग्रीष्मेण ऋतुना देवा रुद्राः पञ्चदशे स्तुता ।
बृहता यशसा बलं हविरिन्द्रे वयो दधुः ॥

Yaj.XXI.24

Grīṣmeṇa ṛtunā devā rudrāḥ pañcadaśe stutāḥ ।
Bṛhata yaśasā balaṁ havirindre vayo dadhuḥ ॥

Let the summer season, *grīṣam ṛtu,* enter; let the Rudra devata worship the Deva in different prayers throughout the fifteen times of the moon. By his immense fame and strength, the *havi* or the offering will go directly to Indra. With the fulfilment of this Yajña, the divine king gives fame and strength.

वर्षाभिर्ऋतुनादित्याः स्तोमे सप्तदशे स्तुताः ।
वैरूपेण विशौजसा हविरिन्द्रे वयो दधुः ॥

Yaj.XXI.25

Varṣābhirṛtunādityāḥ stome saptadaśe stutāḥ ।
Vairūpeṇa viśaujasā havirindre vayo dadhūḥ ॥

Welcome to the rainy season, *varṣa ṛtu.* Let the Sun worship Deva in seventeen different ways. By these prayers, the greatness goes as an offering directly to Lord Indra. With the fulfilment of this Yajña, the divine king gives pure and powerful beauty to the body.

शारदेन ऋतुना देवाऽ एकविंश ऋभव स्तुताः ।
वैराजेन श्रिया श्रियं हविरिन्द्रे वयो दधुः ॥

Yaj.XXI.26

Śāradena ṛtunā devā' ekaviṁśa ṛbhava stutāḥ ।
Vairājena śriyā śriyaṁ havirindre vayo dadhuḥ ॥

Let in the autumn, *śārad ṛtu*. Let the Ṛibhavas worship Deva the Truth in different prayers divided into twenty one parts. Through these the beauty of the body increases and it goes as an offering to the Lord Indra. As the fulfilment of the Yajña, the divine king provides divine beauty.

हेमन्तेन ऋतुना देवास्त्रिणवे मरुत स्तुताः ।
बलेन शक्वरीः सहो हविरिन्द्रे वयो दधुः ॥

Yaj.XXI.27

Hemantena ṛtunā devāstriṇave maruta stutāḥ /
Balena śakvarīḥ saho havirindre vayo dadhuḥ //

Let the dewy season the *hemanta ṛtu* in, let the Marut worship Deva, through his manifold prayers. Through these his power increases and it goes as an offering to Indra. As the fulfilment of that Yajña, the divine King replaces it with divine power..

शैशिरेण ऋतुना देवास्त्रयस्त्रिंशेऽमृता स्तुताः ।
सत्येन रेवतीः क्षत्रं हविरिन्द्रे वयो दधुः ॥

Yaj.XXI.28

Śaiśireṇa ṛtunā devāstrayastriṁśe'mṛtā stutāḥ /
Satyena revatīḥ kṣatraṁ havirindre vayo dadhūḥ //

Let in the winter season, the *śiśira ritu* and let the thirty three Gods worship Deva Immortal, with manifold prayers. Through these the power increases immensely and goes to Lord Indra as an offering. At the completion of that Yajña, the divine King bestows on us the achievement of Truth.

In short, these are the six *ṛtus*, seasons.

Vasanta-spring, Grīṣma-summer, Varṣā-rain, Śarad-autumn, Hemanta-dew and Śiśir-winter. The Godhead Upava has established them on the royal road of Truth "Devāyaṇa" and has opened the path completely, so that Truth could descend on the Earth and the seasons are there to welcome it.

21

SATYADEVA LEADS US TO IMMORTALITY

When Upava acts to open the royal road for the manifestation of Deva on the earth, the Ṛtus identify themselves with the several Godheads to sing hymns to the Lord of the Truth to invite Him on the earth. Then Time takes a turn towards the period of immortality. As a result the Human Will becomes eager to aspire for the Truth. It discards all vital enjoyment that it was engaged in as well as the lower mental formations. At that moment, when the sacrificial offerings from the earth reach the Deva, Time then makes a union with the Power of Truth.

This is the Age of Truth, the Golden Age. We, the Ṛṣis, chant the Hymns to the Satyadeva to strengthen the human will to form an increasingly closer identification with the Truth for the complete manifestation.

Agñeya Sauciki, the Priest for the birth of Satyadeva, commences the new Age of Truth at the beginning of each Kalpa by influencing the Human Will by chanting the mantras for Deva. We also join with Sauciki to chant the Hymns to the Mystic Fire so that His Advent is hastened.

Today, our aspirations, thoughts and meditations are similar to what we experienced before. What we had commenced before is now being realised in the present. We are again meditating on the all desirable Deva, whom we had seen for a moment and whom we are worshipping in our Yajña.

O Offerer of Your Own Self! Offer yourself without any hesitation and with a firm determination in this divine sacrifice, the Abhi Yajña, which was kindled by me. Offer all your activities to the Divine. Through this the great power of the divine sacrifice, the Ilā Devi, prays for us and takes our offerings to fulfill and accomplish our yogic effort to invoke our ever desirable Deva, the Lord of the Truth.

Also let the power of ardent aspiration, the Sādhavi Gauribiti, disclose the secrets of Truth. She is our voice and through her all Godheads can realise Deva, the son of Abhivarta. Let this divine sacrifice illumine the five planes of the Divine Mother Aditi (the mind, vital, physical, in the father and in the son) and let this sacrifice, Yajña be successfully completed.

For the successful completion of my self offering, allow that all the five planes of Aditi attain the light and consciousness of the Truth. Let our earth, through the sacrifice of the material, vital and mental, become receptive to attain the Supreme Truth.

तन्तुं तन्वन्रजसो भानुमन्विहि ज्योतिष्मतः पथो रक्ष धिया कृतान् ।
अनुल्बणं वयत जोगुवामपो मनुर्भव जनया दैव्यं जनम् ॥

Ṛg.X.53.6

Tantuṁ tanvanrajaso bhānumanvihi jyotiśmataḥ pathо rakṣa dhiyā kṛtān /
Anulbaṇaṁ vayata joguvāmapo manurbhava janayā daivyaṁ janam //

O Dawn-Red Sun like the luminous Truth! From the subtle body you take the physical body and protect us on the illuminated path. Establish us on the path leading to the journey of Truth, the Devāyaṇa and talk with us in a soft and sweet voice. With this, let the Manurbhāva people, created by Manu, manifest as the divine race and progress from the mental to the supramental. We aspire and meditate for that.

O Tvaṣṭā, you know all the secrets of Māyā. Remove this obscurity and ignorance and pour soma, the divine drink, in the mouth of Truth. Empty the whole drinking pot. Hold your axe to hew the forest like darkness of this earthly creation and remove the obscurity of this Earth. Let this land become illuminated with the Light of Truth and become joyful. In the accomplishment of this task, allow Brahmaṇaspati to become a helper.

Prajāpati described the appearance of Deva thus

यस्मात् कोशादुदभराम वेदं तस्मिन्नन्तरव दध्म एनम् ।
कृतमिष्टं ब्रह्मणो वीर्येण तेन मा देवास्तपसावते ह ॥

Ath.XIX.72.1

Yasmāt kośādudabharāma vedaṁ tasminnantarava dadhma enam /
Kṛtamiṣṭaṁ brahmaṇo vīryeṇa tena mā devāstapasāvate ha //

The Vedas exist in the Deva as cells of His Body and they have manifested themselves from there. With His knowledge and Consciousness, the Vedas have become luminous or in other words, He, the Deva, has become enlightened with the knowledge of the Vedas. With the power of Brahmā, He is the most efficient doer of all works. He is Satyadeva, the Supreme Soul. We meditate on Him and offer our yogic sacrifice to realise Him.

O Jātaveda, Fire! Today you light yourself in this human society by which Satyadeva may manifest with the other Godheads. O Great Mitra-Varuṇa! You are the Poet and the Herald of Truth. Bring the Light of Truth to this world.

Let Tanunāpāt be kind enough to clean, the Fire enlighten and facilitate the advent of Truth. Let Him increase the power of the will and meditation in men. Let Him remove all opposition and power from the demonical powers, which are against sacrifice. Allow our sacrificial offering to reach straight to the Truth.

The Vasus, with all their powers, are meditating with their constant call and prayer and are prostrating to the Satyadeva. O Fire! For the manifestation of the Truth, be the Yajña-hota, the Manifestor of Truth. Be the remover of all opposition and become the Luminous Priest for the manifestation of the Truth.

The eternal and ancient seat for the manifestation of the Truth is our heart. In the whole creation, this Earth was meant for that purpose. O Fire! Take your place there and remain seated down there. Call the Supreme Truth on this Earth. Let the call of Truth be spread throughout this Earth so that Satyadeva, together with the Gods – the sons of Aditi, manifests here.

O Fire! Make the restless and peaceless heart of the Earth conscious and tell her the news of the Truth. Satyadeva will give her rest, shelter and protection. Be the Discloser of the Divine Path of the Deva, to establish divine beauty in mankind, to open the door of the greater creation with the help of Goddesses for identification with the Truth

O Fire! Adore the Supreme Truth for His manifestation. Call down his daughter, the Divine Dawn, Uṣā, who is the Conqueror of Night to manifest a new race upon Earth. That divine girl has enlightened the eternal heaven. That pure white light is the best. She is the symbol of Truth, bring It down on this Earth.

O Fire! You are the divine priest. Tell us about the Truth. This is the Yajña, which has been kindled and maintained by men. Give them the consciousness to achieve their divinity together with the knowledge of the ancient creation, art and the radiant light that spreads around the Earth. Let it be enlightened with ānanda.

Bhārati fulfils in many ways our divine sacrifice and makes our human world conscious. Three goddesses, Ilā, Bhārati and Sarasvatī, appear first in the seat of the soul which is the human body. Sarasvatī is the architect, who gives a beautiful artistic shape to this human home.

With the identification of Earth and Heaven, the divine appearance of this universe is secured. In this sacrifice, the divine priest performs a sacrificial rite by pulling down the Power and Light of Truth and the wise artist Tvaṣṭā gives the artistic touch to this creation so that it appears divine.

In this divine creation, Upava devata was encouraged to open the wide road of Devāyaṇa, for Deva the Truth. On that road he established the six ṛtus (seasons) to call down and worship the Deva on the Earth. Vanaspati gave the sacrificial offering with ghṛta, clarified butter, and madhu, honey, to increase the power of Agni, the Lord of Fire, in this divine sacrifice through which Deva manifested.

Agni, the Lord of Fire, is the Priest to call down Satyadeva, with the other Godheads at the Yajña where the Earth becomes united with Heaven. The Fire chants the mantra of Truth and gives the sacrificial offering with the help of Svāha, his power, for the fulfilment of the sacrifice and to manifest the Deva.

We know Satyadeva, who is the Lord of All. We heard that He is completely liberated and exists above all. We came to know about these secrets. Our ancient Ṛṣis invoked the Deva and offered him the portion of Time where he is all-powerful. We are now invoking him to offer Him that portion of Time.

The Light of Truth touches this Earth with the constant aspiration of the seekers of Truth and Kali sees that his days in power are coming to an end, his rule is ending and that the Earth is approaching the time when she will be under the control of Truth. At the moment of transition, the hostile forces become more active under the guidance of Kali. They work incessantly to diminish the Light of Truth in human beings. They create an elegiac chant in the heart of the Earth by which the sufferings of humanity increase enormously. It rotates aimlessly with evil doers committing insane acts, resulting in no peace. That is the moment when Kali withdraws from this Earth. On hearing the elegiac chant of the Earth, Truth acts with redoubled force to drive out Kali together with all the hostile forces. Then the Kingdom of Truth is established on the earth.

O People of Earth! Remember the conqueror of the negative forces and the antidivine, the Lord Indra. In former times, also, He undertook this battle to re-establish the light of Truth upon the earth. Now again His time has come. All of you meditate on Lord Indra, the conqueror of all evils and enemies. We chant the mantras to Indra as mentioned in the Vedas:

O Indra! We pray to you as you have conquered the Asuras, the anti-divine, in former times. Now once again, O Truth-Seer Śakra! Conquer our enemies on this Earth, the hostile forces, by your indomitable heroism and be victorious. Let the divine victory come upon the Earth.

O Lord Indra, as you conquered the evil forces and destroyed them, the Vedas have highly praised you in thousand ways. Your supreme character and your brave deeds are mentioned in several thousand mantras. O eternally adored Śatakratu! Conqueror of all our enemies, let the divine victory come upon our Earth.

Remove all the divisions on the Earth and lead her into unity. Destroy and remove all opposition and diversities. We aspire and meditate on the all-powerful Satyadeva. Let Him protect us by surrounding our inner self with His supreme protection.

We have heard about Satyadeva from the mantras of Bharadvāja. He appeared from the divine flame and was established in the sacrificial Yajña. The enemies, the hostile forces, have covered us with their ignorance and folly, always influencing our mind and allowing contrary thoughts to make their home there. Let them be removed and let us become enlightened and peaceful with the presence of Deva.

Deva is the remover of all pains and sufferings. O Father Heaven! O Mother Earth! Look at the Time Wheel, which is revolving between happiness and sorrows. There Satyadeva has re-appeared and is showering His purity, like rain, to remove the heat of suffering and give us peace.

Our Deva is seated in the chariot of śrava, the chariot being surrounded by the golden screen, the divine Māyā. He is the conqueror and remover of Māyā, ignorance and Moha, attachment which is like a powerful monkey. He is the remover of all pain; he appears like a great friend to establish us in the supreme ānanda.

The Deva provides us with our food. He supports the base of our head that is the neck. He also controls the oceans, the huge expanses of water. He is the one who has opened the path of immortality to mortality. This food, anna, holds Deva. It has served the Deva, attracted his love, served the Vaisvanara, Fire and achieved a glorious position. He has become famous. He also served Śiva and attained the maximum sweetness.

O Truth! Once before you announced yourself before the Earth; as the Atharvaveda said:

सत्यमहं गभीरः काव्येन सत्यं जातेनास्मि जातवेदाः ।
न मे दासो नार्यो महित्वा व्रतं मीमाय यदहं धरिष्ये ॥

Ath.V.11.3

Satyamahaṁ gabhīraḥ kāvyena satyaṁ jātenāsmi jātavedāḥ /
Na me dāso nāryo mahitvā vrataṁ mīmāya yadahaṁ dhariṣye //

With the help of Jātaveda, the Fire, I manifest myself. I am the Truth that appears through the great epic. There is none above me. I am the unique Truth, I take birth in the Epic. O Earth! I constantly protect you and receive your worship and deeds through my indomitable power.

We have realised: Truth is the anna, matter; Truth is the antarikṣa, life or the vital plane; Truth is the manas, mind; Truth is the mahas-vijñana, supermind; and finally, Truth is transcendental.

22

TWO GREAT POWERS FOR THE MANIFESTATION OF TRUTH

There are two great powers, one is in the inconscient matter and the other in the superconscient void; both are combinedly manifesting Deva. The inconscient, which becomes conscious and conquers the attachment – *māyā*, stupidity-*moha* and death; the other, the superconscient brings peace, purity and the nectar, *soma*. One aspires for the Truth and awakens the immovable Puruṣa, who remains unconscious in matter, and conquers death by calling and embracing Truth. The other brings Truth down upon the Earth and fortifies the aspirant power of immortality (Vitihotra) and gives to mankind, the children of the Earth, eternal *ānanda* and immunity.

The inconscient great power was called Aśmanvatī, the power residing in the mountain, stone. This power also received the name of Pārvatī, the daughter of the Mountain who was offered to Lord Śiva as the symbol of Truth. She is also named Mahākāli or Mahādevi when she assumes her violent form and with irresistible force goes towards truth consciousness by conquering all antidivine forces. In her relationship with Lord Śiva, she represents the inconscient matter. In response to her movement from below, the transcendental Truth Power descends from above and touches the power of the inconscient.

When the super-conscient power, Suhavā, descends on the Earth and touches the inconscient force, Aśmanvatī, these two powers combine and become united in one and mortality disappears from the world. Then we observe immortality reappearing in the world. This is the time for the manifestation of the Truth. The Ṛgveda says that Truth-Power remains in matter as well as in the transcendent. One remains in the inconscient matter and the other in the superconscient void. Truth exists at both ends. When these two powers amalgamate, Truth manifests fully in this world.

The inconscient power was worshipped as Pārvatī, Durgā, Mahākāli etc. In the present Iron Age, the Sages and the Seekers (Yogis) did their yogic austerity individually and entered into a trance. They united themselves with the superconscient power. With her violent power, Pārvatī, Mahākāli shatters into pieces the stupidity and ignorance existing on the Earth and destroys the deadly lethargy of matter and the warped human never-ending desire for vital enjoyment. The Sages then enter into the divine consciousness and individually become liberated as a Mahatma or an enlightened Puruṣa.

However, without an individual effort or sadhana, there is no visible push for the entire humanity towards the supramental status, even when the power of Aśmanvatī is acting through the individual yogi. Humanity remains at the same level of ignorance. Even the capacity to understand a Yogi is missing due to want of receptivity. The question arises why such a condition is present in the world. The reason is that in the Iron Age, Time does not allow the general spread of divinity. However, Time allows an individual to achieve the divine, only under the condition that he or she forsakes all earthly enjoyment. That individual cannot return to normal life even when wishing to do so. This is the condition of Kali. If you enjoy being in the world then you cannot enter into higher consciousness. Once the Yogis achieve that stage then they are not allowed to mingle in human society as they might spread these divine ideas in the world.

As a result in the Iron Age, we all have the capacity individually to realise the Truth, by becoming fully detached from earthly enjoyment. If one prays and meditates on the divine advent, the hidden divine power awakes in each individual from the yogic cakra at the bottom of the being. This power is called Mūḷadhāra and it elevates the human consciousness to a higher level to be absorbed there. This inconscient power when it awakens has four aspects. The Yoga Shikha Upaniṣad says that these are Mahāmāyā, Mahākāli, Mahālakṣmi and Mahāsarasvatī. Sri Aurobindo describes these four aspects as Maheśvari, Mahākāli, Mahālakṣmi and Mahāsarasvatī. Their functioning takes place through individuals according to their varying aspirations.

When the question arises for the whole Earth, then the inconscient power acts to uplift the general mass of humanity to the divine truth consciousness. To achieve this goal, the power and activities come from four sides. (1) From the inconscient power, (2) from Time, (3) from the Earth's aspirations and the power of the Ṛṣis and (4) from the work of the superconscient power. Their names are (1) Aśmanvatī, the inconscient power, (2) Śiva, (3) Gauribiti and (4) Suhavā.

(1) Aśmanvatī is the inconscient power. She awakens humanity from the sleep of attachment and ignorance and takes us towards the Truth.
(2) Śiva is Time. He remains in a dormant condition in a deathlike trance. As Rudra, He gave a boon to Kali to manage the activities of this universe for a certain period. Thus, at this time all happenings are under the influence of negative forces. To bring back the auspicious Time, the Gods and the Ṛṣis take action.
(3) Gauribiti was established by the Ṛṣis to keep the memory of Truth on the Earth during the Iron Age, the Kaliyuga. Gauribiti has a direct contact with the Truth. As a result the power of the Transcendental Truth comes down on the Earth.
(4) Suhavā is the superconscient power. She comes from the transcendental plane and is always identified with the Deva. Whenever she descends on the Earth, Truth follows.

The Ṛgveda said:

अश्मन्वती रीयते सं रभध्वमुत्तिष्ठत प्र तरता सखायः ।
अत्रा जहाम ये असन्नशेवाः शिवान्वयमुत्तरेमाभि वाजान् ॥

Rg.X.53.8

Aśmanvatī riyate saṁ rabhadhvamuttiṣṭhata pra taratā sakhāyaḥ /
Atrā jahāma ye asannaśevāḥ śivānvayamuttaremābhi vājān //

Aśmanvatī, the power of the mountain, pulls down Deva the Truth and embraces Him with a deep love; and rises after rejecting immobility. O Aśmanvatī! Make Truth your beloved friend. By meditating on your beloved Deva, you can conquer death, where the immobile Puruṣa, Time as Śiva is lying dormant in sleep and is inconscient like a dead body. Wake him up so that he becomes conscious for the Truth. Let the inconscient matter become the Truth conscient Śiva. Let matter manifest as Truth.

Through his inconscient power, Kali is existing on this Earth and guiding humanity towards vital enjoyment and materialism. For this reason, mankind remains immersed in the vital plane and is attracted towards materialism. Matter is considered to be the only reality. In reality, Truth is transcendental and superconscient – Deva. When He touches the mind it becomes supermind. The upper reaches of the mind become illumined with this light but the lower portions remain still covered with darkness. This sombre obscurity remains for the whole period of Kali. At the end of this Age, Deva starts his adventure towards the Earth. When He conquers the forces of diversity and appears in the mind, He embraces the purified truthful Heaven. When Deva defeats the vital cravings, then life becomes peaceful and full of joy. Then Earth embraces Heaven. When the ignorance of matter is conquered, the Earth appears suffused with a lovely beauty and Truth manifests.

This describes the journey of Devāyaṇa, from Satya to Kali and from Kali to Satya. Kali spreads his influence from the inconscient plane on life and mind. Satya starts his journey from the supramental plane and conquers plane after plane. This is the work of Devi Suhavā, the power of truth, *Deva-patni*, the power of immortality. The *Amṛtasya-patni* influences the mind and life up to the matter and everything appears truthful and immortalised.

श्वात्रा स्थ वृत्रतुरो राधोगूर्ताऽ अमृतस्य पत्नीः ।
ता देवीर्देवत्रेमं यज्ञं नयतोपहूताः सोमस्य पिबत ॥

Yaj.VI-34

Śvātrā stha vṛtraturo rādhogūrtā' amṛtasya patnīḥ /
Tā devīrdevatremaṁ yajñaṁ nayatopahūtāḥ somasya pibata //

The Devi, who embodies the power of immortality, conquers the antidivine, removes diversity and establishes unity. She appears with the Deva, as a result of the Yajña made on the Earth by the Ṛṣis, called *Vitihotra.* She opens a New Age and worshippers of Truth drink *soma* by her grace and attain immortality.

The Devi Kuhu, *Amṛtasya-patni* comes down from the superconscient plane straight to the Yajña, the sacrificial flame, called Vitihotra, which consists of the aspirant power of the Ṛṣis. She appears together with Deva. From beneath rises Aśmanvatī by removing Kali from the Time Wheel. This she accomplishes in the form of Mahākāli who conquers all Earthly attachment and ignorance and liberates Time from hostile powers such as diseases, infirmity and death. She pushes Time to become conscious of Truth. She herself throws away all the garments of Kali and becomes ready to embrace Truth. She approaches *Vitihotra* and embraces the Devi Suhavā before touching Deva. Then Suhavā covers her with the garment of Truth. Dressed in this garment, she appears as the Power of Truth and Devi Durgā establishes herself in the Vitihotra.

(The Devyupaniṣad said: *Vidyakar samyuktaṁ Vitihotra samwitaṁ.* In other words, she identifies with the sky like unmanifested Truth, representing *ṛtaṁ* and establishes herself in the *Vitihotra.*)

The *Vitihotra* is the place for the union of two great powers – the power of the superconscient Truth, Devi Suhavā and the power of Inconscient Time, Śiva. Aśmanvatī appears as Mahādevi Durgā as she removes all sufferings of humanity by bringing Time, Śiva together with Deva. Time appears then as *Devaṁ Śivaṁ Satyaṁ.* Without Deva, the Time, Śiva, leans towards the negative forces and is known as Rudra, the destructive face of Śiva. At that time, Kali, the Lord of the Iron Age, appears and it becomes Kaliyuga, the Iron Age. With Deva, Time becomes favourable for divine deeds and He is then called Piṅgala Maheśvara, the creative aspect of time. Then appears Satyadeva and we have the Golden Age. In short, eternal Time is divided into two parts and appears as two Maheśvaras (Gods).

Piṅgala Maheśvara assists the activities of Gods and gives immortality to men while Rudra Maheśvara is for the activities of the Asuras, to bring mortality, death and diseases to mankind. At present, we are approaching the end of one era of Time, after which the next period would start. Rudra Maheśvara is now withdrawing his epic, full of pathos and pains, sufferings and sorrows as well as death and diseases. The days of tears, depressions and mortality are passing away. Piṅgala Maheśvara has already started his new divine Epic. Now, the Earth and Heaven will be full of *ānanda*, peace and unity with the purity of Heaven. The days of gaiety, divine joy and immortality are approaching us.

Aśmanvatī was also called Prakṛti, the Nature, but her activities are divided in two, called para and apara. Śiva is the creator for this Earthly creation. He is the father of beings with *jivas*, souls. For this reason, he is called *Jagatpitā,* the Father of the Universe. Aśmanvatī is Prakṛti. As she has delivered this Earthly creation, she is the Mother of all the *jivas*. She is called *Jaganmata*, the Mother of the Universe.

When this Prakṛti-Aśmanvatī acts under the influence of the dark forces, Nakta, she becomes *Apara-Prakṛti* at the time of Kali. She creates people, who lead their lives without having any feeling for *Deva*. They live in ignorance and folly, continuously suffering from diseases and death. When she comes under the influence of Deva, she becomes Para Prakṛti. This happens during the period of Deva, the Golden Age. She creates beings who are supramental. They lead their life in a divine manner with the knowledge of Truth, they enjoy immortality and immunity in their lives.

Although, we, as human beings, always suffer from ill-health, diseases and death, we still remember our Mother, *Pārvatī-Durgā,* as we are the sons of Śiva. As their divine creation included their sons Ganeśa, Kārtikeya etc., we human beings meditate on them as our brothers. The same parents have two creations, one divine and the other undivine. The divine children are created in the Light of Truth and they exist in Heaven; others are created in the Night of Kali - namely the human beings who exist on the Earth and experience both light and darkness, and are at the same time divine and mortal.

Then Śiva enters into the womb of Prakṛti and becomes the being or the child. As the father enters into the womb of the mother, he himself becomes the child. Consequently, the father of these children is the immortal *Śivaṁ, Satyaṁ, Sundaraṁ*. Similarly, the son is the same immortal *Jivaṁ, Satyaṁ, Sundaraṁ.*

23

BEING ATTAINS ŚIVA – THE SUPRAMENTAL CONSCIOUSNESS

The Time, *Kāla*, is the creator of these *jivas*, human beings. When Nature, *Prakṛti* identifies with *Nakta* she appears as the *Apara Prakṛti*, delivers children who have an undivine nature influenced mainly by hostile forces. When *Śiva's Prakṛti* identifies herself with Deva, then she appears as *Para Prakṛti*. She delivers children who have a divine nature, influenced by divine forces. At that time, the Goddesses *Aditi, Bhārati, Ilā, Sarasvatī, Sinibali* and others act for the divine creation upon the Earth. And the supramental race manifests on the Earth.

These beings, *jivas*, appeared on the Earth as *Śiva's* children, but as they are under the influence of the dark and negative forces they are unaware of their immortality. Now the time has come to make them aware of their real nature. They have to become conscious that they are like *Śiva, Satya, Sundara* by rejecting diseases, infirmity and death, which destroy the immunity in their lives and make them weak. By chanting the mantras from the Vedas, we the Ṛṣis remind them and re-acquaint them with their thoughts concerning immortality. As Yajurveda said:

यज्जाग्रतो दूरमुदैति दैवं तदु सुप्तस्य तथैवैति ।
दूरङ्गमं ज्योतिषां ज्योतिरेकं तन्मे मनः शिवसंकल्पमस्तु ॥

Yaj.XXXIV.1

Yajjāgrato dụramudaiti daivaṁ tadu suptasya tathaivaiti /
Duraṅgamaṁ jyotiṣāṁ jyotirekaṁ tanme manaḥ śivasaṁkalpamastu //

The luminosity of Satyadeva is approaching us. This light is the most excellent of all. O unconscious mind! Regain the memory of your former truth consciousness. Awake with these recollections and become conscious of Truth. Be peaceful, quiet and achieve your Śiva status.

येन कर्माण्यपसो मनीषिणो यज्ञे कृण्वन्ति विदथेषु धीराः ।
यदपूर्वं यक्षमन्तः प्रजानां तन्मे मनः शिवसंकल्पमस्तु ॥

Yaj.XXXIV.2

Yena karmāṇyapaso manīṣiṇo yajñe kṛṇvanti vidatheṣu dhīrāḥ /
Yadapūrvaṁ yakṣamantaḥ prajānāṁ tanme manaḥ śivasaṁkalpamastu //

In former ages, the wise people rejected all other efforts excepting the Yajña. Through the divine Yajña, they became quiet and peaceful. This was considered the most propitious. Remember, O mind be conscious, peaceful, quiet and achieve your divinity.

यत्प्रज्ञानमुत चेतो धृतिश्च यज्ज्योतिरन्तरमृतं प्रजासु ।
यस्मान्नऽऋते किं चन कर्म क्रियते तन्मे मनः शिवसंकल्पमस्तु ॥

Yaj.XXXIV.3

Yatprajñānamuta ceto dhṛtiśca yajjyotirantaramṛtaṁ prajāsu /
Yasmānna' ṛte kiṁ cana karma kriyate tanme manaḥ śivasaṁkalpamastu //

Enlightened with that light, the wise people attained their knowledge and entered into immortality. Remember, O mind the memories of the Golden Age and work for the Truth so that you become peaceful, quiet and achieve your divinity.

येनेदं भूतं भुवनं भविष्यत् परिगृहीतममृतेन सर्वम् ।
येन यज्ञस्तायते सप्तहोता तन्मे मनः शिवसंकल्पमस्तु ॥

Yaj.XXXIV.4

Yenedaṁ bhūtaṁ bhuvanaṁ bhaviṣyat
parigṛhītamṛtena sarvam /
Yena yajñastāyate saptahotā tanme manaḥ
śivasaṁkalpamastu //

Past memories and stories remind us of our former achievements namely, immortality in this life. That was the ultimate and supreme realisation. Let these golden recollections become constant in you. In former ages, those seven great priests performed the Yajña. At present, these signs are reappearing for the manifestation of Truth. Do the same for the future. Remember, O mind those golden memories. Be peaceful and quiet and achieve your Śivahood.

यस्मिन्नृचः साम यजूंषि यस्मिन् प्रतिष्ठिता रथनाभाविवाराः ।
यस्मिंश्चित्तं सर्वमोतं प्रजानां तन्मे मनः शिवसंकल्पमस्तु ॥

Yaj.XXXIV.5

Yasminnṛcaḥ sāma yajūṁṣi yasmin pratiṣṭhitā
rathanābhāvivārāḥ /
Yasmiṁścintaṁ sarvamotaṁ prajānāṁ tanme
manaḥ śivasaṁkalpamastu //

The *citta*, the heart of the intellect, remains as the navel of the chariot wheel and to these are adjusted the *aradanda*, like the rods of the wheel, the Ṛg, the Sāma and the Yajurveda. His heart and consciousness has surrounded and embraced us throughout all the creations. Remember, O Mind the golden memory, be peaceful, quiet and achieve your Śivahood.

सुषारथिरश्वानिव यन्मनुष्यान्नेनीयतेभीशुर्वाजिन ऽ इव ।
हृत्प्रतिष्ठं यदजिरं जविष्ठं तन्मे मनः शिवसंकल्पमस्तु ॥

Yaj.XXXIV.6

Suṣārathirāśvāniva yanmanuṣyānnenīyate bhīśurvājina'iva |
Hṛtpratiṣṭhaṁ yadajiraṁ javiṣṭhaṁ tanme manaḥ śivasaṁkalpamastu ||

The life, *prāṇa* is like a horse and the mind, *manas* like a chariot. When the mind chariot guides the five *prāṇas* of this life and these are established in the heart, then men attain immunity from all diseases, infirmity and death. Remember, O Mind! That golden memory, be peaceful, quiet and achieve a Śiva like condition.

While chanting the mantras of the mind, when men become confirmed in the idea of self-divinity, then let them draw their life force towards the Truth. The *prāṇa-śakti*, life force centred in the heart, is to be unified with *Sudeva* who represents *Satyadeva* in the individual being. Thus, O Men! Cultivate your mind by sharing the seed-idea of self-divinity by concentrating on divine ideas. Control those life activities that are attracted towards materialism for vital enjoyment. Let them be channelled towards Truth and Immortality. By the surrender of the vital demand, the *prāṇa* will enter into divinity. Man will then become supramentalised, enjoy immortality and lead the life divine.

24

CONQUEST OF DEATH

O Divine Herald! O Ishaspati! Enlighten us with the light of Abhi to eternal fame. In the shining creation above, announce that He, the Deva, the Lord of Truth is opening the *yuvakośa*, the treasure of youth, to provide us with an immunity for life. Provide them with this prayer:-

O Deva! With the divine purity and supreme light of your body, let the divine manifestation be announced and become evident even in the outer world and let there be complete immortality.

At that moment we chant the Hymns to Death, to banish her influence from this present life. According to the Yajurveda, Prajāpati told Death the following:-

परं मृत्यु अनु परेहि पन्थां यस्ते अन्य ऽ इतरो देवयानात् ।
चक्षुष्मते श‍ृण्वते ते ब्रवीमि मा नः प्रजां रीरिषो मोत वीरान् ॥

Yaj.XXXV.7

Paraṁ mṛtyo anu parehi panthāṁ yaste anya' itaro devayānāt /
Cakṣuṣmate śṛṇvate te bravīmi mā naḥ prajāṁ rīriṣo mota vīrān //

O Death! Stop taking the lives of human beings to the darkest path named *Pitṛyana.* Allow the children of this Earth with their sons and grandsons to take the enlightened path, Devayāṇa, which leads them to truth and immortality. Don't injure and kill them.

इमं जीवेभ्यः परिधिं दधामि मैषां नु गादपरो अर्थमेतम् ।
शतं जीवन्तु शरदः परूचीरन्तर्मृत्युं दधतां पर्वतेन ॥

Yaj.XXXV.15

Imaṁ jīvebhyaḥ paridhim dadhāmi maiṣāṁ nu gādaparo arthametam I
Śataṁ jīvantu śaradaḥ parūcīrantarmṛtyuṁ dadhatāṁ parvatena II

I am Prajāpati. With respect to the people of the Earth, I ask of Thee, O Death! Do not afflict these beings again. When they come to know about Devāyaṇa and their life proceeds on that advanced road, do not come near them for many hundred autumns, in other words, at least ten thousand years. Let them enjoy their life in immunity and immortality. Let their life come to an end according to their own will. Let them be like a mountain and remain immovable even after the withdrawal of their life from their body. O Death! Be present only to help them enter into that immortality.

Prajāpati advised the people of the Earth to respect death and be liberated from her cruelty. The Atharvaveda said to us

नमो देववधेभ्यो नमो राजवधेभ्यः ।
अथो ये विश्यानां वधास्तेभ्यो मृत्यो नमोऽस्तु ते ॥

Ath.VI.13.1

Namo devavadhebhyo namo rājavadhebhyaḥ I
Atho ye viśyānāṁ vadhāstebhyo mṛtyo namo'stu te II

I prostrate before you, O Destroyer of the Divine and Divinity! I bow down before you, O Slayer of Kings and Kingdoms! I bow down again before you, O Killer of Earthly Creations! O Death! I prostrate before you again and again.

नमस्ते अधिवाकाय परावाकाय ते नमः ।
सुमत्यै मृत्यो ते नमो दुर्मत्यै त इदं नमः ॥

Ath.VI.13.2

Namaste adhivākāya parāvākāya te namaḥ /
Sumatyai mṛtyo te namo durmatyai ta idaṁ namaḥ //

I salute you, O Destroyer of human beings! I bow down before You, O Death! Dissolver of divine creations. You are the liberator of revered religious or spiritual men and you are the killer of the notorious. O Death! I bow down to Thee again and again.

नमस्ते यातुधानेभ्यो नमस्ते भेषजेभ्यः ।
नमस्ते मृत्यो मूलेभ्यो ब्राह्मणेभ्य इदं नमः ॥

Ath.VI.13.3

Namaste yātudhānebhyo namaste bheṣajebhyaḥ /
Namaste mṛtyo mūlebhyo brāhmaṇebhya idaṁ namaḥ //

I prostrate before you, O Yātudhāni, Death! Torturer of body and life. O *Anna*! O Plant! I also prostrate before you to protect us from the torture of Yātudhāni. I bow down, O Death! to the root of your birth and also I prostrate before Brahman, the Creator and the Destroyer. I prostrate before Him again and again.

त्र्यम्बकं यजामहे सुगन्धिं पुष्टिवर्धनम् ।
उर्वारुकमिव बन्धनान्मृत्योर्मुक्षीय मामृतात् ॥

Yaj.III.60

Tryambakaṁ yajāmahe sugandhiṁ puṣṭivardhanam /
Urvārukamiva bandhanānmṛtyormukṣīya māmṛtāt //

We worship the Tryambaka (Lord Śiva as Time) who increases the fragrance and the nourishment of our lives, who removes all our bondages, who liberates us from the hand of Death and who takes us to immortality. We meditate on Him.

As the Atharvaveda said, to remove diseases and infirmity, we chant again:-

नमो रूराय च्यवनाय नीदनाय धृष्णवे ।
नमः शीताय पूर्वकामकृत्वने ॥

Ath.VII.121.1

Namo rurāya cyavanāya nīdanāya dhṛṣṇave I
Namaḥ śītāya purvakāmakṛtvane II

We bow down before Ruru and before Cyavana. We bow down before pain and sufferings, before heat and cold. We prostrate ourselves before the Deva and ask him to remove our former vital desires and its effects.

शतं च मे सहस्त्रं चापवक्तार ओषधे ।
ऋतजात ऋतावरि मधु मे मधुला करः ॥

Ath.V.15.11

Śataṁ ca me sahasraṁ cāpavaktāra oṣadhe I
Ṛtajāta ṛtāvari madhu me madhulā karaḥ II

O Devi Madhulā! Curative Power of all Diseases! Be active in us in hundreds or thousands of ways to cure our sufferings. Remember, O Madhulā! You are the daughter of Ṛta, the Truth and you were established by Him to influence, to exist in plants and in grains to remove all diseases from this Earth. Because you are the daughter of immortality, O Ṛtavari! influence our food so that it becomes sweet in taste. Be the all-curative power and give us perfect health and youth.

25

PERFECTION OF LIFE, THE LIFE DIVINE

When the individual mind becomes one and unified with the Truth, it touches the vital being and leads the aspirant's vital powers to the Truth and takes life towards divinity. We chant the mantras of Prajāpati; for life to be divinised with the help of the word, svāhā to achieve perfection as Yajurveda said:

प्राणाय स्वाहऽपानाय स्वाहा व्यानाय स्वाहा ।
अम्बे अम्बिकेऽम्बालिके न मा नयाति कश्चन ।
ससस्त्यश्वक: सुभद्रिकां काम्पीलावासिनीम् ॥

Yaj.XXIII.18

Prāṇāya svāhāpānāya svāhā vyānāya svāhā /
Ambe ambike'mbālike na mā nayati kaścana /
Sasastyaśvakaḥ subhadrikāṁ kāmpīlavāsinīm //

O Kampila Vasini, the vital power – life force – existing in the heart; O Amba, Power of Life and Giver of Fortune. O Ambika, Power of apānā energy! Giver of beauty in the body. O Ambālika, Power of vyānā energy! Giver of modesty and softness. Remove all deformations, impurities and contaminations from the body and replace them with good fortune, beauty, modesty and softness. With this idea, we offer our sacrificial offering by adding the word svāhā, prānāya svāhā, apānāya svāhā, vyānāya svāhā.

Let us pray to the Truth that the vital powers become illuminated with his luminous power.

O Truth, O Sudeva! Nourish and protect our life force through the three vital airs, prāna, apāna and vyāna. Protect and increase our eyesight and the hearing capacity of our ears. O Apas, water! Fall on us as rain and provide pure drinks for men and animals during their lives. Exist as serum in plants to increase their happiness.

O Deva! Increase the length of our life, protect our life breath, our inhalation and aspiration and control the air in our body. Increase our eyesight and provide us with a sharp hearing. Protect our words, control our minds and develop our love. O Sudeva! You are our soul, surround us with your light and nourish our life, mind and body.

To realise the divine in this life and to enter into immortality, *i.e.* to live like Gods on this Earth, it is often not enough to simply offer the vital forces to the Truth. Even though hunger and thirst, together with other desires, are satisfied by surrendering the vital forces, one is not able to enter into the divine life. The reason being that when the vital forces are sacrificed to the Truth, then the human ego is strengthened. The "I" becomes very powerful. The ego feels that it is pure, beautiful, without desires; in touch with the Truth and that it has become divine. In this way, the self becomes strengthened and this feeling or realisation leads us away from the divine directly to the undivine. As long as I and mine remain in the individual nature, it is not possible to achieve divinity on Earth.

The fulfilment of the divine in the human body will come only at that moment when the ego will be completely surrendered to the Truth. The ego is the last barrier in an individual's life. When the ego is surrendered to the divine and the separate identity becomes one with the Truth, the completion of the total sacrifice to the divine takes place. With this step, man enters into divinity and appears as a superman. He achieves immunity and immortality.

Now the next question comes? How will the individual human ego become totally unified with the Truth. In former Ages, when the human race entered into immortality by becoming liberated from the human ego, they attained divine life by chanting mantras for self dedication in the divine sacrifice. Similarly, we are chanting these mantras today which are in the Yajur Veda.

My prāna, apāna, vyāna, will, heart, learning, words, mind, eyes, ears, principles, intellect, strength and power together with my ego are surrendered to the Truth.

Instead of the feeling of "I" in all my organs, let Agni devata become active in the mouth, Vāyu in the nose, Sūrya in the eyes, Candra in the hearing, Vasu in the self, Rudra in the ears, Aditya in the will, Marut in the vital, Viśvedeva in the arms and the legs, Bṛhaspati in the intellect, Indra in the senses and Mitra-Varuṇa in the activities of the life. All those parts where the "I" was ensconced before, let these be occupied by the Godheads. Instead of the ego, let all the godheads act unitedly in a single body as well as at the universal level.

I should still see, feel and realise the activities of God in me for the perfection of my individuality. To this end the mantras should be chanted as the Yajurveda says:

My truth, my faith, my wealth, my universe, my supramental play, my joy, my birth, my creation, my work, my message, my divine activities all these I surrender to the Truth through this divine sacrifice. Let them all be established in the Supreme Truth.

When we have achieved the highest level as a human being, we have still not reached so far that we could establish immortality or the supramental plane in us, as our purity is still far from complete. The pure ego that has achieved divinity will still not be enough for our immortality. To achieve that goal, Gods will have to do tapasya or Yajña for the immortality and the following mantras will be chanted:

My truth, my immortality, my Heaven, my immunity, my life time, my longevity, my all encompassing friendliness, my fearlessness, my happiness and peace, my repose, my happy commencement, my days of fame and good activities; all I surrender to the Truth through this sacrifice. What was undivine in me, I have already offered to the Truth; what is good in me, I also surrender now. My ego is now beyond divine and undivine, good or bad, true or false. All are established in the Supreme Truth.

Life is then totally surrendered to the Deva, has then become truthful and immortal. That inexpressible state of the individual being where no feeling of ego remains, achieved through a total surrender to the divine, has been very well expressed by the Ṛg and the Sāmaveda. This is the condition when a complete identification with Deva has taken place.

यच्चिद्धि शश्वता तना देवं देवं यजामहे ।
त्वे इद्धूयते हवि ॥

Ṛg.I.26.6; Sām.1618

Yacciddhi saśvatā tanā devaṁ devaṁ yajāmahe /
Tve iddhūyate haviḥ //

To achieve the transcendental truth and to attain the divine body and beauty which is the ultimate, I contemplate on Him who provides perfection by uttering these words - *Deva, O Deva* - that brings about a complete surrender. He is the Deva and I am the Deva, till the final and complete surrender from my side is arrived at and then we have one Truth, one Deva.

With the final accomplishment, one enters into –

बण्महां असि सूर्य बळादित्य महां असि ।
महस्ते सतो महिमा पनस्यतेऽद्धा देव महां असि ॥

Ṛg.VIII.101.11

Baṇmahaṁ asi sūrya baḷāditya mahāṁ asi /
Mahaste sato mahimā panasyate'ddhā deva mahāṁ asi //

This beautiful creation, which is the best of all creations, is blazing like the sun. In it you see the larger Sun shining with its greater rays. That is the purest light of the Supreme Truth showering on this earthly creation, by which all hostile powers would be removed and destroyed. That light and power of the Deva was called *Mahas*, the Supramental.

बट् सूर्य श्रवसा महां असि सत्रा देव महां असि ।
मह्ना देवानामसुर्यः पुरोहिता विभु ज्योतिरदाभ्यम् ॥

Ṛg.VIII.101.12

Baṭ sūrya śravasā mahāṁ asi satrā deva mahāṁ asi /
Mahnā devānāmasuryaḥ purohitā vibhu
jyotiradābhyam //

Like the everlasting sun, the Vedas are existing eternally. In there, the Deva, the Supreme Truth, exists. By the movement of the *Vedasūrya*, the Sun, there appears light and darkness, truth and falsehood, divinity and the undivine. This was known as the Mahna ayana. When the *Veda-Sūrya*, appears before this creation for immortality, *ānanda* and peace, at that moment the Supreme Divine himself manifests in an aurora of radiant light. This is the manifestation of the supramental.

But without the ego, the activities of life are carried on normally by Yajña, son of Yaju. Life is then established in Yajña, that is, on this Earth divine life manifests and man becomes superman.

26

TRUTH AND FALSEHOOD

The individual achievement of the divine life or the supramental status is neither very clear to understand nor easy to achieve in our general life. Individually, one can achieve immortality but it is not welcomed by others. People believe that some can achieve this goal, but then they are not like normal mortals. They are Sadhus, who have renounced life. Normal people find this effort impossible as they are occupied with problems faced in day-to-day life. Moreover, they do not possess the will power to reach this stage.

O Children of Earth! When the golden moment arrives, we, the Ṛṣis, will meditate on the Truth for you so that we could bring the general mass of humanity into divinity. Then mankind will become immortal. Those who have the capability to achieve this stage, will make achievement of Truth their ultimate goal. However, for the the general mass, we can say that Truth consciousness realised by an individual would serve as a medium or a base to bring down the higher supramental consciousness into the earthly mass consciousness.

When the mind awakens in an individual being, the vital surrenders to the supramental through the *Vitihotra*, the psychic aspiration; at that moment the Four Ages make this individual an instrument to influence the whole humanity. The Four Ages are the Satya, Trita, Dvita and Kali. They act together with the three powers, *i.e.*

(1) Satyadeva confronts the Lord of Falsehood, Kali, with His power, light and purity while the latter insists on holding on with his power of death and diseases.

(2) Time, Śiva, together with his power Aśmanvatī supports Satyadeva in His attempt to take the Time wheel, the Kālacakra, under His control.

(3) The Ṛṣis through their psychic aspiration decide to accept Satyadeva and to reject Kali.

When the Ṛṣis and Lord Śiva invite Satyadeva to become active and control the Kālacakra, at that moment Piṅgala Maheśvara appears to start the Golden Age. We, the Ṛṣis, chant the mantras to bring clarity into the ideas prevalent in the general mass of humanity, to make them aware of the difference between Truth and Falsehood and to force Kali together with his hostile powers to withdraw completely from the Earth atmosphere.

सत्यमित्था वृषेदसि वृषजूतिर्नोऽविता ।
वृषा ह्युग्र श्रुण्विषे परावति वृषो अर्वावति श्रुतः ॥

Sām. 263

Satyamitthā vṛṣedasi vṛsajūtirno'vitā /
Vṛṣa hyugra śruṇviṣe parāvati vṛṣo arvāvati śrutaḥ //

Vṛṣa was the first Ṛṣi who differentiated between Truth and Falsehood. He was the first Seeker and Seer of Truth upon the Earth and came from the family of Vataraśana. He is like our father who has shown us the secrets between Truth and Falsehood. At first, Vṛṣa himself established the Supreme Truth with his firm faith and he rejected the falsehood together with its ignorance and stupidity. This is mentioned in Sāmaveda, as Ṛṣi Medatithi, son of Kaṇva one of the Uncles of Kali has told us. Medatithi also told us that Kali was chanting hymns to Indra to be established in the Vedas as an immortal Ṛṣi. Among several mantras, we chant one mantra of Kali to show his character and quality of tapasya.

वयेनमिदा ह्योऽपीपेमेह वज्रिणम् ।
तस्मा उ अद्य सवने सुतं भरा नूनं भूषत श्रुते ॥

Sām.272, 1691

Vayenamidā hyo'pīpemeha vajriṇam /
Tasmā u adya savane sutaṁ bharā nūnaṁ bhūṣata śrute //

This is our ignorance and stupidity. Let me be established on this Falsehood. O Vajri! O Indra! You are in a unique position, throughout all the creations. Falsehood was also fashioned by the Creator and for this reason you must not destroy it. Influence this Falsehood and maintain it with your unique power and heroism. Let Nakta with his Falsehood exist eternally and let him be worshipped by the people of the Earth.

Through the power of his yogic sacrifice, Indra was bound to accept Kali's prayer and allow him his position and space in eternity. The activities of Kali and the Deva were divided equally by the Ṛṣis. Thus, Time was divided equally between Kali and the Deva, one half for the Kali and the other half for the Deva. From the half allocated to Kali, the Ṛṣis took away two-thirds and left only one third for Kali. The two-third portion was influenced by the sons of Aptya Ṛṣi, Trita and Dvita. They are worshippers of Truth. They also appeared in this golden moment to invoke the Deva upon the Earth and to banish Kali from the Earth. First of all, Trita came in front of Kali to oppose his portrayal of Falsehood as reality. He worshipped Deva for immortality as he chanted the mantras of Sāmaveda and the Ṛgveda.

ऋचं साम यजामहे याभ्यां कर्माणि कृण्वते ।
वि ते सदसि राजतो यज्ञं देवेषु वक्षतः ॥

Sām.369

Ṛcaṁ sāma yajāmahe yābhyām karmāṇi kṛṇvate /
Vi te sadasi rājato yajñaṁ deveṣu vakṣataḥ //

We chant the mantras of the Ṛgveda and the Sāmaveda, to Him through whom all works are accomplished. He is the Truth who is standing in the sacrificial flame and was called Deva by the Ṛṣis.

अभि ब्रह्मीरनूषत यह्वीर्ऋतस्य मातरः ।
मर्जयन्तीर्दिवः शिशुम् ॥

Sām.870

Abhi brahmīranūṣata yahvīrṛtasya mātaraḥ I
Marjayantīrdivaḥ śiśum II

O Abhi! Let the unmanifested power of Brahmā manifest. She is Yahvī, the Mother of Truth. By worshipping Her you will achieve the enlightened child for the immortality of this Earth.

अभिमृतस्य विष्टपं दुहेत पृश्निमातरः ।
चारु प्रियतमं हविः ॥

Ṛg.IX.34.5

Abhīmṛtasya viṣṭapaṁ duheta pṛśnimātaraḥ I
Cāru priyatamaṁ haviḥ II

O Abhi! Maintainer of the enlightened Truth. Milk the power of the Night like a cow. With that milk prepare the best *havi*, clarified butter, and offer to the Truth for the unification of the Earth with the Heaven.

समाचीने अभित्मना यह्वी ऋतस्य मातरा ।
तन्वाना यज्ञमानुषग्यदञ्जते ॥

Ṛg.IX.102.7

Samācīne abhitmanā yahvī ṛtasya mātarā I
Tanvānā yajñamānuṣagyadañjate II

O Abhi! Kindle the fire of sacrifice in the human mind in the proper way. Let Yahvī, the Mother of Truth, appear and allow her to transform these human beings into a divine shape. They will then appear in the enlightened pure and beautiful shape of Truth.

After Trita, came Dvita to support his brother, in calling for the descent of Truth and for the removal of Kali. He chanted the following mantra as the Vedas said:

परि सप्तिर्न वाजयुर्देवो देवेभ्यः सुतः ।
व्यानशिः पवमानो वि धावति ॥

Ṛg.IX.103.6

Pari saptirna vājayurdevo devebhyaḥ sutaḥ /
Vyānaśiḥ pavamāno vi dhāvati //

There are seven creations full of riches. Let the purity of Satyadeva flow like a stream over them so that all these creations may attain immortality.

इच्छन्ति देवाः सुन्वन्तं न स्वप्नाय स्पृहयन्ति ।
यन्ति प्रमादमतन्द्राः॥

Ṛg.VIII.2.18

Icchanti devāḥ sunvantaṁ na svapnāya spṛhayanti /
Yanti pramādamatandrāḥ //

I aspire for the all beautiful Deva for us all, not in a dream state nor in a deep meditation. I aspire to realise Him here on this Earth, in the present state of deepest ignorance, as a living consciousness and in an active condition.

न हि त्वा शूर देवा न मर्तासो दित्सन्तम् ।
भीमं न गां वारयन्ते ॥

Ṛg.VIII.81.3

Nahi tvā śūra devā na martāso ditsantam /
Bhīmaṁ na gāṁ vārayante //

There is no other hero or warrior greater than you, O Deva! O Truth! Remove Death and enter into this Earth with your unique power. Remove our ignorance and folly, with a powerful attack similar to Bhīma.

At the same time, the Vedas ordered the son of Yaju, Yajña, to take the place on the human ego and work under the guidance of Truth to allow humanity to enjoy immortality in this mortal world. Then the human ego will be dissolved. The human existence will become divinised and totally identified with Deva the Truth.

. . . सुम्नहूर्यज्ञ ऽ आ च वक्षत् ।
यक्षदग्निर्देवो देवां आ च वक्षत् ॥

Yaj.XVIII.62

...Sumnahūr yajña' ā ca vakṣat /
Yakṣadagnirdevo devāṁ ā ca vakṣat //

O Yajña! With your modesty and humility make a union with the Deva. By your constant conversation you will appear as the pure light of Truth. As a result, let this human being appear as the Deva.

In this way, there will be one Deva throughout this Earth. Among the many divisions, there will be the one united consciousness for all, by the activities of Yajña. Through the dissolution of diversity, Kali will withdraw from this Earth.

27

THE DIVINE PERSON – IMMORTALITY

When Yajña, son of Yaju, establishes himself in the place of human ego and works constantly under the guidance of Deva, then the divine personality is visible in all activities of men. Men then become immortal as supermen.

As in former times, a man, conscious of his immortality, represented the divine personality. He was called Darbhya, the divine man or superman upon this Earth. By his actions, the Age of Truth commenced on this Earth and the divine kingdom, the divine society and the divine or supramental race was established. The divine artist Viśvakarmā worshipped him as the Yajurveda mentioned:

चित्तिं जुहोमि मनसा घृतेन यथा देवाऽइहागमन्वीतिहोत्रा ऽ ऋतावृधः ।
पत्ये विश्वस्य भूमनो जुहोमि विश्वकर्मणे विश्वाहादाभ्यं हविः ॥

Yaj.XVII.78

Cittiṁ juhomi manasā ghṛtena yathā devā'
ihāgamanvītihotrā' ṛtāvṛdhaḥ /
Patye viśvasya bhūmano juhomi viśvakarmaṇe
viśvahādābhyaṁ haviḥ //

When one offers one's mind as the offering for the fulfilment of the divine sacrifice, there the *Vitihotra*, the psychic aspiration, rises high, touches the Heaven and embraces the Truth. Then the Deva appears. This is the individual appearance of Deva. Thus, Darbhya, becomes the Lord and the Leader of this Earth.

At that time, Viśvakarmā offers to the Deva his artisitic offerings and brings to the world a divine beauty.

In this way, the divine empire comes down again on the Earth suffused with an imaginable beauty, love and purity of Truth. Darbhya appears as the divine King and Emperor, adored by the people of the world. He establishes unity, peace and brotherhood. During the Iron Age, the concept of imperialism was abolished due to the misuse of this power. The self-centred and corrupt Kings used their position, power and wealth for their self-enjoyment. Under that proud, egoistic government, the divinity among the people of the Earth suffered greatly. At that time, Truth calls upon them to rise up and re-establish their inherent divinity. With this divine call, men rose, but through their ignorance, they became part of many isms and parties. They removed the kings from the Earth, but they did not know how to rule or maintain the government. Their efforts resulted in creating increased disunity and discord amongst themselves. They became more and more confused due to the activities of their own created parties.

When the people of the Earth became very disheartened and suffered greatly without any peace or unity, at that moment Truth descended to provide relief to humanity. Deva appeared through the Vitihotra under the name of Darbhya, as Indra upon the Earth, to establish a divine empire. He treated all human beings as Gods and immortal beings and gave full respect to each individual divinity. Just as Lord Indra dispenses Truth and justice in Heaven, similarly Darbhya manifested a divine rule on the Earth.

Following Darbhya, appeared the seven Vasus (one after another) to disclose the seven riches of Truth, which make the Earth similar to Heaven. The seven riches are:-

(1) One united empire throughout the world, with mankind enjoying divinity without diversities and conflicts.

(2) One peaceful divine race throughout the whole world, with no strife, quarrels or war.

(3) One divine language to converse with others.
(4) Eyes that can see the whole universe from one place.
(5) Ears that can hear and receive vibrations of all conversations.
(6) A body that can change according to their will.
(7) The human body of any size, that can grow big or small according to their own choice.

Then appeared seven Great Godheads who disclosed seven lights and consciousness of Truth.

(1) The light of Indra encouraged the all conquering heroism and consciousness, in a unique position to maintain all.
(2) The light of Sūrya destroyed the night, the darkness and the ignorance, bringing consciousness to beings that breaks their deep sleep. It is also the provider of creative activities of truth.
(3) The light of Candra purified contaminations and gave consciousness of *ānanda* and joy of purity of truth.
(4) The light of Bṛhaspati dissolved all disorder and provided consciousness of the justice of truth.
(5) The light of Vāyu invoked the all clarifying heroism and consciousness for spreading the pure fragrance of Truth.
(6) The light of Agni invoked the divine will and sacrifice as well as consciousness to adore Truth.
(7) The light of Mitra-Varuṇa spread unity and harmony and consciousness of the order and rule of Truth.

After the Great Godheads, the seven Goddesses come who represented the supreme and active power of Truth.

(1) Yahvī, the Mother Power of Truth, acts for the unification of Earth and Heaven.
(2) Suhavā, the consort of the Deva. Also called Uṣati and Kuhu. She is the soul power of Truth. She brings Truth down on the Earth and establishes Him through the divine sacrifice in the *Vitihotra*.
(3) Mahāyāni and Sinibali – Sister Power of Truth. They act for the new creation of Truth.

(4) Aditi, Bhārati, Ilā, Sarasvatī, Aśmanvatī, Āśā, Mahī, Madhulā, Uṣā – Daughters of the Power of Truth. They act together for the manifestation of Truth upon Earth in the activities of human life that transform the lower nature of mankind.

(5) Juhu and Dakṣina – Power of Truth *ānanda*. They act for the joy of immortality.

(6) Saci, Saṇgaṇa, Rohiṇi, Svāhā, Marudini, Mitrani, Varuṇi – Powers of Truth-Purity; they work for the purification of the people of the Earth.

(7) Vaiṣṇavi – Lakṣmi – the Power of Truth – Love. She promotes harmony and beauty of Truth to manifest here in these people.

Finally, there are the various emanations of Truth, that were worshipped on this Earth in different periods of time. One continues to think that they are the Truth. The realization of the Eternal Truth brings about a confusion to these human beings. They quarrel among themselves as to who has seen the greater Truth. But the Veda declares that the various appearances of Truth were in fact not the Deva himself, also known as Ṛta, Amṛta, Satya or Satyadeva.

(1) Hari, Viṣṇu, Prajāpati, Sarasvāna and Śiva are the Brothers of Truth and appear like him.

(a) Hari comes, when any opponent of Truth arises with the wish to dominate all creations as if he is the Lord of All. He wishes to crush the devotees of Truth by forcing them to ignore the Supreme Truth. Then Hari appears as the Truth himself to crush the opponent.

(b) Viṣṇu acts, when the Asura gains power through the power of yogic endeavour and tries to gain dominance over Heaven by driving out all God-heads from there. He also troubles the sages and the seers by causing disturbances in their Yajña, places hurdles in their knowledge and hurls insults at their religion. At such times, Viṣṇu appears as the Truth himself to destroy them.

(c) Prajāpati acts for the creation of Truth, for the manifestation of Vedas. He appears as Truth as the proverbial Brahma-Satya.

(d) Sarasvāna acts to protect, preserve and develop the creations fashioned by Prajāpati. He is like the Protector or Truth himself.

(e) Śiva as Time, acts for the physical manifestation of Prajāpati's creations. He destroys the old creations to replace them with new. In this he appears as the destructive Rudra and the creative Piṅgala. Both of his forms are like Truth, like the proverb, *Śivaṁ, Satyaṁ, Sundaraṁ*.

(2) Anna, Apas, Dakṣa and Pūṣan are Sons of Truth, having the appearance of Truth. They look like him.

(a) *Anna*, food, is responsible for the physical formation, to provide stability in life and to return to the static condition of this earthly creation as matter. He represents matter as the Truth, the *Anna-Brahmā*.

(b) *Apas*, water, acts for the vital formation, to ensure that life returns in stability and to return back to the static condition of this earthly creation as the life. He represents life as the Truth himself, the *Prana-Brahmā*.

(c) *Soma* acts for the mental formation to provide a stability in life and to return back to the static condition of this earthly creation as the mind. He represents the mind as the truth, the *Mana Brahmā*.

(d) *Dakṣa* creates the Heavens, connects the greater Heaven with the Earth. He himself represents the truth as Prajāpati.

(e) *Pūṣan* acts for the manifestation of the divine dawn upon the Earth. He himself manifests as the Truth before the actual manifestation of Deva.

(3) Then there are the voices of Truth, the seven Ṛṣis, the Great Creators with the seven Chandaṣ.

(a) Kaśyapa, Kaṇva, Aṅgirā, Atri, Gautama, Bharadvāja, Mitra-Vasiṣṭha. These seven great Ṛṣis have been considered as the *Akṣarabrahman.* They brought this creation from akṣara, in other words, from the non-formative eternity to an earthly formation. They are the originators of *jivas*, the people of the Earth. For this, they are also called *Gotrapati*, father of peoples.

(b) Gāyātri, Uṣṇik, Anuṣṭubh, Bṛhatī, Panktī, Triṣṭubh and Jagati are the seven great chandas, metres, power of the *akṣaras,* words. They originate from the non-formative eternity appearing here with the invisible souls to give them the necessary formations through the creator Ṛṣis. Therefore, they were called Mothers of the beings on the Earth.

Subsequently, the soul of the world wakes up, called Viśvedeva, by Devāyaṇa. He became conscious by the touch of Uṣā, the Dawn – the Light of Truth and then became active for the manifestation of Truth. He embraces Dawn's Light of Truth and creates with the Dawn to appear as the Truth. Viśvedeva, the world soul represents the Deva on this Earth. He was the son-in-law of the Deva. He has a son by Uṣā, the Dawn, named Taranta, the grandson of Deva. Also Pūṣān has two sons called Bhaga and Aryaman. Taranta has two sons called Vaidadaświ and Purumihla. With the three grandsons and two great grandsons of Deva; the Viśvedeva appears as the active Truth himself.

(1) Viśvedeva, son-in-law of Deva, acts to promote the activities of Truth in human beings. In front of them, he appears as the Truth himself, mainly as the soul of the Immortal Puruṣa. The Yogi realises him as the Divine. He gives guidance to Truth in the individual being to understand what is right or wrong, divine or undivine and true or false. He also gives them the consciousness to understand each other and to remove all misunderstandings.

(2) Taranta, grandson of Deva, promotes true thoughts and ideas in individuals. He works for unifying all individual separate minds. With the help of Taranta, the individuals understand themselves even without words. Thus, Taranta brings Truth into individual thoughts.

(3) Bhaga, the bachelor grandson of Deva, acts for true enjoyment in life and gives each individual, divine joy and fulfilment. With these, people enter into a contented peaceful condition.

(4) Aryaman, the second bachelor grandson of Deva, works to promote true feeling for each other. With this all misbehaviour vanishes, all quarrels subside and people have one united peaceful heart.

(5) Vaidadaśvi, great grandson of Deva, is active in the physical senses and the body. His power assists the individual in obtaining a transformation in the body. He provides good health and increases strength.

(6) Purumilha, second great grandson of Deva works for the divine beauty and youth and in increasing longevity.

Another true self-existence is the Nārāyaṇa Ṛṣi who did a yogic austerity to achieve the *Ātmā-Puruṣa*, the soul-being, realised the divine in himself and identified himself with the *Paramātmā-Puruṣa*, the Supreme Truth. He became the shining example of Truth on the Earth. He symbolises the eternal truth consciousness in the individual personality, the ideal form of humanity on the path of spiritual adventure. Through this, the individual being can hope for the perfection of life in Truth and be immortalised. Nārāyaṇa demonstates to us how through the Supreme Truth realisation, one can appear as the divine himself. This idea remains as a firm belief among the people of the Earth. Before worshipping other Gods, they worship Nārāyaṇa as He is the Truth himself. He manifests to guide mankind towards Deva, through his own example.

Then appear the divine artists, the servants of the Deva, the divine singers and dancers, who are responsible for the decoration and cleaning of the ways, the roads, the paths and the home of Truth. For welcoming the Truth, they create their beautiful divine music and dances. First appear the two artists, Tvaṣṭā and Viśvakarmā.

(1) Tvaṣṭā takes care of the construction of the royal road and the House of Truth. He repairs the damages and gives them a new shape with his workers. During the long absence of Deva, those places were misused by Kali. He rearranges them for the use of Deva. Also, he keeps the garments and dresses ready for the Truth.

(2) Viśvakarmā gives an artistic touch to the constructions and repairs of Tvaṣṭā. He beautifies the road with his artistry, as well as the inner and the outer parts of the dwelling of the Truth to increase the pleasure of Deva.

(3) Prastoka keeps the treasury of divine riches, as well as the arms and weapons ready in the home of Truth. He looks after the health of people and protects them from diseases, infirmity and death. He also ensures peace in their lives. In ten areas, he settles his necessary suppliers and workers to protect the divine wealth and gems, arms and weapons, dresses, garments and foods and drinks.

(4) Sarjaya forms a reception committee to receive, call and invite Deva in his earthly home. Then the Deva comes with his whole divine family to make the Earth his own for several thousand years. Sarjaya is responsible for making all the arrangements and to inform Deva about the time to commence his journey to the Earth.

(5) Vanaspati takes care of the gardens and the fields of the home of Truth, where the Deva will come to stay with his family. He ensures a rich harvest of fruits, flowers etc.

(6) Tanunāpat is the personal servant of Deva, who recognises all the antidivine and asuric forces as well as Deva. He opens the door of the royal road and

keeps it clean. He keeps ready the honey and milk for the Deva.

(7) Apānapāt increases divine fragrance in the land, in the trees, plants and creepers, in the flowers and fruits, in paddy and barley, in the water and the air for welcoming the Deva. By this the people of the divine land become happy and enter into the purity and meditation of Deva. They thus attain their immunity and longevity.

(8) Draviṇoda opens the door of the royal road on the other side, *i.e.* from the Earth so that the people of the Earth become fulfilled with the Advent of Truth; he cleans it by sprinkling divine water on it and decorating it with divine flowers, incense and lights.

(9) Upava constructs the wide royal road from Greater Heaven to the Earth and establishes the six seasons besides it to sing the welcoming songs to Deva.

The six melodies of Truth then appear. These are the *Gandharvas*, the celestial musicians, a class of demi-gods who are the creators of the divine melodies for the Truth. Their names are Mudo, Ayuvo, Mekuraya, Urjo, Stava and Eshtayo. With them appear, the ten powers of the divine tunes, the *Apsarās*, a class of celestial damsels, who are proficient in dancing. Their names are Punjikasthala, Kratusthala, Menaka, Sahajanya, Pramlocanti, Anumlocanti, Viśvaci, Ghṛtaci, Urvaśi and Purvacitti. They dance in front of Lord Indra in Heaven. To please him, they are chanting the Hymns to the Deva. The Ṛṣis have also assembled in the divine assembly to hear their Chant of Truth. Some of these *Gandharvas* and *Apsarās* are famous amongst mankind, as there are many stories about them in the Puranas, the Rāmāyaṇa and the Mahābhārata. The others are not known. Now, Devāyaṇa discloses stories about all of them with the manifestation of Truth. Their existence is fully dedicated to the service of Truth. They work for the manifestation of Truth. They charm the hostile forces and sing with joy the songs of Truth.

When Truth manifests in the home of Truth (Vaṅga or Bengal), he covers the whole Earth with his

- Seven riches (as there are eight Vasus)
- Seven lights and consciousnesses (of the eight great Gods)
- Thirteen powers of Truth-Action (one mother power, two sister-powers, one soul-power, nine daughter powers)
- Two powers of Truth – *ānanda*
- Seven powers of Truth – Purity
- One power of Truth – Love
- Five brother existences of Truth
- Five existences of Truth – Son
- Seven voices of Truth (from the seven great Ṛṣis)
- Seven powers of the Voice of Truth
- Six tunes of Truth
- Ten powers of the Tunes of Truth
- Three artists of Truth (Tvaṣṭā, Viśvakarmā, Rhibhus)
- Seven servants of Truth with the servant maids

Altogether, there are ninety-four special appearances of Truth together with the manifestation of Satyadeva. Along with them, many workers, assistants and army personnel accompany them. He descends on the Earth, settles down and establishes his empire which is the one united government instead of the many separate governments. With his coming, all the mental *isms* and parties disappear. His Truism spreads over the whole world and the world becomes one united whole with peace, love and unity. He provides everyone with food for the body, fulfilment in life and satisfaction of mind. People on the Earth live like Gods on the Earth. This is the glorious manifestation of the eagerly-awaited supramental race.

28

THE AGE OF TRUTH – TIME AS PIṄGALA MAHEŚVARA

When *Vitihotra*, the human psychic aspiration drew down the Deva upon this mortal Earth, we chanted the relevant mantras. Subsequently Darbhya established a link between the human and the divine existence. He, Darbhya, performed the sacrifice upon this Earth for human beings to become divine. As a result of that divine sacrifice, Satyadeva, together with the other Gods, Goddesses and Ṛṣis manifested in a subtle form, resulting in a full and complete manifestation of the Vedas. But all these manifestations were still in a subtle form. For them to appear in the physical form, they required the right time. It is only with the sanction of Time that the manifestation of Truth with the complete Vedas in a physical form can take place.

As mentioned before, Śiva, the Lord of Time has a creative form, called the Piṅgala Maheśvara. He appeared to give a physical form to Deva. He influenced the nature – where the six seasons – the *ṛtus* – chanted mantras for the physical manifestation of the Deva. As the Yajurveda said:

तं पत्नीभिरनु गच्छेम देवाः पुत्रैर्भ्रातृभिरुत वा हिरण्यैः ।
नाकं गृभ्णानाः सुकृतस्य लोके तृतीये पृष्ठे अधि रोचने दिवः ॥

Yaj.XV.50

Taṁ patnībhiranu gacchema devāh
putrairbhrātṛbhiruta vā hiraṇyaiḥ /
Nākaṁ gṛbhṇānāḥ sukṛtasya loke tṛtīye pṛṣṭhe adhi rocane divaḥ //

There is an enlightened third plane, above the great Heaven, which was called the *Mahas*, the plane of Truth. There Deva remains with his full family, which includes Yahvī, his mother, his powerful wife Suhavā, with his sister, daughters, brothers, sons, grandsons etc. O Truth! Descend upon this Earth with your whole family and manifest here.

The Ṛgveda gives a wonderful description of the Lord of Truth, Satyadeva in the following *mantra*:

हिरण्यकर्णं मणिग्रीवमर्णस्तन्नो विश्वे वरिवस्यन्तु देवाः ।
अर्यो गिरः सद्य आ जग्मुषीरोस्राश्चाकन्तुभयेष्वस्मे ॥

Ṛg.I.122.14

Hiraṇyakarṇaṁ maṇigrīvamarṇastanne viśve varivasyantu devāḥ /
Aryo giraḥ sadya ā jagmuṣīrosrāścākantū bhayeṣvasme //

We adore the Deva with the beautiful body, who has golden ears, with gems and jewels glittering around his neck. We would be delighted to receive him here in this world. Whose head is so high that it touches the sky with the crown, who is shining with a divine light and who removes the ultimate fear of death from us and gives us peace, purity and immortality. We bow down before him.

उद्वयं तमसस्परि ज्योतिष्पश्यन्त उत्तरम् ।
देवं देवत्रा सूर्यमगन्म ज्योतिरुत्तमम् ॥

Ṛg.I.50.10

Udvayaṁ tamasaspari jyotiṣpaśyanta uttaram /
Devaṁ devatrā sūryamaganma jyotiruttamam //

The indescribable and unsurpassed light is visible now, appearing over this earthly obscure night. O Deva! O Truth! Shine like the Sun to remove darkness and death. O most beautiful light! We prostrate before you.

From there Piṅgala Maheśvara starts his creative work. He tells Rudra Maheśvara to withdraw his undivine Epic, the

Pitṛyana, from this world. That epic is full of pain and sorrows. It welcomes the *Ṛpus*, as well as unholy foes like diseases, infirmity and death. This Epic made the people of the Earth unconscious and filled them up with ignorance and folly. In the Pitṛyana, individuals are caught in the cycle of birth and rebirth without any hope of change. The soul goes from one life to another without any knowledge of the divine. The departing souls through their ignorance are not aware of their goal. They fear death as an unknown adventure and do not know where they go afterwards. They cross this darkest path with an immense fear and are doubtful of rebirth. People are conscious of their birth only as a result of sex. From Death they have the utmost fear as they consider that it snatches them away from the known due to cessation of their heartbeats. They consider their lives full of struggle with tears and laughter, loss and gains which ends finally in defeat.

Piṅgala Maheśvara announced that he must now open his divine epic Devāyaṇa in the world. Then the Earth and Heaven will become full of happiness, *ānanda* and love due to the influence of Gods. The epic would have an immense impact on the health, youth and immortality of mankind. This Epic would make the people aware of divinity in their life by the light and consciousness of truth. The new creation will follow the rules of Heaven according to the Devāyaṇa, exist here on the Earth in their nature-gifted form and remain as an immortal guest of earthly parents, at the same time increasing their joy in being conscious of their immortality. The being will come to the Earth willingly as there will be no birth. Impelled by nature, he will lead his life on the dramatic stage on Earth. As there is no death, he exits willingly to take rest from the earthly drama. He is an immortal guest visiting the Earth, he is the Heaven-born child. These beings live always in light, *ānanda* and purity. They come to the Earth to play and for their rest they return to Heaven. Between their birth and death, they remain in constant joy and eternal bliss. Their life is full of *ānanda*, heavenly bliss. Their life being full of playful enjoyment, there are neither tears nor laughter, neither gain nor loss, neither victory nor defeat. In short, their life is aimed to enjoy the joy of Truth.

Listen, O Nature! I am here to tell you that Satyadeva has descended on the Earth with all Gods, Goddesses, Ṛṣis and the others to effect the complete manifestation of the Vedas. I have brought these seeds to sow in Earth's vast womb, as at present they are existing in subtle forms. The divine nature, the Para-Prakṛti, delivered them in subtle bodies. Hear, O Nature! as the Sāmaveda says,

प्रास्य धारा अक्षरन्वृष्णः सुतस्यौजसः ।
देवां अनु प्रभूषतः ॥

Sām.-1765

Prāsya dhārā akṣaranvṛṣṇaḥ sutasyaujasaḥ /
Devāṁ anu prabhūṣataḥ //

In the same way as the *akṣara*, the words, have come from the pure saliva of the Creator, Satyadeva has appeared through His power in an infinitesimal form on the Earth. He was existing in the Supreme Heaven.

I brought him down here in the physical sky above the Earth. Until now, O Earth, you have been influenced by Nakta and Kali. Moreover, your creation was under the control of Rudra. This was the undivine nature or in other words the *Apara – Prakṛti*. Now, I, Piṅgala Maheśvara, have come to manifest the new divine creation. Identify yourself with Heaven and be one with nature to receive your divine children upon this Earth. O Earth! Be ready to conceive seeds of the Truth and to preserve them in your womb to deliver the divine instead of the human beings.

The Deva is ready to assume his physical form with the Gods, Goddesses, Ṛṣis and others. They are all waiting for this event in the Antarikṣa in subtle forms, where the *Vitihotra* is flaming high. Look at the *Vitihotra*, where the Satyadeva together with his consort, Suhavā is standing. Above them is Yahvī, the Mother of Truth. All Godheads – brothers, sisters, sons, daughters, grandsons etc. as well as servants, maid-servants, artists, musicians and dancers – all divine beings are surrounding the *Vitihotra*. In front, all Ṛṣis are chanting hymns to the Deva for achieving immortality and immunity of the Earth. Hear the chants and imagine Truth with his whole family descending in the physical form. Look at Time, Śiva, and observe his power unifying now with Satyadeva. I have come to tell you to receive these divine beings in your womb as I am the Father of this divine creation. O Earth! Be ready to be worshipped as the Divine Mother by your divine children.

Listen, O Nature! The Ṛṣis are chanting the Vedic mantras for your immunity.

आ ते अग्न इधिमहि द्युमन्तं देवजरम ।
यद्ध स्या ते पनीयसी समिद्दीदयति द्यवीपं स्तोतृभ्य आ भर ॥

Ṛg.V.6.4

Ā te agna idhimahi dyumantaṁ devajaram /
yaddhasyā te panīyasī samiddīdayati dyavīpaṁ
stotṛbhya ā bhara //

Since eternity, Agni has come down on the Earth and is radiant with Truth and Immunity. He destroys and removes the forces inimical to the divine and eliminates darkness by the Power and Light of Truth. With the hymns of Satyadeva, he enlightens and fills up the whole world with the joy of Truth.

सहस्रधारं वृषभं पयोदुहं प्रियं देवाय जन्मने ।
ऋतेन य ऋतजातो विवावृधे राजा देव ऋतं बृहत् ॥

Ṛg.IX.108.8; Sām.1395

Sahasradhāraṁ vṛṣabhaṁ payoduhaṁ priyaṁ
devāye janmane /
Ṛtena ya ṛtajāto vivāvṛdhe rājā deva ṛtaṁ bṛhat //

O enlightened Puruṣa! O shining Vṛṣabhaṁ Heaven! Milk your beloved Earth Cow in a thousand flows. Let the milk nourish the divine birth in man. Let them be born by the Truth and in

Truth let them grow up. The Truth is the Deva, the King and Emperor of all. He is immense and eternal.

> स भक्षमाणो अमृतस्य चारुण उभे द्यावा काव्येना वि शश्रथे ।
> तेजिष्ठा अपो मंहना परि व्यत यदी देवस्य श्रवसा सदो विदुः ॥
>
> Sām.1424
>
> *Sa bhakṣamāṇo amṛtasya cārūṇa ubhe dyāvā kāvyenā vi śaśrathe |*
> *Tejiṣṭhā apo maṁhanā pari vyata yadī devasya śravasā sado viduḥ ||*

When the Earth and Heaven unify and become one or when they embrace each other in the consciousness of Truth, both drink the nectar, *amṛta.* At that moment the life ocean becomes enlightened and powerful. Then death leaves us. We attain our immortality, identifying ourselves completely with the Truth. We become Seers of Truth.

O Heaven! Hear the chant of the Ṛṣis. They are invoking you on the Earth. Embrace the Earth for the manifestation of the divine race! O Father of human beings! Let them become conscious that they are children of immortality.

O Vedas! Influence the lower nature with the power and light of all Godheads for the new creation. I am Piṅgala Maheśvara, I have come to be identified with the Lord of Time, Śiva, for a new creation, a new divine or supramental race upon this Earth. Help my activities. O Vedas! Guide the Godheads one by one towards the wide womb of nature as I call them.

O Vasus! Enter with my power through the ether into the water of nature, the womb for the divine creation. Exist in the water with all the riches of Truth and manifest upon Earth one by one. O Nature, the Vasus have entered in your womb with my power; protect, develop and give them a complete physical shape with life.

O Earth! Deliver those Vasus as your children and take them on your lap. Nourish them with your breast milk. The Vasus will worship you as their Mother with the divine riches. You will become healthy and prosperous with heavenly wealth.

Then O Adityas! Enter with my power through the ether into the water of nature. That is the Earth's womb for the divine creation. All exist there in the water with the light and consciousness of Truth and manifest upon the Earth one by one. O Nature! The Adityas have entered in your womb with my power; protect, develop and give them full physical shape with life.

O Earth! Deliver those Adityas as your children, take them on your lap to feed them with your breast milk. Nourish these divine children! When these Adityas worship you as their mother, you will become the divine mother and appear with the light and consciousness of Heaven.

Enter, O Dakṣāyanis! Through the ether into the water of nature, the womb of nature, with my power. All the divine creations exist in the water with the all purifying power of Truth. Manifest upon Earth one by one. O Nature! The Dakṣāyanis have entered into your womb with my power: protect, develop and give them full physical shape with life.

O Earth! Deliver those Dakṣāyanis as your children, take them on your lap, nourish the divine children with your breast milk. When those Dakṣāyanis will worship you as their Mother, then you will be the divine mother and appear as the all powerful Mahādeva-Mahāśakti.

Awake, O Viśvedeva! Be unified with *soma*. O Taranta! Be unified with Apas. O Vaidādaśvi! Be unified with Anna. O Jivas! You feel that the *Anna*, matter is truth, the *Apas*, life is the truth and *soma*, mind is the truth. Look at the mind, it is already identified with the *Mahas*, the supermind. O People of the Earth! Open this channel for the supramental creation in yourself. Be a *vrittan*, true existence for the divine child, for the birth of Darbhya. That will herald the physical manifestation of Truth amongst yourselves. With the birth of Darbhya, the supramental race will replace the present mental race upon the Earth.

29

DARBHYA, THE SPIRITUAL SUPERMAN

The birth of Darbhya took place through the true existence as the divine man or what one can call the superman. As the Veda says, "Cittiṁ juhomi" the sacrifice of self in the fire of the heart. At this stage, the mind serves as the *ghṛta*, clarified butter and offers all individual thoughts as a sacrifice. This results in a person, neither interested in intellectual ideas nor in using his intellectual judgement, who understands and works with either his senses or the feelings of his heart, where the *Sudeva*, the truth-consciousness exists. He is Darbhya, who is guided directly by observing the situation or the work he has to do, who does not depend on others but who sees the facts himself. He does not imagine but observes the facts clearly. His activities are governed by free and correct perception of right relations and their inevitable execution is based on the actual condition of matter. He has dissolved totally his ideas, imagination and thoughts in the fire of the heart. He connects through the eternal truth with the heart, with the Vedas, with all Godheads and with eternal Time.

He does not work through any mental theories, plans or any *isms* to guide people to accomplish his works. He works and provides welcome guidance through the eternal truth activities in his heart. People are astounded by receiving such an advice from a man and they consider him a superman.

That is the prime reason why automatically humanity accepts the suzerainty of the superman as his invaluable peaceful guidance and selfless activities are highly esteemed. Man surrenders willingly to the superman. For these reasons, they elected Darbhya as their leader. With this election begins the divine government. Men happily accept to remain under his leadership. With full faith, they agree to be guided by him for obtaining better prospects in the future, which on their own they cannot obtain. With individuals willing to accept his supremacy, a divine empire spreads upon this Earth.

Darbhya alone can judge right from wrong, divine from undivine, truth from falsehood and people gladly accept his decisions without any hesitation. In fact they accept the decisions with pleasure knowing their good fortune. They happily accept any punishment or honour which comes directly from him because they realise that what they receive is for their own purity, health and beauty.

Darbhya, who unlocks the divine in each individual and who respects all people under him as he considers them all divine and equal to him. The only difference being that they are engaged in different tasks. He is working like the Leader to lead these people towards Truth and Immortality by conquering all dissensions. His subjects support him for their own fulfilment. By his attractive rules, guidance and behaviour with these people, all opposition melts away. All happily chant the songs of his victory. The people are so full of joy that they pray constantly for his health, longevity and eternal presence.

Under his reign, there is no taxation. Taxes were collected by human governments to increase their treasury. But in his supramental reign, the treasury increases through collection of wealth from places which are out of reach of common dwellers. These are places like the deep forests, high mountains, vast oceans and areas where no one lives, which are lonely and far from inhabited localities.

He provides sufficient space for the people to live as they need to maintain their daily lives. He does not levy taxes on the place of residence or on the fields where the people grow their food grains. All these are for free. Everyone can enjoy that what they earn or have. They do not have to contribute to maintain the government. The only task of the government is to ensure that there are no quarrels and dissensions amongst people and that peace reigns over all.

People are allowed to have material earnings from their own labour. Only if they have more than what they need, they can contribute. If they wish, they can offer a portion of their wealth to the Government for sharing the costs of administration. At the same time, they have the liberty to keep it for themselves. The main concern of the government is to maintain a constant communication between Truth and the Earth. Darbhya is the channel or bridge between the Deva and humanity. His main task is to prevent the influx of hostile forces in the Earth atmosphere where the Power of Truth reigns supreme. As a result, people enjoy peace, purity and bliss coming from the Truth Consciousness. That is how the Empire of Truth or the divine peaceful government commences on the Earth.

Darbhya's powers are used only to control beings who wish to harm or hurt others, or those whose natures are such that they wish to do injury to others. This is to ensure protection of the liberty of the general public. Excepting this, there are no other controls or punishment. All are free and liberated as they are the children of immortality with the aim of achieving the life divine.

He educates these people that their Mother is the Earth and their Father the Heaven. As they themselves are the immortal children of one creator, they should love the whole humanity. They are brothers and sisters enjoying the life divine on the Earth. They must learn to reject this present human civilization which has brought them only sufferings. Instead they should enter into the divine or supramental civilization which represents peace, purity and *ānanda* with immortality.

30

THE DIVINE VAṄGA – BENGAL

Piṅgala Maheśvara continued. Some years ago, I was attracted by a brilliant light emanating from the Earth to look at Vaṅga. Through out the Earth, the obscurity of Nakta and Kali was widespread. Only this flame was burning and aspiring for Truth amongst thousands of other desires. A Ṛṣi in human form, Sri Rāmakṛṣṇa, had forsaken all human desires. Even his own wife he worshipped as the Divine Mother. He offered his feelings and desires as a sacrifice in the fire of his heart. With that was kindled the sacrificial flame, which the Vedas called the rekindled *Vitihotra* upon the Earth.

Then came another Ṛṣi to fan the flames of the *Vitihotra* still higher. He also offered his sacrificial rite in the fire of the heart. With that the *Vitihotra*, the psychic aspiration, became very powerful and it spread wide to promote awareness amongst others. He was called Swami Vivekānanda.

Another Ṛṣi followed him who also performed his sacrificial rite in the fire of his heart. Then the *Vitihotra* flame rose higher and the fire roared. The people of Bengal were awakened. He was called Sri Aurobindo. With him, the people started to worship their motherland. They chanted aloud –

वन्दे मातरम्
सुजलां सुफलां मलयज-शीतलां
सस्य-श्यामलां मातरम् ।

Vande mātaram
Sujalāṁ, suphalāṁ, malayaja-śītalāṁ
Sasya - śyāmalāṁ mātaram ।

I was very pleased to receive these strong feelings and vibrations from the people of Bengal. The song continued

शुभ्र-ज्योत्सना-पुलकित-यामिनीम्
फुल्ल-कुसुमित-द्रुमदल-शोभिनीम्
सुहासिनीं सुमधुर-भाषिणीम्
सुखदां वरदां मातरम् ॥

Śubhra-jyotsnā-pulakita-yāminīm
Phulla-kusumita-drumadala-śobhinīm
Suhāsinīm sumadhura-bhāṣiṇīm
Sukhadāṁ varadāṁ mātaram ॥

It was thrilling for me to hear the long-awaited words worshipping their motherland when they raised their fist and sang:-

सप्तकोटि-कण्ठ-कलकल-निनाद-कराले
द्विसप्तकोटि-भुजैर्धृत-खरकरवाले
के बोले मा तुमि अबले ।
बहुबल-धारिणीं नमामि तारिणीं
रिपुदल-वारिणीं मातरम् ॥

Saptakoṭi-kaṇṭha-kalakala-nināda-karāle
dvisaptakoṭi-bhujairdhṛta-kharakaravāle
Ke bole mā tumi abale ।
Bahubala-dhāriṇīṁ namāmi tāriṇīṁ
Ripudala-vāriṇīm mātaram ॥

I was astonished to hear from their song the long hidden secret that was now revealed. They worshipped their motherland as the divine mother. Immediately, I sent them an additional force of Truth. Then they were charged to sing further.

तुमि विद्या तुमि धर्म
तुमि हृदि तुमि मर्म
त्वं हि प्राणाः शरीरे ।
बाहुते तुमि मा शक्ति
हृदये तुमि मा भक्ति
तोमारइ प्रतिमा गडि
मन्दिरे मन्दिरे ।

Tumi vidyā tumi dharma
Tumi hṛdi tumi marma
Tvaṁ hi prāṇāḥ śarīre /
Bāhute tumi mā śakti
Hṛdaye tumi mā bhakti
Tomārai pratimā gaḍi
Mandire mandire /

त्वं हि दुर्गा दशप्रहरण-धारिणी
कमला कमल-दल-विहारिणी
वाणी विद्यादायिनी
नमामि त्वां
नमामि कमलां अमलां अतुलां
सुजलां सुफलां मातरम् ॥

Tvaṁ hi durgā daśapraharaṇa-dhāriṇī
Kamalā kamal-dala-vihāriṇī
Vāṇī vidyādāyinī
Namāmi tvāṁ
Namāmi kamalāṁ amalām atulāṁ
Sujalāṁ, suphalāṁ mātaram //

With that force, Bengal arose to drive out the hostile powers from its land. The force of truth spread out from Bengal and woke the whole of India. However, Kali took advantage of the interests of the British Government and managed to portray that awakening as criminal. The ruling power, within a short period and with the help of Kali, controlled this movement and it died out. Then the Ṛṣi was unable to stay in Bengal. He enquired from the Lord in his heart and received the direction to go to Pondicherry where the work would be continued.

That force however was still in action. The people of India together with Bengal continued their endeavour under Mahātma Gandhi and with his non-violent policy secured their national freedom. However, that movement was followed as a policy only without any inspiration or guidance from the heart. As a result, the divine force could not act as the activities of the government were guided from the mental plane. The inspiration from the heart which had arisen from Bengal by the sacrificial rite of the Ṛṣis died down by rejecting the active force of Truth. Under the policy of non-violence, an inertia set in and India suffered severely under the influence of the quarrel of the *Ṛpus.* Constant fighting and violence continued under the shadow of non-violence. Then Sri Aurobindo asked the higher consciousness, the Supramental Truth, to act instead on the mental plane. Afterwards I, Piṅgala Maheśvara, found that the moment had arrived for my intervention. I saw the suffering of the people and the helplessness of the leaders due to the failure of the policies directed from the mental plane. Therefore, I opened the path of immortality, the Devāyaṇa, to initiate the influence of the Supramental Truth upon the Earth.

O people of Bengal! Rise up again by leaving all other activities. Worship your motherland as the Divine Mother. The remaining work for the manifestation of the supramental truth will be done by me. Through the worship of your motherland, you will realise the united Bengal, without fissure. You will then sing more powerfully and peacefully. This message will then spread throughout India. People will start to worship the motherland and then the Earth and Heaven will become united. This movement will then spread throughout the world and it will seem as if the Earth was spreading her arms to embrace the Heaven with all the Gods, the Vedas and the Truth.

O people of Bengal! Realise that the unity and the peace of the whole humanity is depending upon you. With the worship of your motherland, only you can start to bring back peace, unity, purity, *ānanda* and the divine life on the Earth. When you worship your motherland, you will become the leader on the path to peace and unity of the whole humanity. You will be the Guru of the world by this discovery of the supramental truth.

As you have chanted the song of your mother land:

त्वं हि दुर्गा दशप्रहरण-धारिणी
कमला कमल-दल-विहारिणी
वाणी विद्यादायिनी
नमामि त्वां ॥

Tvaṁ hi durgā daśapraharaṇa-dhāriṇī
Kamalā kamal-dala-vihāriṇī
Vāṇī vidyādāyinī
Namāmi tvaṁ //

This means, O Bengal! Thou art the ten-armed Durgā, the Conqueror of Asuras and Diversity. Thou art the Giver of Unity. Thou art Lakṣmi, the Giver of Harmony, Beauty and Peace. Thou art Vani-Sarasvatī; the Giver of Wisdom, Perfection of Activities and Fulfilment of Life. Worship your motherland as she is the divine land, the *Vīda-Vaṅga*, the home of Truth.

O Bengal! Be conscious about your ancient status, when you were called *Vīda-Vaṅga* by the Ṛṣis. Become conscious again, Satyadeva is coming to you. Open your doors to receive Him. O Divine land! Prepare your offering that will be that several millions of your children should worship the Deva and keep ready food and drinks for him.

O Heavenly Earth! Remember your previous reminiscences when you had become the Devi yourself by Satyadeva's touch. You received respect from all. Be conscious now and feel that touch which still remains in each cell of your body. In times long past, Deva, moved in you, took His rest in you and played joyfully with many Gods in your land. He had drunk the nectar of *soma*, the touch that still exists in your heart. Become conscious of the former touch of Truth and look He has come back to you in a subtle form, *anurupam.* He is waiting for you with a smiling face to give you all the boons and shelter. Call and receive Him in your home. Give the seat to the Truth, offer Him your best food and drink. Prostrate before Him to tell the pains and sufferings of the whole Earth. He will be pleased to hear about it from you and He will gladly move throughout the Earth. The whole Earth will respect you for your work and worship you with the Truth.

O Divine Vaṅga! In ancient times you achieved your divinity. Mahādevi Pārvatī was born in you. In you, Lord Śiva and Pārvatī undertook their beloved play. Gods worshipped Aśmanavati-Pārvatī also in your land to conquer the Asuras at the Bank of the Ganges. You yourself worshipped Deva and earned the status of the Supreme Devi. At that moment, all the Goddesses manifested in you. As all Gods manifested on the Earth in Fire, therefore the Ṛṣis worshipped Fire as the symbol of all Gods. Like that, O Truth purified Soil! As all Goddesses manifested in you, therefore O Vīda-Vaṅga ! You were worshipped by the Ṛṣis as the symbol of all Goddesses.

O Vaṅga! O Divine Land! The Devi Suhavā has manifested in you. The Power of Truth will speak through your mouth to receive the Deva – O Deva! O Truth! My eternal beloved. Take Your Seat and feast with milk and honey. Worship the Deva with these sweet words of love. He settled in your land with these words and blessings – O Vaṅga! I shall stay here at least ten thousand years.

O Motherland! The Divine Mother Aditi herself manifested to congratulate and receive all Godheads in you. She spoke to the Gods in these sweet words of affection – O Gods! Come here to stay on this soil and conduct your divine activities through the human beings. Let men be the divine workers to establish my divine kingdom and cultivate this vast field of Earth to collect the wealth. Then this field will be full of green crops. Cultivate the mountains and forests by which a large amount of wealth together with gems and jewels will be collected. O Gods! Fill up this land with many riches. To this the Gods replied – O Mother Divine! Stay here on this land for about ten thousand years. We shall maintain your divine kingdom to worship this land with divine riches to ornament this land for her fulfilment.

With the Divine Mother, the other Goddesses also appeared and carried out their activities to establish the Truth-Empire. Recall those ancient memories to open the Age of Truth and receive your divine consciousness. We pray before you. O Mother! We are all your children. O People of Bengal! Remember these prayers to worship your motherland as she was the Divine Mother:-

O Vaṅga! You appeared before us as Yahvī, the Mother of Truth, to identify the Earth with Heaven and sanction immortality for the people of this Earth. Be again like that. We prostrate before you to receive your Heavenly grace and blessings.

O Vaṅga! You appeared before as Yahvī, the soul Mother of Truth, brought down the Deva, the Transcendental Truth in the *Vitihotra* and manifested immortality here upon the Earth. Be again like that to bring the Deva back here. O Mother! We bow down before you to receive your Heavenly grace and blessings.

O Vaṅga! You appeared as Aditi, the Divine Mother! Embrace these human children like the divine children of Heaven to re-open divinity here on this soil. You gave nourishment to these earthly children to fill them with the divine heart and engaged them to do your divine work. Be again like that today, to open your divine kingdom to receive heavenly grace and blessings. O Mother! We bow down in front of you.

O Vaṅga! You appeared as the power of great Time, Śiva. The Vedas called you Aśmanavatī, but we say you are Mahāmāyā Pārvati-Durgā, the ten-handed power, remover of all suffering and the destroyer of the demonical and dark forces.

Particularly, those that have influenced your children and made them unconscious, stupid and ignorant. You destroyed them with the sword of the consciousness of Truth. You destroyed them with the javelin of Truth-Light and made this human heart the abode of the Truth. Then Deva, with the other Gods, appeared. Be again the same today and remove the hostile forces, clean the abode of Deva and receive your share of the heavenly grace and blessings. O Mother! We prostrate in front of you.

O Vaṅga! You appeared before as Vaiṣnavi Mahālakṣmi. Together with the cakra and supreme love, you destroyed the poverty, the desires, the dirt, the disharmony, the quarrels and the jealousy. You established harmony and beauty in these people. You filled their house with your divine riches. They augmented their divine affection by your divine love, unity and peace. Be again like that to remove all poverty and disharmony and be identified with each other. To receive your supreme love and blessings, O Mother, we bow down in front of you.

O Vaṅga! You appeared before as Sarasvatī, the giver of success in works by removing all misunderstanding in words, inertia and negligence of activities. You replaced it with the contemplation of constant work. You gave us the encouragement to achieve Truth consciousness and to enrich ourselves on the Earth with the true attitude, enthusiasm and inspiration. Be the same again and remove our lethargy, our inactivity in the works to attain divine contemplation. O Mother! We prostrate before you.

O Vaṅga! You appeared before us as Sureśvari Saci with the thousand eyes. You glance at us from all sides while holding the Vajra, the unique divine weapon. You conquered all anti-divine forces and established a peaceful united divine empire upon the Earth. O Mother! All your children are Heaven born. They are sons of immortality. You looked at them, nourished them with your thousand divine eyes. You helped your children to realise their self-divinity. Today, be again like that and remove the anti-divine forces to establish the divine empire. To receive your divine grace and blessings, we prostrate in front of you.

O Vaṅga! You appeared before us as the Rohiṇi Someśvari, the power of *soma*, the nectar, that flowed from the golden pot into the mouth of your children. By that, O Mother, they entered into divine purity by the removal of all *ṛpus*, enemies, such as hunger and thirst and achieved immortality. Today, be again be like that. Remove all the *ṛpus* so that we can attain immortality. To receive your divine grace and blessings, O Mother, we prostrate in front of you.

O Vaṅga! You appeared before us as Savitṛ Sūrya, giver of truth consciousness. You woke up your children from their deep sleep of unconsciousness with this message - Awake, O my children and enter into divinity. Behold the Truth, whose name is *amṛta*, the Deva immortal. Look! He has appeared before you and see you also form part of Him in the Truth consciousness. Like your soul, call and draw him inside you: O Truth, descend upon us, enter into our bodies and be unified with our cells. With this prayer, realise your total identity with Deva, the transcendental truth. Be as truthful as the Gods by entering into immortality and conquer death. O Mother! With this voice of affection, all your children entered into Truth consciousness and appeared as the immortal truth. Today, be again like that. Conquer death and become conscious in the immortality of Truth. For obtaining your divine grace and blessings, O Mother! We prostrate in front of you.

O Vaṅga! You appeared before as Agñeya Svāha, the power of the *Vitihotra* and you burnt high in every heart to call Deva with the soaring aspiration to achieve immortality, which is the only aim of human life. Diseases, infirmity, death, pains and all other sufferings are forms of falsehood and ignorance. O Mother! Teach those who are suffering from diseases, fearing infirmity and death and feeling the pains and sorrows, that this suffering is due to ignorance. Make them conscious of their divine immunity. Announce that the Truth and Immortality is for the entire Earth. Teach us to aspire for the

Truth and to receive your divine grace and blessings. O Mother! We prostrate in front of you.

O Vaṅga! You appeared before us as Pavamani Vāyāvi, forcefully, with a great noise to destroy falsehood and stupidity. You announced the withdrawal of Nakta and Kali. You also gave the news of the advent of Deva. The whole world looked at you with great attention. With your sweet message of Truth, the entire Earth was purified. Mankind was eager to hear more about this event and inspired to attain Deva. Be again like that now. The moment has once more come to announce the withdrawal of Kali with his dark forces, the arrival of Deva with his divine light and the commencement of the Deva Yuga. O Mother! We pray for your grace and blessings and we prostrate again and again in front of you.

O Vaṅga! You appeared before as Maitra-Varuṇi Apeśvari. You embraced the children of the whole Earth so that they are harmoniously united and peaceful. You made them eager to attain the Deva by the announcement of Truth's advent and bound them in a chain of brotherhood. They became totally unified without losing their individuality. At that time, mankind looked like a necklace which was hung around the neck and chest of the Deva as they were all luminous with their unique individuality. O Divine Mother! The whole Earth became united into one through your adoration of Truth and it had a heavenly glitter. Be again like that, for the unity and peace of the mankind. O Mother! We pray for your divine grace and blessings and prostrate again and again in front of you.

Let the divine singers, the Gandharvas sing with their divine tunes and the divine dancers, the *Apsarās*, dance with their divine gestures. Let them manifest their divine beauty in music as they did before on this divine Earth with these chants.

O Vaṅga! O Divine Land! You are the supreme Devi and all the Goddesses appear in you. All the Goddesses become one in you. You are Yahvī, the Mother of Truth; who unites Earth with Heaven. You are the Deva Patni Uṣati, the Power of Truth, who manifests Deva, on the Earth. You are Aditi, the

Divine Mother, the Mother of Gods, who manifests the Gods on the Earth. You are the Brahmani, the Power of Brahmā the Creator, who creates the divine creations. You are Vaiṣnavi, the Giver of Wealth, who protects the divine creations. O Mother! We bow down before you again and again. You are Durgā, Reliever of all Sufferings. You are Sarasvatī, the Provider of all Accomplishment of Work. O Mother! We prostrate before you constantly.

O Vaṅga! You are the Mahāśakti. In your eyes exists the Savitṛ-Sūrya, in your heart the Rohiṇicandra, in your ears the Rudra, in your nose the Pāvamani, in your life Sarasvatī, in your abdomen the Varuṇi, in your navel the Dharma, below the navel the Aśvinīs, in your senses the Indraṇi and in your skin the Vanaspatini. In this way, all the Goddesses are appearing in your body. You appeared as Devi-Vaṅga on this Earth and as the Devi Suhavā on the transcendental plane.

O Devi! Your immortal children will be fully transformed and will enter into divinity by meditating on your divine features and by chanting your hymns, because they were born from your cells, grew up on your milk, developed with the feasts given by you and nourished by your divinity. They will regain their divine life and you will appear wonderful with your children in the pure, sweet, peaceful and enlightened land.

O Vaṅga! Listen to the voice of the Yajurveda:-

सुगा वो देवाः सदनाऽ अकर्म य आजग्मेदं सवनं जुषाणाः ।
भरमाणा वहमाना हवींष्यस्मे धत्त वसवो वसूनि स्वाहा ॥

Yaj.VIII.18

Sugā vo devāḥ sadanā' akarma ya ājagmedaṁ savanaṁ juṣāṇāḥ /
Bharamāṇā vahamānā havīṁṣyasme dhatta vasavo vasūnī svāhā //

In this divine land, which is the *devāḥ sadana*, the Abode of Truth, let the Deva come back again to perform his pure activities for peace in the place of the activities of the hostile or negative forces. He will lead the entire humanity to fulfilment. We worship him with the word svāha and offer our sacrificial offering for our perfection. O Deva! O Truth! Manifest and establish yourself with divine riches on this Earth.

O Divine Land! Listen to the voices of Truth.

31

THE VOICE OF TRUTH: SATYADEVA

When Vaṅga becomes conscious and eager with her children to see Satyadeva and attain immortality, nature together with time will call down Deva upon the Earth; the seasons, the Ṛtus, will chant the hymns to Ṛta, the Truth. The Gandharvas will adjust their divine tunes and the *Apsarās* take their dance positions to solicit Satyadeva.

य एतं देवानामेकम् वृतं वेद ।

Ath.XIII.4.22

Ya etaṁ devānāmekaṁ vṛtaṁ veda /

There is only one Deva, who exists throughout the Vedas.

यस्मात् कोशादुदभराम वेदं तस्मिन्नन्तरव दध्म एनम् ।
कृतमिष्टं ब्रह्मणो वीर्येण तेन मा देवास्तपसावते ह ॥

Ath.XIX.72.1

Yasmāt kośādudabharāma vedaṁ tasminnantarava dadhma enam /
Kṛtamiṣṭaṁ brahmaṇo vīryeṇa tena mā devāstapasāvate ha //

From Satyadeva's body cells the four Vedas appeared as they exist in his cells; with his self-knowledge the Vedas are shining like the Sun. In other words, with the knowledge of the Vedas, He is himself glowing. He is our Satyadeva, the Supreme Soul existing everywhere, who is doing all the incomparable activities. We adore Him and solicit Him to manifest here.

हिरण्यकर्णं मणिग्रीवमर्णस्तन्नो विश्वे वरिवस्यन्तु देवाः ।
अर्यो गिरः सद्य आ जग्मुषीरोस्राश्चाकन्तूभयेष्वस्मे ॥

Ṛg.I.122.14

Hiraṇyakarṇaṁ maṇigrīvamarṇastanno viśve varivasyantu devāḥ I
Aryo giraḥ sadya ā jagmuṣīrosrāścākantūbhayeṣvasme II

We adore the Deva with the beautiful body, who has golden ears, gems and jewels around his neck and would be overjoyed to receive him here in this world. Whose head is so high that with the crown it touches the sky, who is shining with a divine light and who removes the ultimate fear of death from our innermost soul and gives us peace, purity and immortality. We bow down before him.

सत्रस्य ऋद्धिरस्यगन्म ज्योतिरमृताऽअभूम ।
दिवं पृथिव्या ऽ अध्यारुहामाविदाम देवान्त्स्वर्ज्योतिः ॥

Yaj.VIII.52

Satrasya ṛddhirasyaganma jyotiramṛtā' abhūma I
Divaṁ pṛthivyā' adhyāruhāmāvidāma devāntsvarjyotiḥ II

Appear here, O Deva! Increase the riches of the divine sacrifice by showering your immortal and purest light for the unification of Earth and Heaven and for the unity and peace of the whole humanity. O Truth! Manifest with your pure and heavenly light.

यज्ञो देवानाम् ।

Yajño devānām I

The sacrifice is only for the Deva.

The Deva holds the sacrificial plants and by his power the Aśvinīs become the Healers of all Diseases and Remover of Falsehood. Sarasvatī became the Giver of Power of immunity in words by holding all the senses.

अनुष्टुभेन छन्दसा ।

Anuṣṭubhena chandasā I

The manifestation of the Deva is by the Anuṣṭubh chanda.

So far the creator Brahman has described and indicated the forms of Deva in the sacrifice, that is the Supreme Truth existing everywhere. On his chest the sacrificial thread is hanging. On this thread the creations are shining like gems and jewels.

ऋतं सत्यममृतं सत्यम् ।

Ṛtaṁ satyamamṛtaṁ satyam I

Truth is truth-immortality and immortality is the Truth.

The Deva, who is greater than all Godheads, appears before all Gods and gives us his power, light and purity to be enlightened, powerful and purified.

उदुत्यं चित्रं देवानाम् ।

Udutyaṁ citraṁ devānām I

Let the magnificent picture or the wonderful appearance of the Deva be disclosed.

देवं बर्हिरिन्द्रं सुदेवं देवैर्वीरवत्स्तीर्णं वेद्यामवर्धयत् ।

Yaj.XXVIII.12

Devaṁ barhirindraṁ sudevaṁ devairvīravatstīrṇam vedyāmavardhayat I

The Deva, who himself is established on the Indravarhi, the sacrificial seat of the heart is called Sudeva or Vasudeva. He is Satyadeva, who is manifesting His Light like a hero by conquering the obscurity of night. He increases our self-knowledge and our self-consciousness.

अद्या देवा उदिता सूर्यस्य निरंहसः पिपृता निरवद्यात् ।
तन्नो मित्रो वरुणो मामहन्तामदितिः सिन्धुः पृथिवी उत द्यौः ॥

Yaj.XXXIII.42

Adyā devā uditā sūryasya niraṁhasaḥ pipṛtā niravadyāt /
Tanno mitro varuṇo māmahantāmaditiḥ sindhuḥ pṛthivī uta dyauḥ //

Today the Deva, the destroyer of Asūrya, the sunless deep obscurity, has appeared before us by his own power. He is the giver of fulfilment with love and beauty. Along with him appeared the Gods, Mitra-Varuṇa to control conflicts and egoistic pride. Immerse yourself in the Aditi-Sindhu, wherever it is visible for being unified with Heaven. O Earth, become conscious of yourself, the Truth has manifested before you.

देवं देवं वोऽवसे देवं देवमभिष्टये ।
देवं देवं हुवेम वाजसातये गृणान्तो देव्या धिया ॥

Yaj.XXXIII.91

Devaṁ devaṁ vo'vase devaṁ devamabhiṣṭaye /
Devaṁ devaṁ huvema vājasātaye gṛṇanto devyā dhiyā //

With the Deva, all the Godheads have developed themselves further and attained their self fulfilment, that is why all the Gods are always aspiring for a union with the Deva. The disciple of Yaju, Vājasātaya, has decided upon this meditation for the Deva on the Earth that the Deva increases the effects of our meditation and fulfils us with his divine riches. We call on Him constantly – Deva, O Deva! Come to us.

O Deva! You are in the heart, in the mind, in the Heaven and in the Sun. The Seers of Truth, those seated in the higher planes, gave us this meditation.

यत्पुरुषेण हविषा देवा यज्ञमतन्वत ।
वसन्तोऽस्यासीदाज्यं ग्रीष्म इध्म शरद्धविः ॥

Yaj.XXXI.14

Yatpuruṣeṇa haviṣā devā yajñamatanvata /
Vasanto'syāsīdājyaṁ griṣma idhma śaraddhaviḥ //

When we aspired for the Truth and kindled the fire to call the Deva down, it was Ṛṣi Nārayāna, who established the Deva-Yajña in the cyclic movement of years. Nārāyaṇa described the Ṛtus, the seasons, as sacrificial materials. Vasanta, the spring for the sacrificial wood; Griṣma, the summer for the fire, Śarad, the autumn for the sacrifice.

This is the Deva Yajña, the sacrificial fire for the Truth, kindled and established in the Nature by the Nārayāna himself, for the new creation and immortality. The Deva comes according to the cyclic movement of aeons, which I have named ayana. When the Ṛṣis aspire to call, to receive and to attain the Deva; then Satyadeva appears with all the Gods and Goddesses and thus manifests the entire Veda. The path of the Deva, the Devāyaṇa, opens the way to the immortality of the Earth and then starts the Age of Truth upon the Earth.

Nārayāna said that the Earth had higher possibilities than all the other physically manifested planets. Thus, it is the Earth only that achieved immortality and realised the Truth and the children of Earth entered into divinity. The Yajur Veda disclosed to us that those who think that there is a superior creation in the other planets are confused. Amongst all planets only the Earth attained her divinity as the Nārayāna Ṛṣi claimed.

अद्भ्यः सम्भृतः पृथिव्यै रसाच्च विश्वकर्मणः समवर्तताग्रे ।
तस्य त्वष्टा विदधद्रूपमेति तन्मर्त्यस्य देवत्वमाजानमग्रे ॥

Yaj.XXXI.17

Adhbhyaḥ sambhṛtaḥ pṛthivyai rasācca
viśvakarmaṇaḥ samavartatāgre /
Tasya tvaṣṭā vidadhadrūpameti tanmartyasya
devatvamājānamagre //

Amongst all physical manifestations, Viśvakarmā chose and decorated this Earth, surrounded her with water, with divine beauty; Tvaṣṭā fashioned the divine figures of human beings; the same beings then entered into divinity and immortality. None of the other planets have such fortunate manifestations.

Here on the Earth, Satyadeva manifested once before and told the people of the Earth:

अहं परस्तादहमावस्ताद्यन्तरिक्षं तदु मे पिता भूत ।
अहं सूर्यमुभयतो ददर्शाहं देवानां परमं गुहा यत् ॥

Yaj.VIII.9

Ahaṁ parastādahamāvastādyantarikṣaṁ tadu me pitā bhūt |
Ahaṁ sūryamubhayato dadarśāhaṁ devānāṁ paramaṁ guhā yat ||

I am above all creations, I am beneath all creations and also in the heart of all creations. I was my father in the former and I am the son at present. I have seen the Sun from both its sides. I am seeing both past and present. I exist in the secret cave under the name of Deva.

That home of mine, the Prajāpati Supreme Creator called *Deva Sadana*, the home of the Deva and the Ṛṣis named that as the Vīda Vaṅga. In the beginning of the creation I manifested here in my home, the Vīda Vaṅga. To come back here again and again, Prajāpati said these words to the Agni,

यॉ२ आवहऽ उशतो देव देवांस्तान् प्रेरय स्वे अग्ने सधस्थे ।
जाक्षिवांसः पपिवांसश्च विश्वेसुं धर्मं स्वरातिष्ठतानु स्वाहा ॥

Yaj.VIII.19

Yān āvaha'uśato deva devānstān preraya sve agne sadhasthe |
Jākṣivāṁsaḥ papivāṁsaśca viśvesuṁ dharmaṁ svarātiṣṭhatānu svāhā ||

Appear again, O Deva, with your soul power Devi Ūṣati in the home that you occupied before. O all purified Supreme

Puruṣa! Come back again on this divine soil and let the Heaven be manifested here in Vīda-Vaṅga. O Fire! I am joining Svāha with you to carry the self-offering of this land to the Supreme Puruṣa, Satyadeva. On reaching before Him chant the needful prayer by which He will be encouraged to come here. By the Will of Prajāpati and by the call from Agni, Fire, ask Him to manifest again.

देवस्याहं सवितुः सवे सत्यसवसो बृहस्पतेरुत्तमं नाकं रुहे यम् ।
देवस्याहं सवितुः सवे सत्यसवसऽ इन्द्रस्योत्तमं नाकं रुहेयम् ॥

Yaj. IX.10

Devasyāhaṁ savituḥ save satyasavaso
bṛhaspateruttamaṁ nākaṁ ruheyam ।
Devasyāhaṁ savituḥ save satyasavasa'
indrasyottamaṁ nākaṁ ruheyam ॥

I am Deva, who appeared like the greater Sun, the Savitṛ Mandala when I rose on the greater Heaven; Bṛhaspati recognised me as the Supreme Truth, when I appeared on the sky of Maharloka, the supramental plane like a greater Sun, the Savitṛ Mandala. Indra recognised me as the Supreme Truth.

अहमस्मि प्रथमजा ऋतस्य पूर्वं देवेभ्यो अमृतस्य नाम ।
यो मा ददाति स इदेवमावदहमन्नमन्नमदन्तमक्षि ॥

Sām.IX.594

Ahamasmi prathamajā ṛtasya pūrvaṁ devebhyo
amṛtasya nāma ।
Yo mā dadāti sa
idevamāvadahamannamannamadantamakṣi ॥

I am the Truth. I was born before the creations, even before the birth of the Godheads. The Ṛṣis called me *Ṛta*, the Truth and they gave me the name *Amṛta*. For this reason, I call myself *Ahaṁ Ṛtaṁ*, in other words, I am the Truth that converts into *Amṛta*, the Heavenly nectar. I am the immortality. I am He, the Deva and I give willingly food, drink, rest, growth, beauty, love and knowledge to those who have surrendered everything to me.

सत्यमहं गभीरः काव्येन सत्यं जातेनास्मि जातवेदाः ।
न म दासो नार्यो महित्वा व्रतं मीमाय यदहं धरिष्ये ॥

Ath.V.11.3

Satyamahaṁ gabhīraḥ kāvyena satyaṁ jātenāsmi jātavedāḥ I
Na me dāso nāryo mahitvā vrataṁ mimāya yadahaṁ dhariṣye II

I am Satya, the Truth. I manifest myself in the great epic. I appear as the Truth through the Jātaveda fire. None is above me, I am the ultimate. O Earth! Your worship and true action I hold with the indomitable power of mine.

In short, I am Satya, I am the Deva. This the reason behind the Ṛṣis calling me Satyadeva. I am *Ṛtaṁ*, *Ahaṁ-Rtaṁ*, that is why the Prajāpati called me *amṛtaṁ*.

The Veda said,

saschad deva devam satya Indu satyamindraṁ.

This verse means that there is a Deva, who is the Truth and consciousness himself. O Indu! We call on him, He is the Satyadeva. O Indra! He is the Supreme Truth. Those who are calling me, by the name of Satyadeva, Ṛta or Amṛta, I manifest before them. I give them my power, light, consciousness and purity and then they enjoy immortality.

I am the One who gives immortality. All the Godheads, Goddesses, as well as Ṛṣis in Heaven did an immense sacrifice for me. As a result, I gave them immortality. Those who want only me, who do not hanker for power, position, wealth, or fame, I give them immortality. In addition, I give them power, position, wealth and fame. The Gods were like that. I gave them immortality. The Asuras all undertook a long yogic austerity and made an intense sacrifice for power, position, wealth and fame. They did not desire me so I did not appear in front of them. For this reason, they did not realise immortality. To reward them for their prolonged sacrifice, Prajāpati gave them the chance to acquire power, position, wealth and fame. They received boons for that. I did not tolerate their power, position and subjugation of Heaven. Thus, in course of time, I had them destroyed through Hari, Viṣṇu or Indra. These are the three forms with which I confront the evil forces. Those who do not welcome me have to disappear in the abyss.

There is no power above me, no position above mine, no existence above me. Those, who understand this crucial fact, become wise. For this reason, the Seers worship me alone, without seeking anything else and I give them immortality.

O Earth! I come in the course of the cyclic movement of Great Time to you as you aspire for me only after undergoing great sufferings. I have come to relieve your pains and to give you peace, purity, ānanda and immortality, which you will realise.

O Earth! Remember that I came here before, to open the Age of Truth and to make the Earth immortal and heavenly. I appeared in Bengal and stayed there to give peace, purity and immortality to the whole humanity. That is why Vīda Vaṅga was called the home of Truth by the Ṛṣis. I had manifested before in Bengal through the great epic Devāyaṇa.

सत्यमहं गभीरः काव्येन सत्यं जातेनास्मि जातवेदा ।

Ath.V.11.3

Satyamahaṁ gabhīraḥ kāvyena satyaṁ jātenāsmi jātavedāḥ ।

Now, I have appeared again through the great epic, the Devāyaṇa, in the Bengali language. I will manifest now again in Bengal, my home. I ride on the chariot to come here from the transcendental plane through the Anuṣṭubh chanda, the power of the Anuṣṭubh metre.

I descend here in Bengal in the Deva Yajña, the sacrificial fire. This sacrifice was established by the Nārāyaṇa Ṛṣi in the previous Deva Yajña with the worship of the six seasons, the

Ṛtus. Look at Bengal, the six seasons are appearing fully in their ideal form worshipping me. In no other part of the world are they appearing in full formation.

I am Deva, the ultimate Truth. I am the source of light, power, consciousness and purity. I am Satya, the source of all beauty, love, peace and unity. My justice, my rules and orders, my protection and guidance are above all. I am *Ṛta*, my conquest and my victory is ultimate. I am the Immortality, in other words, *Ṛtaṁ Satyam Ṛtaṁ Satyam.* I am Truth, I am Truth Immortality, I am the Truth.

My manifestation with all beauty, glory, position and fame is ultimate. I am the Immortality. Those who are seeing me, touching me, attaining me or attending on me, they will receive immortality.

Among the people of the Earth, both influences are present – divine and undivine, light and dark, deva and asura –

द्वे सृती अशृणवं पितृणामहं देवानामुत मर्त्यानाम् ।
ताभ्यामिदं विश्वमेजत्समेति यदन्तरा पितरं मातरं च ॥

Yaj.XIX.47

Dve sṛtī aśṛṇavaṁ pitṛṇāmahaṁ devānāmuta martyānām I
Tābhyāmidaṁ viśvamejatsameti yadantarā pitaraṁ mātaraṁ ca II

Mankind has two choices in front of them, two roads for their life journey. They can either choose the path of their fathers and ancestors, Pitṛyana, the dark obscure road, or the other, the path of the Gods, Devāyaṇa, the pure enlightened road. Both are visible to them. I remain as the protector and maintainer of the world through the outward creators, the fathers and the mothers.

Among those who follow the enlightened path of the Gods, Devāyaṇa, are the beings who can see me and enter into immortality. Those who are taking the dark obscure path Pitṛyana cannot see me and they vanish in the nether abyss.

Those who see me, they chant –
ude tvam citraṁ devanām.

They say, look at the magnificent appearance of the Deva, the ever desirable Truth. See He has manifested in front of us. We hear his beautiful words.

One who sees me even once, he conquers the diseases, infirmity and death. I am the Truth, I am the Immortality.

I remain in the transcendental plane, which the Ṛṣis called the plane of Truth. In my triangular home, Viṣṇu, Hari and Prajāpati go to purify themselves; Viṣṇu after his unique battle, Hari after his final conquest and Prajāpati after his creations. When they feel impure and fatigued, they enter my home and drink *soma*, the nectar, which removes their impurity and tiredness, they again feel full of purity and power.

On the Earth, I remain in the sacrificial fire, established by the Nārayāna with the cyclic movement of seasons. There in my home, the wise devotees enter, who became impure and tired of worldly activities. They regain their purity and power.

I remain as *anna*, food, before them to relieve their sufferings from diseases, infirmity and death. With this Truth-consciousness, when human beings take food, they enjoy health and immunity.

I remain in the *apas*, water. Those who drink or consume water with Truth-consciousness, they become fulfilled with satisfaction of hunger and thirst.

I always support and hold the base of the head of all living beings. Amongst them those Yogis who are conscious about my touch at the base of their head, they drink *soma* and enter into immortality.

O Men! I, alone, come from the transcendental plane to the physical plane. Be conscious about your food, your drink and the base of your head. I exist there constantly. I am the Truth. I have come to give you the gift of immortality.

32

THE MANIFESTATION OF PEACE

O Earth! May you be blessed with ample food, much more than your needs! May you have more sweet juice flowing than the number of people ! Let water become the sweetest drink.

Let human beings realise the Truth at the base of their head and let the Truth be fully manifested upon this Earth. Let the Earth enter into unity and harmony. We, the *Ṛsis*, pray for the Earth:

स्वस्ति न ऽ इन्द्रो वृद्धश्रवाः स्वस्ति नः पूषा विश्ववेदाः ।
स्वस्ति नस्तार्क्ष्यो अरिष्टनेमिः स्वस्ति नो बृहस्पतिर्दधातु ॥

Yaj.XXV.19

Svasti na' indro vṛddhaśravāḥ svasti naḥ pūṣā viśvavedāḥ ।
Svasti nastārkṣyo ariṣṭanemiḥ svasti no bṛhaspatirdadhātu ॥

O Indra! Ancient Seer of Truth, provide us with rest, unity and harmony. Give us rest, O Pūṣā, who knows the soul of the world. Give us unity, O Tārkṣya! Bring harmony in us, O Ariṣṭanemi! O Bṛhaspati! Give us rest and unity throughout all mankind.

वेदः स्वस्तिर्द्रुघणः स्वस्तिः परशुर्वेदिः परशुर्नः स्वस्ति ।

Ath.VII.29.1

Vedaḥ svastirdrughaṇaḥ svastiḥ paraśurvediḥ paraśurnaḥ svasti ।

O Vedas! Give us rest with the knowledge of Truth. In the present turbulent condition of the Earth, provide us with respite; O Vedas! Shine with the Truth-Light like an axe. O Veda-axe! Dissolve and remove all ignorance and let us rest in Truth Consciousness. Om Svasti! Svasti! Svasti!

> पृथिवी शान्तिरन्तरिक्षं शान्तिर्द्यौः शान्तिरापः शान्तिरोषधयः शान्तिर्वनस्पतयः शान्तिर्विश्वे मे देवाः शान्तिः सर्वे मे देवाः शान्तिः शान्तिः शान्तिः शान्तिभिः ।
> ताभिः शान्तिभिः सर्व शान्तिभिः शमयामोहं यदिहघोरं यदिह क्रूरं यदिह पापं तच्छान्तं तच्छिवं सर्वमेव शमस्तु नः ।
>
> Ath.XIX.9.14
>
> *Pṛthivi śāntirantarikṣaṁ śantiḥ dyauḥ śāntirāpaḥ śāntiroṣadhayaḥ*
> *śantirvanaspatayaḥ śantirviśve me devāḥ śāntiḥ sarve me devāḥ śantiḥ śāntiḥ śāntiḥ śāntibhiḥ* ।
> *Tābhiḥ śāntibhiḥ sarva śāntibhiḥ śamayamohaṁ yadiha ghoraṁ yadiha krūraṁ*
> *yadiha pāpaṁ tacchāntaṁ tacchivaṁ sarvameva śamastu naḥ* ।

Let peace be established on the Earth, in life, in mind and in the Heaven. Let there be peace in water, in plants, in trees and in the forests. Let all Gods enjoy peace in the world. In the land where complete peace reigns, let Deva the Truth manifest: peace, peace, peace is the final attainment of Truth. That is the Truth, the peaceful Truth, the all peaceful Truth, which removes all of our egoistic turbulences. Even though we are furious, even though we are cruel, even though we are sinful: still we shall be peaceful, we shall be like the self-entranced Śiva in a quiet peaceful condition, we shall enter in the presence of the Deva. Peace, peace, peace is the ultimate goal.

> ॐ शान्तिः शान्तिः शान्तिः
>
> Om śāntiḥ śāntiḥ śāntiḥ.

O Lord, let peace prevail everywhere.

Mantras to Welcome the Golden Age

To welcome the approaching Golden Age and to prepare ourselves for the intense golden light that will immerse us, the regular listening and chanting of the following mantras compiled by Dr. Hajari, author of the Devāyaṇa, will purify and strengthen our inner being.

यच्चिद्धि शश्वता तना देवं देवं यजामहे ॥

Yacciddhi śaśvatā tanā devaṁ devaṁ yajāmahe – to be chanted 12 times

To realise the Truth and to attain a divine body, I meditate on Him who is The Ultimate. By uttering the words – Deva, O Deva, we attain a total identification. He is the Deva and I am the Deva. With this I am one with the Truth.

देवं देवं यजामहे ॥

Devaṁ devaṁ yajāmahe – to be chanted 12 times

Let me be one with God.

देवं देवं ॥

Devaṁ devaṁ – to be chanted from 10–100 times

I call on Deva time and again. Then chant the holy word of Om

आनन्दं आनन्दं केवलानन्दं ॥

Ānandaṁ ānandaṁ kevalānandaṁ – to be chanted 6 times

Let the Divine bliss alone prevail.

आनन्ददेव खल्विमानि भूतानि जायन्ते ।
आनन्देन जातानि जीवन्ति ।
आनन्दं प्रयन्तं संविशंति ॥

Ānanddev khalvimāni bhutāni jāyante
Ānanden jātāni jīvanti
Ānandaṁ prayantaṁ sanviśanti – (to be chanted 3 times.)

From Delight all things are born, in Delight they exist and grow, to Delight they ultimately return.

आनन्दं आनन्दं ॥

Ānandaṁ ānandaṁ – (to be chanted 6 times)

Let Divine Joy surround us.

आनन्दं ब्रह्म ॥

Anandaṁ Brahma – (to be chanted 12 times)

Delight Is the Divine Creator.

ब्रह्म सत्यं ॥

Brahma Satyaṁ – to be chanted 12 times

The Creator Is the Truth

सत्यं देवं ॥

Satyaṁ devaṁ – to be chanted 12 times

Truth Is God.

देवं देवं ॥

Devaṁ devaṁ – to be chanted from 10–100 times

I call on Deva time and again.

तत्सवितुर्वरेण्यम् भर्गोदेवस्य धीमहि ।
धियो यो नः प्रचोदयात् ॥

Tatsaviturvareṇyaṁ bhargo devasya dhīmahi
Dhiyo yo nāḥ pracodayāt – to be chanted 3 times

Let us meditate
On the most excellent Light
Of the Divine Truth
That it may impel our minds
Without reserve.

ॐ भूर्भुवस्वः महः ॥

Om bhūrbhuvarsvahāḥ mahāḥ – to chanted 3 times

O Lord, let us meditate on the physical, vital, mental and the Supramental planes

तत्सवितुर्वरेण्यम् भर्गो देवस्य धीमहि ।
धियो यो नः प्रचोदयात ॥

Tatsaviturvareṇyaṁ bhargo devasya dhīmahi
Dhiyo yo nāḥ pracodayāt – to be chanted once

Let us meditate
On the most excellent Light
Of the Divine Truth
That it may impel our minds
Without reserve.

देवं देवं ॥

Devaṁ devaṁ – to be chanted from 10–100 times

I call on Deva time and again.

ऋतं सत्यं अमृतं सत्यं ॥

Ṛtaṁ satyaṁ amṛtaṁ satyaṁ – to be chanted 12 times

Truth is immortality and immortality is Truth

देवं देवं ॥

Devaṁ devaṁ – to be chanted from 10–100 times

I call on Deva time and again.

अमृतं कुरु कुरु स्वाहा ॥

Amṛtaṁ kuru kuru svāhā – to be chanted 12 times

Do noble deeds and offer them to the Divine

देवं देवं ॥

Devaṁ devaṁ – to be chanted from 10–100 times

I call on Deva time and again.

ॐ क्रीं क्रीं क्रीं ह्रं ह्रं श्रीं श्रीं दक्षिणे कालिके ·स्वाहा

Om krīṁ krīṁ krīṁ hriṁ hriṁ śrīṁ śrīṁ dakṣine kālike svāhā – to be chanted 12 times.

Secret sounds to invoke the powers of Goddess Kāli into our being that will demolish erroneous zones of our nature.

ॐ क्रीं क्रीं क्रीं हुं हुं श्रीं श्रीं दक्षिणे कालिके स्वाहा

Om krīṁ krīṁ krīṁ huṁ huṁ śrīṁ śrīṁ dakṣine kālike svāhā – to be chanted 12 times.

Secret sounds to invoke the powers of Goddess Kāli into our being that will demolish erroneous zones of our nature.

GLOSSARY

A

Abhivarta	Son of Ṛṣi Aṅgirā, the King of Ṛṣis
Adharma	Ungodly, Anti-dharma (irreligious), Śani
Adharma-Śani	Manifestation of the dark force under the influence of the Sun, Opposing the Gods
Adhyāya	A chapter. A canto in the Mahābhārata
Aditi	The Divine Mother, the Mother of the Great Godheads, Daughter of the Power of Truth
Āditya	The Sun
Ādityaloka	The plane of the Sun
Agni	The Lord of Fire
Agni devatā	Aspirant God, the Lord of the Aspirant Force
Aiteraya Upaniṣad	Name of an Upaniṣad
Akṣara	Soul, a word
Ākhyāna	Story of the past
Akṣarabrahman	Brahman as sound
Akṣrāpa	The Sea of the Brahman, Ocean of the Vedas
Ambhṛnī-Ṛṣikā	A female Seer, mother of Vāk, Dvitā and Tritā, wife of the Creator Aptya
Amijaspati	Satyadeva, the Lord of Truth
Amṛta	Divine wine
Amṛtasya putrāh	Children of Immortality
Ānanda	Bliss
Aṅgirā	One of the seven Ṛṣis, created from the mind of Parabrahman

Āṅgirasa	Sons of Aṅgirā
Animal-Śatarūpa	Śatarūpa as an animal, the evolutionary force in the form of an animal
Antarikṣa	Vital plane existing between the mental and the physical
Anusvāra	Nasal sound
Anuṣṭubh	A Sanskrit metre of 32 letters
Apānapāt	Godhead who prepares for the Golden Age
Apāra prakṛti	Nature under the influence of evil forces
Apasabaraṇa	A cover of water
Āptya	One of the seven Ṛṣis, created from the mind of Parabrahman. Also, creator of the worlds and of the two Ages, Dvitā and Tritā.
Apsarā	Dancing girl of heaven
Arbuda	Snake king
Arjuna	The third Pāṇḍava, the intimate friend of Divine Kṛṣṇa
Aryaman	The grandson of Deva
Āśā	Daughter of the Power of Truth
Aśokvana	Garden house of Rāvaṇa
Aśmanvatī	Daughter of the Power of Truth
Aśvathāmā	Son of Droṇacārya, the teacher of the Kauravas and the Paṇḍavas, one of the immortals who reincarnated in Kaliyuga to bring spiritual awakening to mortal souls
Aśvinī devatā	Son of Sūrya (the Sun)
Astika	Son of Jaratkāru, nephew of Vāsuki
Asura	Undivine being, Titan, Demon, hostile, opposing the power of God
Asuraloka	Plane of the Demons
Ātmā	Soul
Atharva Veda	One of the four Vedas

Avatāra	An Incarnation of the Divine
Ayana	A time cycle, to come to the same point by encircling
Bali	Descendent of Prahlād. Due to Brahma's boon, he obtained supremacy over the three worlds. When the Gods wished for help, then Viṣṇu descended as the Vāmana Avatāra and expelled Bali to the nether worlds. Bāli Sugrīva's brother, who was destroyed by Rāma.
Bālkhilya	A boy Ṛṣi, who achieved supreme knowledge
Balrāma	Brother of Kṛṣṇa
Bhaga	God of Joy, son of Pūṣan
Bhāgavata	One of the 18 Purāṇas, describing the life and works of Lord Kṛṣṇa
Bharadvāja	A Ṛṣi, one of the seven Ṛṣis who came out from the mind of Parabrahman
Bharata	Son of Duṣyanta. He was a king of India who ruled over the whole world
Bhārata	A short name of Mahābhārata, the second epic of India
Bhārati	Powers of Truth-Purity working for the purification of humanity
Bhāva	Source of thoughts
Bhāvana	Thoughts
Bhāvayavya	Name of the thought holder, who controls and guides thoughts
Bhīma	Second Pāṇḍava
Bhīma (2)	King of Vidharbha, father of Damayantī
Bhīṣma	Grandfather of Kauravas and Pāṇḍavas, Son of Gaṅgā and Śantanu
Bhojraja	King of Bhoja
Bhṛgu	Son of Pragatha, brother of Kali
Bhuvanas	Worlds, sons of Āptya Ṛṣi
Bhūr	The physical plane

Bhuvar	The vital plane
Bimbisāra	A famous king of India Bird Demi god power
Biti	A short form of Gauribiti, daughter of Śakti
Brahmā	Creator of all
Brahman	The Supreme
Brahmaṇaspati	Another name of Gaṇapati
Brahmāṇī	Power of Brahmā
Bṛhaspati	Teacher of the Gods
Bṛhatī	A metre of 36 syllables

C

Cakra	Wheel
Caṇḍī	A portion of the Mārkaṇḍeya Purāṇa, which contains the glorious description of the Divine Mother "Ambikā"
Candra	The Moon, Lord of Ecstasy
Candra-Vaṁśa	The Lunar Dynasty
Chanda	Rhythm, Metre
Chandasa	One who was born with the Vedas, Sūrya
Chāyā	Wife of Sūrya, the Sun, shadow
Caturdaśa Bhuvanas	Fourteen worlds or planes of existence
Caturtha Sanvarga	Fourth canto
Cow-shaped Śatarūpā	Śatarūpā in the shape of a cow

D

Dakṣa	A Creator of the Goddess "Devi-Śakti" who had hundred daughters, married to many of the Gods
Dakṣāyaṇi	Daughter of Bṛhaspati – married to Putadakṣa
Dakṣina	Daughter of Parabrahman – married to Bṛhaspati, Power of Truth
Darbhya	Incarnation of Indra to bring the Divine Kingdom on the earth

Daśaratha	King of Ayodhyā, Father of Rāma, Lakṣmaṇa, Bharata and Śatrughna
Dasyus	Hostile forces, thieves
Devakī	Mother of Sri Kṛṣṇa, wife of King Vasudeva
Deva	Incarnation of the Supreme Truth, born as a son of Abhivarta
Devatā	God, divine being
Deva Sūrya	Deva the Truth as the Sun
Deva Yajña	Sacrificial flame kindled by Satyadeva, for the Golden Age.
Devāyaṇa	Third Epic of India, describing the four Ages, together with the movement of the Gods towards humanity and of humanity towards the Gods for the manifestation of the Golden Age.
Devī	Goddess
Devī-Sūkta	A portion of Ṛgveda, 125 Sūkta of the tenth Maṇḍala
Dhiṣaṇā	Daughter of Agni
Dharma	Son of Sūrya (Sun)
Dharmeya	Sons of Dharma
Dhruva	On receiving the advice from his mother that for everything one has to work hard, he did such an intense meditation and austerity that he became one of the immortals. He reincarnated in Kaliyuga to bring spiritual awakening to mortal souls
Dinamaṇi	The Sun
Dīrghātamā	A Ṛṣi
Diti	Mother of the Demons
Divya-deha	Divine body
Drobinoda	Son of Ritaba
Droṇa	Teacher of both Kauravs and Pāṇḍavas. He disclosed the secret of the divine weapons to Arjuna.

Drupada	King of Pañcāla
Dundubhi	Divine drum
Durgā	Power of Śiva, wife of Śiva
Durvāsā	A Ṛṣi, who took birth under the influence of Rudra, and thus was always having a violent temper
Dvaipāyana	Another name of Vyāsa
Dvandva	Diversity, dispute
Dvāpara	Bronze Age
Dvārakā	Capital of Kṛṣṇa's kingdom
Dvita	Director of the Time Wheel during the Bronze Age

G

Gadādhara	An incaranation of Ṛṣi Aptya, later on known as Rāmakṛṣṇa, the priest of the Dakṣinesvar temple
Gaṇapati	Son of Śiva
Gaṇeśa	Another name of Gaṇapati
Gandharva	Demi-Gods, celestial musician
Gadā	Club
Gaṅgā Devi	Goddess of River Gaṅgā
Garbha Upaniṣad	Name of an Upaniṣad
Gathini	Daughter of Kushika, wife of Pragatha. Mother of Kali, Lord of the Iron Age
Gauribiti	Daughter of Śakti, Vasiṣṭha's son
Gāyatrī	Source of all metres, Mother of all chandas or Vedas
Guṇa	Three essential properties of nature Sattva, Rajas, Tamas
Guru	Spiritual Teacher

H

Hanumān	Monkey devotee of Śrī Rāma
Hari	A name of Viṣṇu
Hariścandra	King of the Solar Dynasty

Havyāhūti	Sacrifice
Havyavāhu	Fire
Hayagrīva	A Godhead with a horse's head
Heramba	Son of Śiva
Hiraṇyākṣa	A Demon who dragged the earth under the waters and who was then destroyed by Viṣṇu in his Varāha Avatāra
Hiraṇyakaśipu	A Demon King, brother of Hiraṇyākṣa, who due to Brahmā's boon, achieved supremacy in the three worlds. He tried repeatedly to kill his own son Prahlāda, for worshipping Viṣṇu instead of himself. Finally Viṣṇu in his Narasiṁha avtāra killed him.
Hindu	Aryans of India, name given by the Moslems

I

Ilā	Daughter of the Power of Truth
Indra	The Divine King, Supreme Being
Indu Devata	Moon God
Indraprastha	Capital of the Paṇḍavas's Kingdom
Ishaspati	Divine Herald
Iva	Mother of mankind

J

Jaganmātā	Mother of the world
Jagatī	A Sanskrit metre of 48 letters
Jagatpitā	Father of the world
Jagat-Sūrya	Sun of the three worlds
Jana	Holder of life, who controls and guides the life movement
Janaka	Rājarṣi, father of Sita, father-in-law of Sri Ram
Janārdana	A name of Viṣṇu
Japa	Chanting a mantra

Jaraktkūru	Son of a Ṛṣi names Jaru
Jātaveda	Name of Agni
Jīva	A living being
Jīvātmā	Mortal soul or human soul
Juhu	Power of Truth

K

Kāla	The Time
Kālacakra	Time Wheel, the holder of the three worlds
Kālarātri	An inauspicious night
Kāli	The power of Rudra
Kali	The Lord of the Iron Age, the Kaliyuga
Kaliyuga	Period of Time influenced by Kali
Kalpa	A day of Brahmā consisting of the four ages, an aeon
Kāma	Short form of Kāmdeva, also desire, passion
Kāmadeva	Creator of the physical birth
Kāṇḍa	A section of the Rāmāyaṇa or the Veda
Kaṇva	One of the seven Ṛṣis, who came out from the mind of the Parabrahman.
Kaṇveya	Son of Rṣi Kaṇva
Kardama	Father of mankind
Karma-phala	The results of our actions
Kaśyapa	Father of the Gods, who also came out from the mind of Parabrahman.
Kaśyapa-mārīca	Kaśyapa as an enlightened body
Kavi	The Seer, Poet
Kirtya	Incarnation of Candra
Kṛṣṇa	Viṣṇu's incarnation during the Bronze Age
Ksamā-śakti	Power of forgiveness
Kṣatra	The warrior, fighter

L

Laksmaṇa Brother of Rāma
Lakṣmī Daughter of Bṛhaspati, Power of Truth
Love
Laya Universal cataclysm. At this time, the spiritual culture disappears.
Loka Plane, world

M

Madhulā Daughter of the Power of Truth, curative power for all diseases
Magadha Capital of Jarāsandha
Mahābhārata The Second Epic of India
Mahācamasya A Rṣi, who discovered the supramental plane (*Mahas*) above the mental plane and introduced the mantra, Bhūr, Bhuvar, Svar and *Mahas*. He also preserved the memory of the Golden Age.
Mahākāla The Great Time, Śiva
Mahākāla Piṅgala A creative aspect of Śiva, a poetic form
Mahākāla-Rudra A destructive aspect of Śiva
Mahākāli The destructive power of Maheśvara
Mahā Kavi A Seer who attains the consciousness of Brahman. Great poet
Mahā Kāvya Great epic
Mahālakṣmī Power of Viṣṇu
Mahāmāyā Great attachment, Durgā, Maheśvarī
Mahas The mantra Vyāhriṭi, the Supermind
Maharloka Plane of Sun, the Supramental plane
Mahā Sarasvatī Power of Sarasvana
Mahāyāni Sister power of Truth
Maheśvari Power of Maheśvara
Mahī The Earth, Daughter of the Power of Truth
Manas The mind

ınasā	Mother of Āstīka, Jagatgaurī
ānava	Man, Father of Man
lantra	The words which when repeated constantly help in attaining inner consciousness, power, peace, ānanda, etc.
Manu	Creator of Mānavas
Marut-vāyu	Same as Vāyu
Maṇḍala	An orb, gathering of many things, persons etc. In Devāyaṇa used to divide volumes
Māṇḍūkya	Son of Maṇḍūka. A Ṛṣi who gave the Māṇḍūkya Upaniṣad
Manu	Creator of Mānavas
Markandeya	A Ṛṣi who spoke a Purāṇa, the worshipper of Divine Śakti and the devotee of Śiva who conquered death
Marudini	Powers of Truth-Purity working for the purification of humanity
Māyā	Attachment
Meghapurī	High peak in the Himalayas
Mohini-māyā	An attachment that charms
Mitra	God of life, water
Mitrani	Powers of Truth-Purity working for the purification of humanity
Mitra-Varuṇa	God of life
Mṛdaṅga	A musical instrument
Mṛtyu	Death, daughter of the Sun from Sandhyā-chāyā
Muṇḍaka	Paijavana, son of Parjanya – the God of rain – when cursed remains a frog (Maṇḍūka)

N

Nāda	Sound
Nakta	The dark existence

Nārada	Ṛṣi, son of Kaṇva
Naraka	Hell, Son of Saturn
Nārāyaṇa	The manifested cosmic existence, who exists throughout all creations.
Narendra	Like God Indra amongst men, King
Naṭarāja	Rudra, An aspect of Śiva at his destructive dance
Nirvāṇa	To obtain release from the cycle of birth and death, eternal peace

O

Om	The primal sound, Akṣarabrahman

P

Padma	Lotus
Pāṇḍavas	Sons of Pāṇḍu – Yudhiṣṭhira, Bhīma, Arjuna, Nakula, Sahadeva
Paṅkti	A Sanskrit metre of 40 letters
Para Prakṛti	Nature under the influence of the divine forces
Parāśara	Son of Śakti
Parabrahman	The unmanifested eternal existence
Paramātman	Supreme Soul
Paramvyom	The supreme heaven
Parvata	Mountain
Pārvatī	Daughter of Parvata Himālaya. Wife of Śiva.
Pāvaka	Pure
Piṇḍa	Name of an Upaniṣad
Piṅgala	The Poetic existence, the poetic form of Maheśvara
Pīṭhasthāna	Places of religious purity, where Viṣṇu let parts of Satī's body fall down on the earth
Pitṛloka	Plane of the fathers
Pitṛviya	Guide of ancestors for creation

Pitṛyana	Path of obscure mortality
Praceta	A Godhead
Pragatha	Son of Kaṇva, father of Kali, the Lord of the Iron Age
Prahlāda	Son of the Demon Hiraṇyakaṣipu, who worshipped Viṣṇu
Prajāpati	Brahmā, God of the universe
Prakṛti	The Nature
Prāṇa	Life
Prāṇa śakti	Life force
Prastoka	Godhead to prepare for the Golden Age
Preta	The Evil Spirit
Pṛthivi	The earth
Purāṇa	Religious mythology
Purumilha	Son of Taranta, Ruler of the physical plane
Puruṣa	The male form
Puruṣa-Vedamāyā	Who holds the Vedas, who lives in the Vedas, Satyadeva
Pūṣā	Son of Satyadeva, the Power of Light of Truth,wars against the dark forces to manifest the dawn
Punya phala	Effect of virtue

R

Rājarṣi	The King who remains as a Ṛṣi, detached from worldly enjoyment
Rājasāya Yagña	Royal sacrificial ceremony
Rākṣasa	Anti-divine, Titan, Demon
Rakṣasi-force	Power of the anti-divine, hostile forces
Rāma	An incarnation of Viṣṇu, the son of Daśratha
Rāmāyaṇa	First epic of India written by Vālmīki
Rāvaṇa	King of Laṅkā and of the Demonṣ, killed by Rāma

Ṛbhu	Son of Ṛbhaba
Ṛk	Mantra
Ṛgveda	One of the four Vedas
Rodasi	Earth and heaven
Ṛpus	Enemies, hostile forces
Ṛṣi	A seer
Ṛṣika	A female seer
Ritaba	Son of Aśvini-devatā
Rohidaśva	Incarnation of Aśvadeva. An aspect of Sūrya
Rohiṇi	Powers of Truth-Purity working for the purification of humanity
Ṛtā	The Truth
Ṛtaṁ	Divine Truth
Ṛtāyana	Change from day to night
Ṛtavari	Power of Truth
Ṛtus	Seasons
Rudra	The destroyer, a destructive form of Maheśvara
Rudrāṇī	The female form of Rudra

S

Saci	Powers of Truth-Purity working for the purification of humanity
Sādhana	Son of Svar-bhuvana, worship, effort
Sādhya	Sons of Sarasvatī
Sāmaveda	One of the four Vedas
Sanatkumāra	A Ṛṣi – a Brāhmaṇa
Santāna Dharma	The eternal religion
Sangana	Wife of Sūrya
Saṁvarga	Smaller form of Varga. In Devāyaṇa, it is used for a canto
Saṁnyāsin	A person who has given up normal life, and becomes a seeker of God
Saṅkalpa	Will, volition
Sarasvāna	God of words, the male part of Sarasvatī

Sarasvatī	Goddess of learning, daughter of the Power of Truth
Sarga	A canto in the Rāmāyaṇa
Sarjaya	Godhead to bring down the Golden Age
Sarpa	Snake
Satī	Daughter of Dakṣa, married to Śiva
Satya	Truth
Satyadeva	Lord of Truth
Satya Yuga	Golden Age
Sauciki	A Ṛṣi, who kindled the sacrificial flame for the Deva
Sāvitṛ-Sūrya	Power of the Sun, wife of Sūrya
Śakti	Son of Vasiṣṭha, power
Śānti	Peace, daughter of Yama
Śaṅkarācārya	A South Indian philosopher who propagated the concept of the one Brahman
Śaṅkha	Conch
Śani	Saturn
Śanti-yamāyāni	Same as Śanti
Śatakratu	Indra, the King of Gods
Śāradāmoni	Sri Rāmakṛṣṇan's wife, whom he revered as mother
Siddhidātā	God of poetic realisation for the Truth. Other names are Heramba, Gaṇapati, Ganesh, Brahmaṇaspati
Sinibali	The creator in the mother's womb, Sister Power of Truth
Sinibalya	The puruṣa part of Sinibali
Sītā	Daughter of Janaka and the wife of Rāma
Śloka	A verse
Snake	One with undivine power
Soma	Divine nectar Soma devata
Soma devata	The Moon God, Lord of the nectar

Śuci-svarga	The pure heaven
Suhavā	Queen of the Lord of Truth
Śukrācārya	The teacher of the Asuras
Śukadeva	Son of Vyasa
Sukṣma-śarīra	Subtle body
Sukta	Canto or a section of Veda, a chapter
Supramental	Sri Aurobindo's name for Maharloka of the Upaniṣads
Suraloka	Plane of the Gods, heaven
Sūrya	Sun, Lord of Mental Truth
Sūrya Saṅga	Power of the Sun, Power of Sūrya also known as Saṅga
Suṣamma	Ocean, absolute beauty and light
Svāhā	Powers of Truth-Purity working for the purification of humanity
Svar	Heaven
Svarga	Heaven

T

Taittirīya Upaniṣad	An Upaniṣad
Takṣaka	The snake who bit King Parīkṣit and killed him
Tanunāpat	Godhead to prepare for teh Golden Age
Tapasyā	Religious austerity, penance, discipline for the achievement of spititual power
Taranta	Son of Viśvedeva, ruler of the vital plane
Tīrthasthāna	A place of religious merit or virtue
Tittiri	Name of a bird
Trita	Director and holder of the Time Wheel. Under his guidance we have the Silver Age, (Trita Yuga)
Tritayuga	The Silver Age
Triṣṭhubh	A Sanskrit metre of 44 letters

U

Udyama	An effort to start the work
Upaniṣad	A discussion of Vedic hymns with disciples
Upava	Godhead who opens the path for the Truth
Uṣā	Divine Dawn, daughter of Satyadeva
Uṣā-Saṅgana	Power of the Sun on the mental plane, an awakening conscious power
Uṣati	Another name for Yahvī
Uṣṇīk	A Sanskrit metre of 28 letters

V

Vaidadaśvi	Son of Taranta, ruler of the physical plane
Vaiśampāyana	Disciple of Vyāsa
Vaiṣṇavī	Power of Viṣṇu, Power of Truth-Love
Vaiśvanara	The Fire
Vaiśyas	Those who increase riches in the world
Vajra	Weapon of Indra
Vālmīkī	Poet of Rāmāyaṇa
Vanaspati	God of forest
Vaṇga	Bengal
Vāk	Daughter of Ambhṝṇī
Vāk-devī	Saravatī – Goddess of words
Varga	Like the Maṇḍala but shorter. In Devāyaṇa, it contains many Saṁvargas
Varuṇa	God of life, of water
Varuṇi	Powers of Truth-Purity working for the purification of humanity
Varṇa	Caste
Vasiṣṭha	Ṛṣi, son of Mitra-devatā
Vasu	God of riches
Vasukarṇa	The third Divine King ensures the physical transformation of the bodies

	into divine bodies. His power is Vasupriyā.
Vāsudeva	Another name of Kṛṣṇa
Vāsuki	The Snake King who holds the creation on his head in the subtle world
Vasukra	The first Divine King upon the earth. Commencement of the Golden Age where earth became like heaven. Death is removed from the world. Beings, if they so willed, could leave their bodies by calling upon Yamaraja. His power is Indrasnusha, also called Urnavati as she came directly to the world without taking a human birth.
Vasukrīḍ	The second Divine King. Under him, souls could manifest directly upon the earth. Question of birth and death was solved. His power was Vasusaṇgā.
Vasuna	The seventh Vasu King who gifts to the world divine wealth and riches. Greed, passion and jealousy disappear from the earth. His power is Vasundharā.
Vasumāna	The last Vasu King, the eighth, maintains and protects all that was achieved by the Vasus. His power is Vasumati.
Vasurochisa	The fourth Vasu King from the Golden Age who gifted his people with clairvoyance. His power is Vasukanta.
Vasuśruta	The fifth Vasu King. Under his people receive clairaudience. They can hear from vast distances. His power is Vasuvara.
Vasuyuva	The sixth Vasu King of the Golden Age. He brings down divine all-pervading

	love, divine rhythms, art and beauty. Misunderstanding and discord vanish from the world. His power who effects this is Vasulata.
Vāyu	Lord of the Winds, the life force, Commander of the Divine Forces
Veda	The unique spiritual authority
Vedic	Authority of spiritual Truth
Vibhīṣaṇa	Brother of Rāvaṇa, who gave him the right advice, one of the immortals who reincarnated in Kaliyuga to bring spiritual awakening to mortal souls
Vidhu	Moon God
Viḍa Vaṇga	Home of Truth
Vipra	Brahmin
Vināyaka	Son of Śiva, another name of Gaṇapati
Vipāśā	Name of a river
Vipra	A Brahmin, who has knowledge
Virāja	A Sanskrit metre having 10 letters in each foot
Viṣṇu	The Protector, who maintains and protects the world
Viśvakarmā	Son of Svar-bhuvana
Viśvāmitra	Ṛṣi, son of Gādhi Kauśika
Viśvāvasu	King of the Gandharvas, the celestial musicians
Viśvedeva	The son-in-law of the Lord of Truth
Viśvedevas	Gandharvas in Heaven who are the workers in heaven and who sing and dance
Vratta	Spiritual austerities
Vṛṣa	A Ṛsi
Vyādhi	Malady
Vyāhṛti	Plane in mantra

Vyāsa	The poet who wrote Mahābhārata, the second epic of India

Y

Yādavas	Kṛṣṇa's family name
Yahvī	Mother of Truth
Yajña	A sacrifice, the flame of sacrifice
Yajur Veda	One of the four Vedas
Yakṣa	Gandharvas, who increase wealth in Heaven
Yama	The son of Viśwadeva, who is the Sun on the mental plane
Yámaloka	The world of Yama
Yamāyāni Śanti	Śanti
Yajur Veda	One of the four Vedas.
Youvanashwa	Incarnation of Sūrya
Yudhisthir	The eldest Paṇḍava
Yuga	Age
Yuvakośa	Treasure of Youth

BOOKS OF RELATED INTEREST FROM NAB

BEYOND RELIGION: Meditations on Man's True Nature—*Robbert Powell*

True religion or spirituality is nothing other than the reversal of this whole process of chaos, conflict, to a state of simplicity, naturalness, and therefore order....

ISBN: 81-7822-139-x

EMBRACING HEAVEN AND EARTH: The Liberation Teachings for Enlightenment
—*Andrew Cohen*

"...a fresh and profound apprach to spirituality grounded in his own awakened awarness." It is a book of extraordinary spiritual intelligence, challenging the reader to participate in the ultimate revolution: to abandon the security of the known for the thrill of the unknown, which is Enlightenment.

ISBN: 81-7822-218-3

GLIMPSES OF DEVAYANA: A Short Synopsis of the Third Epic of India—*Dr. Hajari*

The Epic is described as a spiritual history from the Golden Age to the Iron Age and again to the Golden Age inaugurated by the descent of the higher consciousness, the supramental, to the earth to unfold the Vedic Truth. The Spiritual history of the race from the early Vedic times onwards....

ISBN: 978-81-7822-284-4

THE HINDU MIND: Fundamentals of Hindu Religion and Philosophy for All Ages—*Bansi Pandit*

The Hindu Mind provides an excellent introduction to the historical, philosophical, ritualistic, social, and ethical dimensions of Hinduism. The major contribution of the book is that it shows the interconnections among these diverse dimensions.

ISBN: 978-81-7822-007-9

ISLAM: An Historical Introduction
—*Gerhard Endress*

"Endress presents an accurate picture of the interplay of religion inspiration and historical circumstances which shaped Islamic history from its inception....It reflects a distinct sensitivity to the nuances of the subject culture, combined with a clear command of the scholarly sources...it is therefore most appropriate for graduate students beginning a middle East or Islamic specialization, for professional scholars with other specializations seeking synoptic treatment of Islamic survey course.

ISBN: 81-7822-156-X

THE MYSTIQUE OF OM—*Jayant Burde*

Om is the most sacred mantra in major Indic religions such as Hinduism, Buddhism and Jainism. It symbolises affirmation, benediction and peace, and is used ritualistically in prayers, invocations and ceremonies, religious as well as secular.

ISBN: 81-7822-281-7

SRIMAD BHAGAVAD GITA—*Kailash Nath Kalia*

Here is a rendering of Srimad Bhagavad Gita into English. The main feature of this translation is that the Sanskrit text has also been given in the Roman script. This enables those readers who do not know Sanskrit to get a fairly correct idea of the spirit of the epic. Before giving the translation of the entire verse, the author has given meaning of each word in it.

ISBN: 978-81-7822-306-3

SUKHMANI SAHEB: Treasure of Bliss
—*Bharat Bhooshan*

Sukhmani Saheb is one of the most revered scriptures of the Sikh faith. It was written by the fifth Guru, Shri Arjun Dev Ji, to make a accessible Divine wisdom to the common man. Its appeal extends beyond the Sikh community and it is widely read by Hindus.

ISBN: 81-7822-258-2

UNDERSTANDING ISLAM—*Frithjof Schoun*

"Islam is the meeting between God as such and man as such.... Islam confronts what is immutable in God with what is permanent in man." These are the opening words of what has become a classic work on Islam, perhaps the most misunderstood of the great Revelations. And yet the purpose of this book "is not so much to give a description of Islam as to explain...why Moslems believe in it."

ISBN: 81-7822-151-9